Praise for
LIVING INSIDE‑OUT

"The beauty of this book is that you don't need to read 18 different books to glean the wisdom of 16 different experts. Eddie Miller brilliantly synthesizes their words of wisdom and his Inside‑Out Philosophy™ to help you discover your own inner compass to break the overwhelmed, overworked and over committed cycle."

— Joe Vitale
Star of the hit movie, *The Secret* and #1 Best‑Selling Author

"Eddie Miller is a Master Student. In Living Inside‑Out *he shares what he has learned from years of his own experience and his studies with some of the world's greatest teachers. Eddie knows that living from the inside‑out works because he practices what he preaches. He LIVES this work as well or better than anyone I know. THAT is what makes Eddie someone you should listen to."*

— Robert MacPhee
Senior Vice President, Canfield Training Group
Author, *Manifesting for Non‑Gurus*

"Living Inside‑Out *is a life changing book with lessons to live by. No matter what your intentions are this book is the perfect roadmap to success. Eddie is heartfelt and has compiled some of the best experts to illustrate his message. It is truly remarkable and is a must read for anyone who is looking to live their best life. No matter where you are today, this book will get you to the next step."*

— Kimberly Mylls
Co‑Author, *Boys Before Business: The Single Girls Guide to Having it All*

"In a world that is simply getting noisier, what a refreshing book that takes you directly to the answers to live your life vibrantly from the inside-out. Eddie Miller has brought it all together in one great read—Inspiring!"

— Allan Milham
CEO, BoldMoves Enterprises, Inc.
Co-Author, *Bold Moves: Inspiring Courageous Action in Uncertain Times*

LIVING
INSIDE-OUT

The Go-To GUIDE
for the
Overwhelmed, Overworked, & Overcommitted

EDDIE MILLER

NEW YORK

LIVING INSIDE-OUT
The Go-To GUIDE for the **Overwhelmed,** **Overworked,** *&* **Overcommittefd**

by EDDIE MILLER
© 2011 Eddie Miller.. All rights reserved.

No part of this publication may be reproduced or transmitted in any form or by any means, mechanical or electronic, including photocopying and recording, or by any information storage and retrieval system, without permission in writing from author or publisher (except by a reviewer, who may quote brief passages and/or show brief video clips in a review).

Disclaimer: The Publisher and the Author make no representations or warranties with respect to the accuracy or completeness of the contents of this work and specifically disclaim all warranties, including without limitation warranties of fitness for a particular purpose. No warranty may be created or extended by sales or promotional materials. The advice and strategies contained herein may not be suitable for every situation. This work is sold with the understanding that the Publisher is not engaged in rendering legal, accounting, or other professional services. If professional assistance is required, the services of a competent professional person should be sought. Neither the Publisher nor the Author shall be liable for damages arising herefrom. The fact that an organization or website is referred to in this work as a citation and/or a potential source of further information does not mean that the Author or the Publisher endorses the information the organization or website may provide or recommendations it may make. Further, readers should be aware that internet websites listed in this work may have changed or disappeared between when this work was written and when it is read.

ISBN 978-1-60037-797-6 (paperback)

Library of Congress Control Number: 2010930181

Published by:

MORGAN JAMES PUBLISHING
1225 Franklin Ave. Ste 325
Garden City, NY 11530-1693
Toll Free 800-485-4943
www.MorganJamesPublishing.com

Book Cover Photo by
Robert Wilson,
PhotoSpaceStudio.com
robert@photospacestudio.com

Cover Design by:
Rachel Lopez
rachel@r2cdesign.com

Interior Design by:
Bonnie Bushman
bbushman@bresnan.net

In an effort to support local communities, raise awareness and funds, Morgan James Publishing donates one percent of all book sales for the life of each book to Habitat for Humanity.
Get involved today, visit **www.HelpHabitatForHumanity.org.**

This book is dedicated to my dad and mom, Ralph and Kelly Miller.
They have always been my biggest cheerleaders.
I'm forever grateful for their unconditional love and belief in me.

ACKNOWLEDGEMENTS

There are a number of people who have encouraged, supported, brainstormed with, and inspired me during the process of writing this book. Each one of their contributions has helped to bring *Living Inside-Out* into being and I'm most grateful.

First and foremost, this book would not be possible without the relentless support and collaboration of one of my closest friends and colleague Pam Mariast. Her insights, enthusiasm, and passion pushed me to go further within. In addition, she helped me to sort though and organize more that 300,000 transcribed words from the interviews of the sixteen experts. I met Pam shortly after I had the idea for this book and she has been an amazing, constant presence ever since.

Another woman who has had a profound influence on my life and this book is Lu Hanessian. Not only is she a featured expert, she has been my writing coach and editor. There is one word I use to descript Lu—Brilliant! From our first conversation she immediately grasped the vision and depth of this book. Lu is one of the most remarkable people I've had the privilege of knowing.

I'm also tremendously appreciative to the other fifteen experts who shared their nuggets of wisdom and personal journeys within in these pages. Each one of them has had a remarkable positive impact on my life. It is because they have enriched my life and have taught me how to further embrace my own strength within that I've included them in this book.

When it comes to mentors, the one that is in the forefront is Jack Canfield. I so appreciate the realness of his character. As a leading expert in the field of human potential and transformation, Jack is one of the most down to earth and insightful individuals I know.

In addition to my parents who this book is dedicated, I want to acknowledge three "salt of the earth women" who from the moment I was born filled my life with unconditional love ... my grandmas Charlotte and Claire and my aunt Virginia. During the process of writing this book, as I reflect on my life's journey, I realized it is their love that nurtured me.

There are seven amazing friends who have been there to lift me up and keep me going and that this book would not be possible without—Diana, Kent, Michael, Linda, Mark, Richard, and Susana.

My buddy Allan, who on a weekly basis keeps me accountable for the vision and contribution I've committed to giving back to those I can help embrace their own radiant beauty within.

And, the most important light in my life, Alekxey. The one who I have the privilege to spend everyday with to explore the journey of life and who consistently loves me for who I am and constantly encourages me to embrace all that I was meant to be.

I am blessed!

CONTENTS

FOREWORD

by Jack Canfield

I've taught people in all walks of life how to realize their dreams and fulfill their potential. But many still ask, "What's my next step? What should I do? How do I do it?" They believe that going through certain motions will create the life-altering changes they so desire.

Yes, they must act; but first they need to be silent and listen to their deep, heartfelt urgings, and then allow those urgings to lead their actions. But in the high-speed pace of daily life, millions feel disillusioned as their own choices pummel their expectations.

Why do we sabotage ourselves? Why do we say we want one thing and then do another? Where can we find answers about how to change our lives?

I've known Eddie Miller for quite a while, so I've had the opportunity to see him adopt an "Inside-Out" philosophy in his own life. He's learned that the key to making our own right choices, finding the answers to our most daunting questions, and uncovering our life lessons consists in listening to our own inner wisdom and allowing that power to guide us.

For many of us, this wisdom becomes shrouded by our perceived fears and the emotional baggage created by overpowering negative self-talk. This pushes our own wisdom out of view, convincing us that we don't know or deserve any better. With *Living Inside-Out*, Eddie explains that the key to real change lies in bridging that internal disconnect and trusting ourselves.

I experienced the power of this inner wisdom years ago and what resulted was the *Chicken Soup for the Soul*® book series. The inspiration came to me on an airplane flight late one night from Boston to Los Angeles, as I sat quietly reflecting on the day and meditating. Suddenly the idea to do this book of stories popped into my mind. Because I was still and ready to listen, I allowed space for something to emerge from deep within my own heart. This initial inspiration evolved into a wonderful book series that has touched the lives of over 100 million people.

Many of us spend a great deal of time and energy working hard to make things happen—all the while focusing on the wrong things. We haven't slowed down enough to allow the idea or inner guidance that can change our lives to come forward.

Living Inside-Out identifies and challenges those internal blocks that hold us back from the life we desire. Within each chapter, Eddie showcases wisdom gleaned from top experts in various life disciplines, who guide us to identify and confront the behaviors that hold us back.

I believe this book will resonate strongly with anyone who wants more out of life but also wants to create balance. Changing your life begins with a decision; *Living Inside-Out* gives you a unique opportunity to embrace that choice in order to create positive, lasting change in your life.

One of the things I've learned about life is if you ask the right questions, you get better answers. Ask yourself what you really want from life, and then use the wisdom in these pages to help you make your decisions for change.

START HERE

"I don't know where to start."

I've heard these words from countless people over the years. They want a better life, a more fulfilling job, or a deeper sense of relationship.

They'd like more time, less anxiety; more joy, less regret.

They feel restless and overwhelmed. Caught in a trap of commitment and exhaustion, wondering when "The Good Life" will reveal itself.

Some want *a whole new life*. As if they could simply replace the old one. But, whether they're faced with this unrealistic task of rebuilding every detail of their lives or just want to re-create certain aspects to better meet their needs, one thing is certain: even the most determined people know what it feels like to stand at a crossroads and not know where to go.

So, they stand there ... stuck.

Everyone knows "*stuck.*"

I know I have. Growing up on a cattle farm in Missouri with an outhouse and no running hot water was part of it. Struggling with dyslexia was part of it too. I was a chunky kid with glasses, not the slightest bit athletic. I didn't have a ton of friends. I often wondered how I'd ever take one step in a forward direction.

As an adult, though, I got tired of feeling stuck. As I studied, read, began my career, and traveled, I looked around and saw a lot of people who were standing in the muck of their lives ... waiting. People who had given up. People who thought they weren't destined to live their best lives—their ultimate life—but rather tolerate the ones they had.

We all know people who inadvertently live their entire lives stuck in the mud of indecision—looking outside themselves for answers, waiting for the right people and circumstances, which never come. Maybe some of us would describe ourselves this way. The state of being stuck takes on a life of its own and can begin to define who we are.

In the past several years, I've encountered people with unfulfilled dreams, broken hearts and promises, financial turmoil, failed businesses, conflicted communication, weight challenges, and low self-esteem—all challenges I've personally faced too. On a deeper level, they're searching for answers. But ask people what they're searching for and they don't exactly know.

For more than 20 years, I've studied the how's and why's of our behavior and our choices. Why do we sabotage ourselves? How do we create our own obstacles? Why do we often fail to see our own solutions? How can we produce real change? Why do we prefer to cling to fantasy instead of embracing reality?

As I paved my own path—bumpier than I ever wanted or expected—I discovered that the biggest hurdle I faced was ... me. I realized I got in my own way, and I saw that others do this too. We come up with all kinds of rationalizations for why we can't do something and all sorts of ways to maneuver around our own best interests.

Although we all want to live better, happier lives and experience more freedom, many of us don't realize how *we unknowingly prevent ourselves from living the very life we say we want.* We're overworked, overcommitted, and overwhelmed ... Miserable as we might be, our lives can become a familiar grind.

At a certain point, we may finally say to ourselves, *"This is it. I want to live my life differently from this moment on and I'm willing to do everything in my power to create a shift to embrace a new way of being."*

Dismantle the Obstacles

In our high-tech, high-demand, fast-paced society, we have cultivated a deep restlessness. We're obsessed with the quick fix—even though it fixes nothing. We look for solutions in how-to books, rah-rah seminars, costly therapy, and fair-weather friends. Yet, in spite of all this searching, I've discovered the answers aren't *out there*—in "Mr./Miss Right," a paycheck, or friends who seem to have much greener grass.

The answers we are seeking lie within us—*in the power of our inner wisdom*.

But we talk ourselves out of listening to it. Our perceived fears drum up a lot of negative self-talk and limiting beliefs that just seize us as we unconsciously convince ourselves we don't know the answers or deserve any better.

The key to significant change lies in understanding how our fears create our internal disconnect so we can ultimately unlock our own innate power.

But how?

I've learned the fastest way for me to break through the very thing that was blocking my path was to identify an expert that had already been down the path I was traveling and follow their lead. So, I began to list the nation's foremost health and wellness, life-balance, and peak performance thought-leaders, people whose perspectives and insights captivated me and had changed my thinking, people whose methods and work have collectively transformed the lives of millions of people, including mine. I interviewed them, some in person and others in extensive phone conversations, analyzed and applied their insight—while consequently discovered my own, and explored the depths of *living life from the inside-out*.

I'm excited to share this process with you on the pages that follow, as you begin your own journey to pave a path to the life you truly desire.

My Intention

My intention is to:

- Help you discover your own right questions and transformative answers within.
- Support you in readily tapping into your innate inner wisdom, your compass.

- Make the changes necessary to live and sustain the ultimate life you desire.

Your Dedication to This Process

If it were easy to do these things, you wouldn't have picked up this book. Something about living inside-out just resonated with you, and I think I know what it is. No doubt you've already tried a lot of different methods, formulas, and strategies. You're better at fixing other people's problems than your own! You've been looking "out there." You've lived "outside-in," using other people's opinions and criticisms as your barometer.

You've turned yourself inside out trying to break out of old habits, to no avail. But you haven't yet *lived* from the inside-out.

How This Book Can Help You

Through investigating the far-reaching effects of your environment and your mind-body-spirit connection, you'll understand how challenges overwhelm you, and why, deep down, you have been *resistant* to change. These insights can help you pinpoint the self-defeating behaviors that have frustrated and betrayed you for so long.

The first six chapters of this book will lay the foundation with key principles that explore and explain our inner scaffolding, so to speak, how we develop self-hindering beliefs, how our minds interpret and our brains re-wire, how we re-write old scripts, and reframe our fears from an energy perspective. The remaining eleven chapters will share insights on the important disciplines of our lives, from health to finances to relationships, and a final chapter on our individual call to action.

At its core, the idea of living inside-out is a *decision* more than a journey or a destination. You'll see that living fully is *worth* the effort of changing old beliefs that no longer serve you, making empowered choices that do, and following through with them.

On the next page I share the Inside-Out Philosophy™ I developed and which this book is based.

THE INSIDE-OUT PHILOSOPHY™

The Inside-Out Philosophy™ is based on the universal premise that, as human beings, we have the *innate wisdom and capacity* to transform our lives, reach our goals, fulfill our purpose, and create the happy, healthy, and prosperous life of our dreams.

Inside-out living consists of essentially two stages:

Stage one involves *knowing*. You become aware—of your truth, your story, and those negative voices in your head that talk you out of the life of your dreams.

Stage two involves *trusting*. You use that awareness to trust, listen to, and follow your intuitive inner voice—your divine wisdom—as it guides you to the authentic life you were intended to live.

As you look within, you discover your *history* and the *story* you played out because of it. You then have a choice. You can make that story your obstacle—your limiting belief, your rationalization, and your chronic disappointment—and continue to live that story your entire life. Or, you can discover how your story has created your ceiling and break through it.

Once you begin to question and change your beliefs and perceptions, you intuitively start to make different choices—choices that reflect your *truth*, not your story. Thus you clear the way to live your potential instead of your unconscious expectations.

In this process of change, you realize your journey, no matter how painful, was perfectly choreographed to bring you to where you are now. When you trust your inner wisdom and have the courage to follow it, you learn to take responsibility, without blame or shame, for the life you've experienced. And in this moment, as in every moment, you are free to dream bigger, willingly accept your heart's desires, and be a positive influence on others and your world. You truly embrace the power of possibility and *be who you were meant to be*.

(For a downloadable version of the Inside-Out Philosophy™, go to www.EddieMiller.com.)

The Seven Living Inside-Out Principles

Focus Your Intention

Embrace Change from Within

Be Present to Possibilities

Know Your Truth

The Questions are the Answers

Awaken to Your Natural Abundance

Move to Action

LIVING INSIDE-OUT PRINCIPLES

1

Focus Your Intention

"Focusing your intention is the key to tapping into your inner wisdom."

— Eddie

I'm about to take you on a journey.

By the end of this book, you will not only know things you didn't know before, but you will understand how to apply that knowledge in real life terms. That doesn't make *Living Inside-Out* a "how-to" book. No, I didn't want to write *that* book, because I don't think anyone can tell you "how to" live your best life, because your "best" life is subjective.

Most self-help books I read, with a few rare exceptions, were based on the premise that I couldn't find answers myself and so I had to seek them elsewhere, outside me. This led me down many garden paths—and winding roads. For a few years, like most of us, I didn't know what I believed in, didn't know what direction I was going, and thought that, if I felt aimless or dissatisfied, it must be because I didn't find the right source yet. The right person's theory or method to plug into and make work for me.

You might assume I lacked concrete direction. But that's not really it. What I have come to realize, after many years, is that I lacked *intention*. Maybe more accurately still, I had intention, but had not yet learned how to focus it.

Our Internal Energy

Many of us get caught up in our daily dramas. That's human. And these days, who isn't overscheduled and overwhelmed? But, often, many of us take this anxiety and spiral. We waste a lot of time worrying about what *might* happen, when most of the time, our fears never become a reality. However, our fears escalate our anxiety, worry, and stressful feelings.

I used to think that if I thought enough about positive emotions and intentions, then, by some magical force, I'd be rewarded with my heart's desires. But over and over again, when I *thought* I was thinking positively, nothing happened. I became disillusioned. You know what that looks like? Impatience. Anger. Frustration. Self-criticism. Self-doubt.

I must not be doing it right, I thought.

My mentor and best-selling author Jack Canfield (and the person who wrote this book's foreword) understood the roadblock. He said, "You will attract into your life whatever you *focus* on. Whatever you give your energy and attention to will come back to you. You are creating your reality in every moment of everyday. You are creating your future with every single thought: either consciously or subconsciously." [Jack Canfield's *Key to Living the Law of Attraction*, Health Communications, Inc., 2007, p. 7]

Focusing our intention is the key.

"But I don't have an intention, or if I have one, I don't know what it is," you might be thinking.

I've come to understand that the antidote to the turmoil we face lies within each of us. When we learn to *access, listen, trust, and follow our own inner wisdom*, we can overcome our mental and emotional blocks, negative self-talk, and perceived fears. We then can more fully focus on our positive intention.

I discovered that, like everything else, the Law of Attraction—which is a sublaw of the Law of Vibration—is an *inside-out* phenomenon. It isn't a magic trick. It isn't about attracting what we desire from the outside or *making* it happen. The Law of Attraction for me is about another process entirely. It's about changing our internal life from the *inside* to match that of what we deeply desire.

Too often, we don't realize how we contradict the very things we believe in, need and want, creating confusion and turmoil by saying one thing and doing another. Millions of people try to will their dreams through pleading prayers, or wish for them as if those dreams were a long list for Santa to check twice. If we don't get what we want, we think we didn't deserve it—or we feel bitter that we didn't get our due.

We bite our nails, but try to convince ourselves that we feel relaxed.

We spend money that we don't have, and then hate that we're in debt.

We criticize and lash out at a loved one, and feel dejected and discouraged that we don't feel connected.

We have a dream for a wonderful new business, and simultaneously worry that it won't work and unwittingly find ways to stall and slow the process of manifesting that dream.

You see, it is not just about changing our thoughts, but about going deeper to connect with the root of what we *feel*. I've learned that in every situation—literally every second of the day—we can choose how to react, how to feel, how to show up, how to be. When we become consciously aware of what we're focusing on and giving our attention to, we discover a wealth of insight about ourselves and the world around us.

If we think of life—or the Universe—as something that we are in *relationship* with, then the Universe will react to our internal energy. We say, "I can't." And we can't. We say, "I'm afraid of becoming too big and too successful because it will demand too much of me." And the Universe agrees.

But, when we say, "I'm ready." When we say, "I want to take my life to the next level and really see what I'm made of. I want to make a difference." The Universe conspires with us to pave that path.

Now, this, I realized, is *not* about a genie in a bottle giving us exactly what we want. No! This is where millions of us get lost. What it's really about is, once we're open and willing and ready, all those unseen forces of life align with our deepest desires to grow us into the next phase of our lives to achieve our highest good. Because we're ready … and because we *consciously choose* to do so.

Living inside-out is not an overnight process; neither is experiencing your heart's desires.

So, what is our relationship with the Universe? It doesn't decide which path is better for us; it responds to whatever energy we're creating and gives us more of the same. It reflects back to us the state of our consciousness.

If we're asleep at the wheel of life, we don't notice all the opportunities passing us by. If we're primed for a fight with every person we meet, we are not open to the kindness of others or the ways in which we can affect others with our own kindness.

Our Emotions are the Key

So, be aware of what you're feeling. *Our emotions are the key to manifesting our desires.* They really are. I'm talking about the stuff that makes us do what we do. We are not automated machines. We feel, and therefore we react! And those reactions can get us further toward our joy and prosperity and good health or not. You might work hard toward a dream, but if you're constantly interjecting negative thoughts and feelings into the mix, your dream won't materialize. Not as easily or quickly as you'd like, anyway.

Once, after telling a close friend how anxious and frustrated I was over a particular circumstance, he looked at me said simply, "Freedom and power."

"What does that mean?" I said.

"You have the freedom to choose whatever you want. That's your power."

If you're feeling stuck, freedom seems out of reach.

If you're feeling powerless, you may reach for power in all the wrong ways.

So, what would you like to *experience* in your life? If your intention is to create positive energy in your life, it's imperative to give your attention to positive thoughts and feelings.

How? The answer is in our cells.

What's Your Vibe?

Have you heard people talk about another person's "vibes?" "He has bad vibes about him." Or, "She has great vibes." You know what I mean, when you sense a situation that doesn't quite feel right or are ambivalent about a decision or a person? These feelings are your intuition talking. Your gut. Your inner wisdom. Your deep sense of who you are and what is life-enhancing—or not.

Our vibes can be measured. Rates of vibration are called frequencies, and the higher the frequency, the more powerful the force. Positive thoughts, feelings, and emotions vibrate at a high frequency, while negative thoughts, feelings, and emotions vibrate at a low frequency.

It's all energy.

Everything, whether solid, liquid, or gas, consists of energy, and all forms of energy constantly move and vibrate. Our entire Universe and everything within it—seen and unseen—is a vibrating mass of atoms and subatomic particles.

The same principles of vibration that operate in the outer, physical world apply to our emotional/psychological world. In other words, our feelings and thoughts consist of energy and have vibrations. Frequencies of *like* vibration attract each other, and herein lies the key to experiencing what you want in your life—what you *intend* to attract.

I've learned to catch myself when I'm in a negative mode—angry, sad, anxious, bored, restless, pessimistic—and shift my energy to the positive. No, it's not a switch I flip. (I wish.) Rather, it's a way of relating to myself, talking myself through a difficult situation, making a note, so to speak, that I am in conflict, and then trying to look at that conflict in me through the most objective and compassionate eyes. That means no judgment, no self-hate, no self-doubt.

So, being aware of our feelings is a major part of making this shift from negative (the Impossible) to positive (the Possible).

The other crucial part of this shift is to be consciously aware of our intention. What's the difference between *knowing* our intention and *having* intentions?

For me, it isn't just semantics. I see intention as our deep, personal goal for the way we want to live. Intention is tied to purpose. It's our lifeblood. Our practical philosophy. It's stronger and more profound than simply having intentions, which I have come to believe, can pay lip service to our goals but not necessarily sustain a good life.

What is Your Intention?

Living Inside-Out helps you realize you can't create happiness if you're caught up in how badly your spouse or friend treated you. Nor can you create a healthy body if you're focused on how overweight (or underweight or sick) you are, or create prosperity if you're thinking about what you lack.

Understanding the power of your *focused intention* can mean the difference between a life of lack, hardship, fear, anxiety, struggle and a life filled with joy, satisfaction, fulfillment, profound peace, limitless prosperity. You can either become stuck in life as a victim of circumstance or shift to discover new possibilities by taking *100% responsibility* for being that which you desire. This is one of the most important inside-out life lessons I've learned.

Six Keys to Maintaining Your Focused Intention

When you're faced with what appears to be a crazy and chaotic world inside your own mind and/or around you, *how can you maintain a positive, focused intention?*

1. **Be aware of your thoughts and actions** regarding your own body image, health, intelligence, and abilities and how you address challenges with your loved ones, co-workers, finances, and career. Know that you're 100% responsible for *how you perceive your life* and *how you show up* as a result. (Chris Waddell's story in the next chapter illustrates the importance of this awareness.)

2. **Focus on the gift.** Look for a silver lining in every situation instead of focusing on the problem. Be open to discovering

not only a solution, but the inherent *gift* that is always born out of your perceived struggle.

3. **Define your purpose and your dreams.** Identify your passion, and from there, you'll find your purpose and how to fulfill your dreams. Understanding your *why* helps keep you focused during difficult or frustrating times. (Brian Biro and I will help you to identify your purpose in chapter 3.)

4. **Create a support team** of those who support and encourage you, and stay away from those who bring you down. Be discerning about who you share your goals and dreams with, because negatively oriented people may unwittingly cause you to sabotage yourself even by giving cautionary advice.

5. **Use "the gap."** Prayer and meditation are essential to help you tap into your inner wisdom and divine guidance. In the silent gap between thoughts is the point in which you are truly connected with Source and where answers emerge that you might never arrive at through conscious effort.

6. **Don't just think, *feel*.** Be aware of and attuned to your feelings. Your emotions reflect what you're creating, positively or negatively, moment by moment. The more you focus on how much you don't want a problem in your life, the bigger and fiercer it grows—in your own mind. (Paul Scheele and I will elaborate on this in chapter 6.)

Your emotions act as your compass. They always create a path to your focused intention. When you become more and more aware of your inner emotional life, you become aware of your predominant focus and what you're "putting out there." Is it positive—or negative? Encouraging—or self-defeating? When you know what you're dispensing to the world, the kind of emotional and therefore vibrational energy, then you can begin to see how it connects to what you're receiving in return.

We're about to explore the many ways in which our perceptions dictate how we approach our life. And once you discern the nature of those perceptions—whether they block, frustrate, confuse, or help you—

you can apply them to better living. More attuned, empowered living—*ultimate* living.

The Living Inside-Out Principles will help cultivate an awareness of the incredible power of your focused intention, develop a way to replace many of the destructive, self-sabotaging thoughts and self-limiting beliefs that hold you in bondage, and provide guideposts to choose again—and, in so doing, reclaim your innate power to consciously create your best life.

"The Inside-Out Philosophy™ is based on the universal premise that, as human beings, *we have within us an innate wisdom and capacity to transform our lives on any level,* be it accepting and loving ourselves, achieving our dreams (health, relationships, family, career, or finances), living with passion, or understanding our divine purpose."

— Eddie

Living Inside-Out Lessons from Chapter 1

- **All of the answers you search for lie within you.**
- **You have the innate wisdom and capacity to transform your life.**
- **Tap into your inner wisdom through prayer or meditation—access the gap.**
- **Become consciously aware of what you focus on in your life.**
- **Use your emotions/feelings as your compass.**
- **Know that you are 100% responsible for your perceptions and choices.**

2

Embracing Change from Within

"One of the biggest impediments to change is that we're unwilling
to let go of those things that are keeping us right where we are."

— Chris Waddell

Chris Waddell defied gravity one afternoon on a snowy mountain in his freshman year of college. While in Vermont with his brother and friends, they decided to do what they always did—ski their hearts out. A trained ski racer, Chris had been on snow skis since he was six years old living in Massachusetts. When he hit the ski hill that day, the last thing on his mind was that a change was about to find *him*.

"I don't remember the actual accident," Chris recalls. "It was a warm day, and we were just skiing and having fun, when my ski popped off in the middle of a turn. You think you'd remember the most significant moment in your life. But even though I was conscious, I was in shock."

Sometimes change is a choice from the get-go. But sometimes *later* becomes *sooner,* whether we planned it that way or not. And sometimes the necessity to change finds *us.*

A crisis can be a turning point or a crossroads that creeps up and pulls you down. At times, a crisis is unexpected, and at others, it arrives after whispering in your ear for a decade as you ignore the signals. I'm talking about the kind of changes that turn you inside out and ask how much you're

17

willing to risk to live the life you want. We often resist change. We're afraid of pain, challenge, or being consumed by hardship, failure, disappointment, or loss. We become good at rationalizing our circumstances and frustrations.

I never really knew how to define change until I met Chris.

"Everything happened very fast from the moment I fell—ambulance to the hospital, helicopter to another hospital, surgery, then two months in the hospital," Chris recalls.

Some changes go deep. They want something more from us. They compel us to take a giant leap of faith that we'll have another trapeze bar to grasp after we've let go of the first one. And those mid-air crises have nothing to do with mid-life and everything to do with surrender—and guts. And they force us into mid-air changes.

Define the Stakes

I had never really talked with anyone who was paralyzed as to how it happened. It was a nightmare for me to imagine, and the thought of a star athlete losing his mobility seemed to me a double tragedy and injustice. But, I was about to have my previously narrow assumption blown wide open by a man who lost everything in a split second.

After his accident, Chris barely got out of bed. He couldn't sit up on his own and when someone helped him, he suffered terrible dizziness. When he finally did get out of the bed, he couldn't sit up for more than an hour without getting a splitting headache. He couldn't dress himself … he couldn't walk.

All he could do was go within.

And in the process became stronger, even as his body wouldn't respond.

"I realized through the process that full recovery didn't necessarily mean walking again," he says. "Full recovery was what I experienced when I couldn't bring myself to indulge any of my negative thoughts. I couldn't indulge any depression. I couldn't allow myself to indulge in those emotions that might affect how I recovered physically. I frequently tell people that the period after my accident was the most important time in my life—though some of them find it hard to believe."

So here's the part where you think his athletics are over, right? You assume he went back, finished his studies, and forgot about his love of skiing. Not even close.

He went *back to college two months after his accident*, in the middle of a snowy February, to a place built on a *hill*. He didn't quit or resign himself to a more physically accessible environment to make life more manageable for him. Why?

"It doesn't sound that smart, I know, but for me it was absolutely the best decision I could have made because that's where my community was. That's where my friends and support system were, which meant I could then get better. In a lot of ways, getting better was about being with the people I loved," he says.

After returning to college Chris stunned everyone when he started ski racing—*disabled ski racing*. He continued on the college ski team and captained the team his senior year. Within two years of his accident, he'd made the disabled ski team. Upon graduation, he went to his first Paralympics Games in Albertville, France, which would become his springboard into an international competitive career. He picked up wheelchair racing along the way to enhance his training, and as he says, "That morphed into another sport." He competed in his first world championship wheelchair racing competition in 1994.

In 2004, after his *seventh* Paralympics, Chris retired with a total of 13 career medals.

However, his remarkable story of triumph doesn't end there. In October of 2009, Chris became the first paraplegic to reach the summit of Mount Kilimanjaro in Tanzania—Africa's highest mountain peak at 19,340 feet.

With a highly trained team, which comprised of his doctor, trainer, guides, a camera crew, and others, he took an important step toward gaining equality for people with disabilities. He gave the world an image that forced them to revisit what it meant to be disabled.

By using his arms, he wheeled himself up the steep and rocky terrain in a special four-wheeled cycle called a Bomba, a highly engineered four wheel mountain bike. The vehicle was driven entirely by Chris's arms and capable of taking on foot-high boulders.

As if he couldn't go any higher, in 2010, Chris was inducted into the Paralympic Hall of Fame.

He continues to defy gravity. He was confronted with a *grave* circumstance, and he defied it. Not because he's superhuman. Not because he's so different from you and me, but because he figured out the key to change: *Choice*.

"One of the most surprising things to me after the accident," notes Chris, "was realizing that could have been the beginning of tremendous depression and pain, and although I *didn't* know how things would turn out, I *did* know I could choose my reaction.

"I think so often people experience an event in their lives and they just react. They may be angry or upset or depressed. They may feel as if they aren't in control—but they *are* in control of how they react. It's amazing that *you do have a choice in how you want to react to change.*"

So, *how do you react to change?*

I'm not referring to ordering something new from the menu at your favorite restaurant, exploring another vacation spot, or getting an extreme makeover. Those kinds of changes don't challenge us to dig deep and confront ourselves when nobody's looking.

I'm not even referring to the bigger, more obvious changes of a move, new job, marriage, baby, empty nest, divorce or other loss, which psychologists call our top life stressors. We can usually find ways to live with such changes, wrestle with them, and cope without having to overhaul our ways, our habits, our attitudes, or thoughts.

But some changes go deep. They want something more from us. What kind of change am I referring to?

You know how you do certain things without thinking—on a subconscious level—and then repeat the same self-impeding pattern over and over again? For example, you get caught up in the same argument at every family gathering. Or, you get completely overwhelmed and go into self-destructive mode by overeating, drinking too much, or allowing your negative self-talk, limiting beliefs, and fears to overtake you.

When Chris shared his story, I was suddenly transported back to the farm where I grew up. In a split second, I was reminded of how I'd perceived my dad as the bad guy for all the frustration and resentment I'd carried well into my twenties. It's human nature to create stories that we carry for decades, unless we become aware and change them.

Although my own change process was very different from Chris's circumstances, the fundamental truth is the same. I too had a choice in how I wanted to react and create change.

Resistance is the Name of the Blame

Hot running water and a bathroom—two things I would have loved as a kid growing up on a mid-western cattle and hog farm in the mid '70s and '80s. Times were tough; my dad was a farmer and truck driver, my mom a waitress. I still remember my grandparents bringing boxes of food every month to help us out.

You might think I was used to farm life as a boy, but, to tell you the truth there were many aspects about it I didn't like. I hated that I had to boil a kettle of water every time I needed to take a bath. I hated that we heated the house with wood. On many cold winter mornings, I'd run to the living room to get dressed by the warmth of the stove.

My dad—my hero—was a good, hard-working man with a big heart. To this day, he hasn't changed much. He still wears blue jeans with pliers hanging from his belt, a button-down shirt, cowboy boots, and his straw cowboy hat. When I was a little guy, I wore jeans with pliers on my belt just like him. I walked like him in my own cowboy boots and trailed right behind him in his footsteps. I admired everything he did and how he did it.

But when I was about ten, I began to realize the other kids didn't live like us. No matter how hard I tried to fit in, I felt like an outcast. At least I created that *story*, which became the central theme of my early teen years. *Why do I have to live like this?* I complained. Resentment grabbed hold of me with a vice grip and didn't let go for more than fifteen years. Oddly enough, the target of my anger and resentment was my biggest hero—that hard-working man in the cowboy boots.

When I was a young teenager, my dad and I began to clash and my mom was caught in the middle. Looking back, I remember how much I wanted my life to change. I wanted him to change. I wanted my luck to change.

I had no idea how to change because I had no clue what change really was. I had yet to understand that we can't create positive, *lasting* change just by altering our environment. In order to change, I had to become consciously aware of how I wanted to react to my situation affecting my feelings about my dad. I could choose to switch my blame, shame, and resentment to openly receiving the gift that awaited me.

In my case, this gift was to rebuild my relationship with him, allowing dad to be my hero again but this time, in a realistic way. A "real" hero because he was a hero who was human, flawed like me. Real because I stopped wanting him to be perfect or different, and learned to accept him for who he was not who I wanted him (myself) to be.

We will likely not face the kind of life altering experience that Chris did—the way he turned a potential tragedy into another opportunity for growth and unexpected (unimaginable) potential.

Most of us will be confronted with the stuff that I grew up with—the family struggles, the limiting beliefs that emerged from dynamics with a parent or someone whose approval we craved, and the years of self-doubt and fence-sitting that makes us want to curl up and give up.

Choice is what saved Chris on that ski slope when he couldn't move his legs.

Choice is what saved my relationship with a dad who I had all wrong.

Choice is what gets us out of abusive situations and into our safety.

Choice is what turns our lives around when our health says so.

Choice is a split second decision—and a lifelong journey.

It's what can spell the difference between joy and despair, freedom and suffering, self-acceptance and self-rejection, life and death of life.

We have not been taught to choose … or how to make a better choice. Our lives are a steady drumbeat of go-go-go achievements, multi-tasking, worry, speed, fatigue and that awful sense that we haven't done a thing with our time. And then, one day, you make a different choice. Either you come up with the idea to change or a choice presents itself and you say yes … or not now.

Look for the Gift

"It's paradoxical in a lot of ways," Chris says. "I lost the use of my legs, but that event pushed me to do things I never would have done before. I never would have been the best in the world at *anything*. But as a mono ski racer, I became the best in the world, and that's a *huge gift*.

"You may think of somebody who's become disabled and believe that person's life is limited. But life is anything but limited. It depends completely on your perception of your situation and your willingness to see the possibilities.

"I faced the greatest requirement for change in my life. I had to save my life—a life in which, prior to the accident, I recognized no limitations, one in which I could *do* and *be* whatever I wanted limited only by my imagination. I now consider the time after my accident to be the most defining. It became a transformation that allowed me to rise higher than I'd ever thought possible."

Learning how to look for the gift is quite different from *trying to find it*. When I searched for the lesson, it eluded me. I fought myself. I felt frustrated by the timing. I even became angry at God, asking "What more do you want from me." And all of this only made me feel more desperate to know the answer—before I even figured out the question.

Looking for the gift means to open your heart to receive the unexpected lessons awaiting you. As Marcel Proust wrote, "seeing with new eyes." This is a key to living inside-out.

Chris explained that change actually found him. "I had to decide what I was going to do with it. Although I originally thought recovery meant walking, I had to change within myself to understand that recovery meant becoming healthy with or without the use of my legs."

Be Open to Change

I've often tried to imagine how I would react if I were in the same situation. I'd probably experience great anger, fear, and resentment. If he did too, how could he move on, make such a powerful transformation, and accomplish so much so quickly?

"You learn a lot about yourself in crisis," he explains philosophically. "It's an opportunity. Sometimes the bigger the problems, the faster you change because change has found you and you must embrace it. However, the little problems—the ones not immediately life-threatening—seem to drain you of your energy and efficiency. *Being open to change* is one of the most difficult things we can master."

So whether we're going through a devastating divorce, a financial crunch, the loss of a job, or even a situation as devastating as Chris's, *we need to look for the possibilities and choose how we want to show up.*

Many of us limit ourselves by fear and the negative thoughts we allow to run through our minds. Instead, we can empower ourselves by looking within for the strength to overcome whatever obstacle we're up against.

Resisting change looks different for each of us. The recurring struggles or conflicts in our lives point to where we most resist change. So we can look at the situations in which we're feeling dissatisfied, wounded, anxious, irritated, or stuck to discover opportunities to break out of our ruts.

Most of us base our choices on emotions related to our past history rather than our mindfulness of the present. Are we making decisions on a conscious level or responding from an unconscious one?

Let Go of Fear, Surrender to Trust

When it came to his biggest goals, Chris learned to always let go and effectively surrender—not to the mountain in his case, but to the work he'd already done.

"As a competitive skier and to climb Mount Kilimanjaro, I had taught my body how to react. I had taught myself what I needed to do. The problem became that the more important I thought something was, the more difficult it was to let go," he recalls.

"In trying to let go, my mind couldn't work quickly enough to keep up with my body. My body knew what to do, but if I stopped to think about each step, it took too much time and I effectively got behind.

"Surrender doesn't mean giving in to 'woe is me, the situation is too difficult, I can't handle it!' It's surrendering to 'I've done my work and now it's time for the performance.' Surrender isn't about giving up or resigning yourself to your fate. It's about the freedom to *trust yourself* and know you will rise above your challenges."

When we don't want to change, we can create a prison. In this perceived prison, we create rigid circumstances and boundaries for what is or isn't possible. We hope life will change, and if it doesn't, then we hope we'll win the lottery. It's like being on a deserted island and hoping for rescue instead of building a raft to save yourself. Hope is not action. Planning is not action. Worry is not action.

Chris says, "It's amazing how a constant state of worry can make us feel we're actually doing something—just by worrying. How much do we let our worrying consume our emotional energy and time? It's as if we say, 'I worry about that so I'm conscious of it.' But worry doesn't move the ball.

"Why do we prefer to worry about something rather than change it? Fear!

"We let our current situation become a comfort zone for us—even if the circumstances are bad. One of the biggest impediments to change is being unwilling or unable to let go of those things that keep us right where we are. For example, it's easy to stay in a bad relationship because, in most people's minds, having a bad relationship is better than no relationship at all—which logically makes no sense. Letting go represents 100% commitment to having what we want, but it also leaves us feeling naked— as if we have no defenses."

The risk doesn't lie in failing, because if we stay in one place, we will, of course, ultimately fail. The risk is in succeeding and *what that might mean*—to ourselves, to our friends and relatives. It's an unknown, and it's camouflaged with preconceived notions about success. Maybe we always sensed that success equaled isolation, loneliness, too much stress, responsibility, loss. For many people, success is far more frightening than failure. Letting go of worry and fear—and surrendering to trust in ourselves—empower us to initiate change.

Create Change that Lasts

Chris's trust in himself and his conscious focus intention not only helped him reframe his idea of what was possible after his accident, but also allowed him to compete soon afterward and rise to great heights. His conscious focus also allowed him to sustain the inner changes he made as a result of the accident.

Embracing change means becoming *consciously aware* of the choices we're making as we're making them and noticing when we fall into old patterns.

We can define the elements of *conscious sustainable change* this way:

- **Conscious**: Having an awareness of one's environment and one's existence, sensations, and thoughts
- **Sustainable**: Capable of being maintained over time
- **Change**: A transformation or transition from one state, condition, or phase to another

Conscious sustainable change isn't as elusive as we might perceive it to be. The key is to remain aware so we can operate out of choice, not subconscious programming. Chris offers his 5 Rs to help us make our changes sustainable, or lasting.

FIVE Rs FOR SUSTAINABLE CHANGE

1. **Have a *reason*.** Knowing *why* you want to create change helps you envision *how* that change will make you better.

2. **Have *reminders*.** Use sticky notes, index cards, or an accountability partner to keep your goal in your conscious mind at all times, thus creating momentum for change.

3. **Develop *resilience*.** Fight the urge to go back to old ways. Make a game out of it. Record what you're doing well to motivate you to go forward.

4. **Give yourself *recognition*** for accomplishments as well as any discomfort you're experiencing during this process. Both mean you're making progress.

5. ***Reward* yourself** for the steps you're making. Give yourself the incentive to focus on a reward while going through the discomfort. Create a similar motivator to preserve the change after you've achieved your initial goal.

The old, self-defeating habits and negative thoughts you want to change may involve your communication style, your waistline, your finances, or how you react to the rest of the world. Whatever they are, you already have what it takes within you to transform them and live the life of your dreams.

Remember, you are 100% responsible for your perceptions and reactions and how those drive your choices.

Chris's experience proves to me that any circumstance or event, no matter how traumatic, can be overcome and still allow us to succeed. It's all a matter of perception, perspective, purpose, and the power to choose.

"Living inside-out to me is the root of change because change doesn't happen unless it comes from within. It's about loving yourself first. When you recognize your own potential and seize your own internal power, you can accomplish anything."

— Chris Waddell

Living Inside-Out Lessons from Chapter 2

- You have a choice in *how you react* to change.

- Wanting security is one of the biggest impediments to change.

- Not accepting 100% responsibility for your own life is another big obstacle to change.

- Be open to see the unexpected lessons in life's challenging situations and receive their gifts.

- When you don't want to change, you create a prison of fear that keeps you stuck.

- Hoping and worrying are not action steps.

- Know *why* you want to create change. Purpose is powerful.

3

Be Present to Possibilities

"Nothing screams so loudly as our presence or lack of presence."

— Brian Biro

I finally realized that one of the hardest things about creating conscious sustainable changes in my life was also one of the simplest. That doesn't mean I should have understood it sooner, but rather that the concept of *presence* is difficult for most of us to grasp.

What do I mean by being *present?*

I figured this out only *after* I had spent all my waking hours either dwelling on something that had already happened, or worrying about something that hadn't yet happened. I realized how much of my life I was missing because I was too busy thinking about the past or future instead of actually living life in the present.

Think about it. How can someone get behind the wheel of a 2,000-pound vehicle and drive from point A to point B without any recollection of having stopped at all the red lights or followed the speed limit? How can people manage to work a 60-plus hour work week and still feel as if they're getting nothing done?

How is it we can talk a blue streak about the dream we want but fail to get even close to it? And then rationalize it as just a fantasy anyway?

Life isn't meant to be lived on autopilot or in a daze. We aren't here to ignore the possibilities and opportunities that come into our daily lives. We were never designed for living at half-mast. So why do so few people live the kind of life they dream of, a dynamic and rich life that invites profound and authentic connection, joy, vitality, vibrant health, and well-being regardless of circumstances?

Good question.

In all of my travels and interviews, one person in particular stood out in my mind with respect to this question. A guy who inspired me to think about the windows of life that I choose to open, close, or look through, and helped me understand how those choices—those windows—could shape the entire trajectory of my life.

Brian Biro is a transformational coach and international best-selling author of *Beyond Success!*. For the past 20 years, he has traveled the world teaching people to break through limiting beliefs, identify their passion, and clarify their purpose to reach their full potential.

Essentially, he transforms people's lives by teaching them to—are you ready for this?—seize their WOOs!

Your WOOs or *Windows Of Opportunity* are all around you, shut tight, waiting for you to jimmy the locks and open them. The only thing is ... you have to be *present* to be aware of them.

Being Fully Present

What's it like to be fully present? You've probably experienced times when you astonished yourself with your productivity. You might have felt this the first few weeks on a new job. In such a situation, you have something to prove, so you focus intently each day, being fully present in your work. This is what being present feels like. It's pure, focused intention. Everything flows.

But then something happens.

Your focus wanes. Your "presence" takes a little hiatus. And then a longer one. Is it a pattern? A habit? Your modus operandi?

Investors and financial advisors assert, "Past performance doesn't guarantee future results." But psychologists declare, "History is the best predictor of future behavior."

What do *you* think? Do you think change is *impossible* when it comes to personality but *possible* when it comes to habits? Does it depend on which habits and how long you've practiced them? Do you believe change is too hard if it requires you to think differently? Do you tend to fear change because it asks too much of you?

Brian has seen the many faces of change—and the many faces of resistance:

The retired person who never realized his potential.

The addict who tried every program, but always failed.

The person who lived in debt for so long, she forgot what it felt like to pay cash and became accustomed to feeling worthless. And countless other cases.

In every life of conflict and confusion and chaos, Brian witnessed people shifting, waking up to their limiting beliefs and the reality those beliefs had helped create. He inspired them to make new choices and remake their lives.

At the core of each change lay a shift in presence—from living in a distracted, complacent, isolated, and anxious state to living fully present. The starting point for changing your life, to living inside-out, is being present in this very moment.

And what does that mean? Think about these situations:

- How many conversations do you have with family members in which you're listening attentively and making eye contact, with your mind only on the present interaction? How often do you notice your mind wandering? Do you feel distracted?

- How many times a day do you actually sit down to eat a meal? How often do you stand at the counter, eat at your computer or in the car, or even forget to eat? How often do you realize you don't recall what you ate or if you ate lunch at all?

- Do you find yourself drifting off in thought while something else is going on around you?

Is it any wonder we don't notice the opportunities all around us and those that cross our path? We're not attuned to them because we aren't attuned to ourselves. We lose connection with ourselves intuitively and emotionally, and we live in a state of either expectation or regret. (More on that in chapter 4 when Lu Hanessian and I explore how and why we create the stories that hold us back.)

But we don't shift from distraction and disconnection to presence and mindfulness simply in one blink.

Brian suggests we start with *awareness*.

Notice your inclinations. Your habits. Your worries. How your anxieties take you off into a distant place where you spin your wheels. Pay attention to what you tell yourself, the way you react to others, the things that set you off, the fears that hold you back from opportunities you choose to reject instead of embrace.

The following Five Components of Awareness is what I use and provides questions to ask yourself in any situation to help you become more aware of what you're doing and why.

Five Components of Awareness

Be Aware of:

1. What is happening within me and the environment/world around me?
2. What emotional triggers (feelings) are igniting within me?
3. What choice am I about to make?
4. Why am I making that choice?
5. And finally, know that I can make a different choice—I can choose again.

We can confront issues only when we consciously choose to be aware of them. That's not to say we usually choose to be *un*aware. But when we're not fully present, we can't be fully aware either, so we make a choice without full awareness.

Choose Your Energy

Awareness takes focus, and focus requires intention. Focused intention creates a powerful energy. As I mentioned earlier, everything consists of energy, including people. This energy is not only the subatomic particles that make up our bodies, but a kind of connective energy.

As Brian explains, "Love-based emotions have extremely high vibrations. So if you keep yourself at a high level of positive emotions, you're maintaining a high level of energy. Gratitude has perhaps the highest vibration of any emotion. Ask the question 'what am I truly grateful for in my life right now?' That causes you to get out of the past and out of the future, and to be here right now with what you're presently grateful for."

When you're in a state of gratitude, fear can't find a foothold.

Your *energy vibration* of gratitude, for example, will allow you to become aware of the positive opportunities and people of a similar vibration that present themselves in your life. I never cease to be amazed by this dynamic phenomenon.

But how do we access that kind of dynamic power when we're riddled with self doubt and anxiety, when we feel powerless to change? Brian says, "*Fear is always about the past or the future.* It's either trying to avoid repeating something that filled you with a negative emotion earlier, or it's negatively anticipating something that hasn't happened yet.

"Fear of abandonment is not a fear that you're abandoned in the present moment, but a fear that you *will* be abandoned. Because in the present, there is no past, there is no future. Therefore, in the present, there is no fear.

Did you get that … *in the present, there is no fear.*

That's why being fully present *right where you are now* is so vital. If you focus on a bad event that did happen or might happen, you're stuck."

As we discussed, getting stuck is the easy part. We *all* get stuck at some point or another. But some of us do it deliberately. Call it procrastination, sitting on the fence, averting perceived risk, lowering the stakes. Or, avoiding our dreams so they can't disappoint us.

Yes, getting stuck is easy. By staying stuck—and accepting it as the only option—we're adept at coming up with all sorts of ways to rationalize our obstacles. All of them have to do with external variables we think caused our problems in the first place. That's *outside-in* thinking that keeps us cut off from ourselves and our possibilities.

How can we recognize that stuck place when our agendas are packed, life is overwhelmingly relentless in its demands, and we feel anything *but* stuck? Miserable, yes, but stuck? We're always *doing* something, aren't we?

But are we moving in the direction we want to go? Do we even *know* where we want to go? And can we conquer the obstacles that block our way?

Our internal obstacles can appear as addictions—even the socially acceptable kind like overspending or overworking. Feeling blocked can manifest in the form of unhealthy and chronic anger. It can rear its head as procrastination, relationship conflicts, loneliness or isolation, lack of self-care and illness. It can be signaled by any form of negative emotion that holds us back from our fully present self and our fully satisfying life.

On the other hand, gratitude, joy, compassion, and giving are born of love. They propel us forward to reach higher while concentrating our concerns and thoughts on the needs of others.

But who can be positive all the time? No one!

Go easy on yourself. Emotions come and go like the wind, be aware of yours and give yourself permission to let them go. Remember, it's not about perfection; it's about progress.

Navigate Your Obstacles

Realizing you have the power to choose doesn't mean you jump for joy if a tree falls on your house, but it does give you the opportunity to be grateful that you're alive and your family is unharmed.

Remember, your focused intention is not what happens but *how you respond* to what happens—how you choose to *be*. You can choose if you will to react with anger or other negative emotions in any given moment, or act with gratitude and kindness to those around you.

Truth is we tend to focus on the negative. It takes conscious persistence to *choose* to focus on the positive. We then begin to realize that all those old fears, hurts, and negative emotions have less and less power over our choices or (ultimately) our lives.

"To really understand how this works, imagine you're a five-year-old child again and you just got a brand new bike," explains Brian. "At first, you're not very good at riding that bike. You're wobbly and unsure, but you're doing it. You're off and you're riding that bike. Suddenly, right on the sidewalk in front of you is a great big rock. What does the five year old look at? The rock! What does the front tire hit? The rock! It's almost like you're *drawn* to the rock. You can't help yourself.

"Now, imagine it's several years later. You've gained confidence and experience, and you've become a whiz on your bike. Suddenly you encounter a much bigger rock. Where do you go? Where do your eyes focus? Around the rock. Over the rock. You pass by that rock like it's not even there. Because what you've done is shift your focus from the obstacle to the freedom, from the obstacle to the breakthrough beyond. You don't give the rock a second glance, and therefore it doesn't present any kind of obstacle."

It's like concentrating so hard on *not* doing something that you wind up doing it anyway. Focusing on what you *don't* want to happen often brings it about.

For many of us, when we hear this we are filled with anxiety. That's *terrible*, I'm going to bring about all these awful things that I don't want to happen to me or the people I love! But remember this isn't a silly superstition like "step on a crack and you'll break your mother's back." It's not that we'd punish ourselves and our loved ones with a crazy spell. It's a scientific fact that our brains act like *radar*. That means they seek out in our external worlds what we create on our internal screens. (I'll discuss with brain expert Doug Bench how our brains do this in chapter 7.)

Brian assures us that this fact provides valuable information. "Once we become aware of being fully present to our WOO," he says, "we increase the positive effects, and before we know it, we're zipping around boulders the size of golf carts."

See how this opens up tremendous possibilities. Once you know and experience this, you'll never view your situation as futile again. You'll understand how much control you have over your life. You'll see that when you decide what you want, focus on it, and become present to your opportunities, your brain zeroes in on how to realize them for yourself.

"*You* are the one who decides whether or not you give up," Brian says. "Nobody can decide to give up for you. *You* are the one who decides if you're going to live life with eagerness and willingness—or lethargy and unwillingness. You choose, and because you can choose at any time, the door to change is always open. You just have to be aware of the opportunities and willing to seize them."

Answer Your Compelling Why

When I began my own search for change and personal growth, I knew I wanted things to be *better,* but I didn't know how to make them better. More so, I didn't know what *better* looked or felt like. What I discovered— and what Brian helps people understand—is that the question of *how* is almost irrelevant.

The most powerful question to ask is *why? Why do I want things to be different?*

Brian Biro uses these three points to help people navigate the breakthrough process and learn to live from the inside-out:

THREE ESSENTIALS FOR A BREAKTHROUGH

1. **Be crystal clear on your compelling *why*.** When your why is strong enough, you'll find the how. First discover your *purpose*—that's the why. Why do you want certain things, and strive toward specific goals?

We may think we have too many obstacles against us that make change impossible. But we just need to be *open to the possibility*, then change can happen instantly.

Some call this their *aha!* moment. That's the second they grasp the idea they can control and change anything they want about their lives.

2. **Your past does not equal your future, so focus on the present.** Not believing you *can* change creates one of your biggest obstacles. Let this sink in: whether you're 15 or 75, you can make positive and lasting changes in your life.

   Granted, it's difficult to get past that internal skepticism, especially if you've had a lot of negative or traumatic experiences. In fact, some of us become so discouraged we lose faith in our own judgment and ability. Change is possible if you focus on the *present,* regardless of where you are today or how long you've lived in your current circumstances. *If you stay in the present and believe you can change, you will.*

3. **Clearly focus on what you want, not what you *don't* want.** A big challenge to breaking through our limiting beliefs is habitually focusing on what we *don't* want. We worry and stress over what *might* happen instead of concentrating on the outcome we want. Or we focus on the obstacle, increasing it to immense proportions. No matter what we say we want, if our focused intention isn't on the outcome we desire, it won't happen.

   What you focus on, you create in your life. This doesn't mean you just take what you get; you decide what you want and give it your attention, trusting you'll receive it. As you tap into your innate wisdom, opportunities and resources will be revealed that you weren't aware were possible.

One of my biggest struggles was figuring out and understanding my purpose. In the process, I worked at various jobs on quite an amazing roller coaster ride. I was an advertising account exec, a waiter and restaurant manager, a network marketing distributor, an operations officer for various nonprofits, and even a construction project manager. Many of these jobs I took out of necessity—to make a living. None fulfilled me. I was driving myself crazy. I yearned to find my purpose, but had no clue how or where to look. I thought my purpose was "out there," as if I was on a big game safari hunt and I'd see it as I came around the next bend in the road—big as an elephant!

Brian says, "The best nugget of truth I can give to help you find your purpose is that you're the only one who knows what your purpose is. No one can give it to you. It's not outside of you. It's in you *right now*. You've just got to access it. Understanding that one fact can make a big difference because people often look outside instead of within.

"You may think that your purpose consists of something you do—like a job. But it's not about winning fame and fortune or receiving accolades and awards. While those may arise from following your purpose, they're not markers, evidence, or hallmarks of it.

"Your ultimate purpose is something you *are*—inspired from the inside, humble in the face of your talents and skills, open to lifelong growth, willing to make the most of the time we have, interested in using your gifts and energies to creating change and possibility for others. Purpose isn't measured by comparisons and competition with others. You don't have to be Mother Teresa to care for others.

"Purpose isn't the engine of our life; it's our fuel."

Get Fueled

"Think back to a time when you felt nearly unstoppable, filled with energy, focus, and excitement," Brian says. "What, specifically, were you doing at that moment? What were you passionate about? What would be the one thing you would do if you knew you couldn't fail—if you had nothing in your way and no one squinting at you in doubt and judgment?"

If an answer doesn't come to you right away, stay with this thought process to tap into the feeling that charges you with the most energy. Don't dismiss or gloss over this part of the process; continue to ask questions. Know that the purpose you're passionate about lies within you. Let it surface. You may even dream about it tonight. Or next week.

One reason we tend to fuss about forever trying to find our purpose is because we're afraid that, if we find it, we might fail at it. We simply don't believe we can accomplish our dreams, so we shrug them off with "I don't know" rather than ask the hard questions.

The solution? Ask the questions and be courageous enough to get quiet with them until some answers begin to appear. Write down what comes to you. Don't judge yourself or censor your thoughts; that's just fear creeping up on you. (In chapter 18 I've provided the *Six Steps to Clarity and Focus* that will assist in this process.)

Incorporate sitting with such questions into your daily routine. Develop a process to evaluate where you are on the path and what steps you need to take to move forward. Don't let days or weeks float by; that time is lost forever. Stay present and purposeful in your life. Then you will be open to endless possibilities.

It's too easy to think you can't be more fully present because you don't have time. So instead of trying to do everything, just *focus on your next step*. This creates momentum for your spirit to grab hold of and run with. Momentum can't build as long as you erode your spirit with lack of confidence. How does this manifest? By looking at others and judging ourselves by how they live, what they do, where they call home, how they dress, and who they know.

Brian sees comparison as a potentially destructive force. "Stop comparing. Comparison is a need of the ego—a destructive need of the ego. We want to measure ourselves through comparison. And when we perceive that we don't measure up to someone else, it shakes the foundation of our belief in ourselves. We feel less than—and it's pure perception on our part, not reality. Comparison breaks down and destroys.

"Most of us have been raised with a definition of success that says there's only one winner. But true success is peace of mind that comes from *knowing* you're focusing on the effort you've put in and not the effect of that effort in the eyes of others. It's the difference between striving to be the best, which is all about comparison, and focusing on *giving* your best."

Giving. Now that's a word we rarely hear when we're talking about success. And yet, that's the most important key to breaking through.

Embrace the Breakthrough

Brian is often called "America's Breakthrough Coach" because he's well known for having his participants—teens to grandparents—break through a one-inch wooden board as a symbol of a personal breakthrough. He uses this tangible prop because the board represents a limit, a fear, an obstacle, a habit, or a doubt. But force doesn't break the board—just as brute force doesn't make problems go away.

"No, the way you break the board is not through force but through *focus*—and not focus on the *board*, but on *moving beyond* the board," he explains.

In our daily living, the way to get beyond obstacles, fears, and limits is by directing our focused intention on what we want regardless if it may seem impossible right now. We focus on something *beyond* our immediate circumstances. In essence, we harness a kind of presence by focusing on something just ahead of us.

This may sound like a paradox—focusing on the future in the present moment—but it's about seeing ourselves *past the obstacle or the fear* and deeply *living in that moment right now by realizing how it looks and feels and sounds*. It's a living energy that we are tapping into, and in that energy, we discover and harness our power. This concept is really a combination of the wisdom you'll glean in the next few chapters, so, I can't emphasize its importance enough.

We live in a highly competitive, distracted, high-pressure world. We're being pulled in so many different directions that it's commonplace to feel overwhelmed. Life is filled with work demands, child-rearing, issues with aging parents, their health issues or our own. We're constantly maintaining a home, exercising our body, getting needed rest—to name a few. That doesn't include fun activities such as keeping up with friends, going to concerts or movies, being involved in a sport, and so on.

We can easily become frustrated because we believe we're only marginally average at any task instead of doing any one thing well. We become task-oriented, and in turn, gauge everything in our lives by those tasks. Are they started? Are there more? Have they been done well? Who noticed? Do I get paid extra? Did someone else do more? What more can I do? ... Whew!

With this line of thinking, it's easy for the underlying message to be *I give up*.

As creatures of habit, it takes a great deal of focused intent to create sustainable change. Why? Because we anticipate something will go wrong, even expect that it will. And when it does, even if we're upset about it, we may feel strangely comforted by having predicted that outcome.

But Brian offers a nugget of wisdom that I have taken to heart. He says, "You need time to recover from the hectic pace of life. Make sure there's a little time in your day, and it doesn't have to be much—perhaps three minutes in the morning and three minutes at night—when you allow yourself to let go of the world. Allow yourself *to enter a recovery stage*.

"During this time, you'll find that you're fresh, you're alive, and your most creative thoughts will surface. You won't have to force them. They'll just come to you. It's perhaps the most important practice to incorporate on a daily basis."

When you throw a pebble into a pond, the ripples don't go from the outside in. They go from the inside out. Their energy radiates in waves, and those waves arrive at the shore and then bounce back—all from the tiniest pebble. We each have the power to choose when and where to toss a rock into our own pond. As Brian says, "No matter what has transpired in the past, you can change in the present and thus open your future to limitless possibility."

To harness that limitless possibility, let's recognize how we keep ourselves from living inside-out. In the next chapter, Lu Hanessian and I will shine a revealing light on the nature of our self-impeding beliefs, paving a path for living our authentic life by knowing our truth.

"Living inside-out is about being present, right here right now. This is the beginning where we tackle everything—limiting beliefs, fears, breakthroughs, clarity of purpose."

— Brian Biro

Living Inside-Out Lessons from Chapter 3

- When in the present, there is no past, no future, no fear.

- When you focus on an obstacle, you grow that obstacle.

- When you focus on your goal beyond the obstacle, the obstacle becomes insignificant.

- Knowing your passion leads to discovering your purpose.

- Discovering your purpose leads to endless possibilities.

- The quality of questions you ask yourself can determine the quality of your life.

4

Know Your Truth

"What is the effect of limiting ourselves in love, joy, in living with heart, purpose, and vitality? The effect is not just that we are shut down, but that we are shut out. A self-limiting belief is not an invitation; it's a rejection slip."

— Lu Hanessian

Alright, so if we can choose to "seize our windows of opportunity" in order to actually create changes in our lives, why do we make this process so difficult? I mean, if change is just a matter of choice and choice is just a matter of overcoming our fears and fear of change is just a story we tell ourselves ... then what's the roadblock?

Fear may be a story we tell ourselves, but it's a *doozie*.

The way we "see" the world around us depends on our story. That means, the way we deal with failure or success, our relationships, our health, our money, every area of our lives, depends on ... our *story*.

For a more in-depth look into how our stories can create blocks to our growth, I reached out to acclaimed author and award-winning columnist Lu Hanessian, whose unique and profound insight into how and why "we tend to derail ourselves in spite of our best intentions" opened my eyes further.

"In a sense, our story is our script, that narrative in our minds—voices from the past, the culture, popular opinion, perceived fears of the future— all comprising the collective voice that tends to drown our own out so we can barely hear it," explains Lu.

43

A veteran journalist, former NBC anchor, and Discovery Health Channel host, Lu is an innovative parent educator and author of acclaimed book *Let the Baby Drive: Navigating the Road to New Motherhood* and *Joyride*. She's the founder of Parent2ParentU, an online integrative parent education series, as well as the founder of one of my favorite new companies WYSH—Wear Your Spirit for Humanity—WearYourSpirit.com, that celebrates our human spirit through empowering phrases, like ... "Know Your Story."

Knowing our story—and embracing *our truth*—is not a task. Nobody puts that on a to-do list! Lu says, "It's one of the reasons so many of us find it easier to remain stuck in our ruts than to muster the courage to blaze new trails. Let's face it, sometimes, we just prefer the status quo. But we can't grow with the status quo."

How Our Stories Get Written

One of the key points Lu makes is that our stories drive our conflicts. That is, she says, our old wounds and unresolved stories determine "where we're going to get stuck" in our lives.

Make sense? It reminded me of one of the old stories I use to play out. As a young boy who thought his dad was to blame for all that was wrong, I focused on everything I wished I could have and kept comparing myself to everyone else who I thought lived where the grass was greener. I got stuck in this mindset for years.

Sure, we all know people who carry on despite harboring memories of childhood struggles, but I didn't just harbor a *memory* of feeling deficient and poor; I had created a whole window on the world that affected how I saw myself and others, the choices I made, and the difficult relationships and work experiences I unconsciously chose as well.

But, as Lu points out, our conflicts are not necessarily the kind between two people who don't agree, but the kind that *live in each of us*.

"Our *own inner war* between growth and gridlock, between the love we yearn for but keep at arm's length, between knowing our strengths and gifts and not using them," explains Lu.

"These conflicts are often multi-generational. This is not just a matter of genes, but *how these family roles are learned and mirrored* from one generation to the next in our family scripts."

What's more, if we go back in our developmental thought process we can typically trace the experience or event in which we first learned the limiting belief that we now hold. The majority of these limiting beliefs were constructed in our earliest years.

Many of the people who have had a profound influence on our lives—including our parents, grandparents, friends, coaches, and teachers—also unknowingly instilled a kind of *doubt* in our minds about our own potential. Ask anyone about the obvious messages they heard growing up and most people can recall them pretty quickly. Those words of warning, the well-meaning and not-so-well-meaning criticisms like *"You can't have it all."*

Some were shaming. *You're crazy! You're just wasting your time! You'll never make that much money! You don't have the talent or brains for that!*

Some were fearful for our success, and tried to protect or even prevent us from becoming too "big" and unwittingly squash our vision and the guts to pursue it.

Some were from physical, emotional, and/or sexual abuse.

"Some of our old scripts are dramas, some are mysteries, others are tragedies," Lu says. "Regardless of the brighter days we may have had along the way, all of us have known loss and suffered disappointment, and some have experienced deep betrayals of trust and security. We've witnessed the failures and successes of those around us, and we've literally taken mental notes.

"When we are young, we internalize our painful experiences, *the pain of a distant or absent or critical or unpredictably hostile, even overprotective parent*, as a kind of emotional blueprint. We physically and emotionally learn to shut down in defense. There's a neurochemistry of shame, of fear, of resistance. As the years pass, we tend to re-live our old, unhealed wounds in the roles we play out with others, the situations we unknowingly create—even if we know, intellectually, that we want something different. They are familiar. And, in that way, they feel safe."

What were *your* powerful limiting messages and the stories you created out of them? It's not an easy question, but it may be one of the most important you'll ever answer. As you recall these messages, and begin to decipher them, you start to uncover clues to your limiting beliefs—your stories. You will then begin to realize how those beliefs have driven and shaped everything you've done—or haven't done—in your life.

Our stories actually represent our own mythologies dressed up as truth. The kind of stories that hold us back from living our best lives.

Lu's brilliant insights into our limiting beliefs and how they can affect both adults and children have truly inspired me. While many experts tend to focus on the how-to, Lu explains *why all of the quick fixes and formulas* we attempt to apply to our lives fall short in spite of our best intentions.

Finding Clues to Our Stories

I've titled the forth principle *Know Your Truth* because most of us live our lives never really knowing ourselves. We'll never find the truth we seek "out there" because it lies within us. All the knowledge in the world won't reveal our truth if our stories block the way. We must look within ourselves. But *where*, exactly? We've created some pretty complicated internal landscapes.

Lu is optimistic however in that she says, "Clues pop up everywhere, from our reactions to our *in*action. We don't need an elaborate ritual or a month off to figure out our truth. If we can become witnesses to our struggles, she says, we can see *patterns of thinking* and reacting that tell us where our blocks are."

"Behind every fear, doubt, anxiety, struggle, conflict, hot button, outburst, rut, disappointment, or fall from grace lies a story," she explains. "Behind every story is a defense we've built internally. We hold ourselves hostage with many of these stories and spend our whole lives buying into falsehoods and fantasies just to keep ourselves from knowing our truth."

This rings so true for me. So you're thinking, why wouldn't we just shake these stories off and write better ones?

Lu explains that we've *practiced* our stories—our beliefs, perceptions, and defenses—for years, and we've learned to react in specific ways. Practice doesn't make perfect, after all! At least not with those things that hinder us.

"In a very real sense, our biography becomes our neurobiology, since our minds and brains are directly affected by our relationships, from the time we're born, and even in the womb."

And since our biographies are all different, we react differently to even the most innocent situations. "Why does one person become enraged after being cut off in traffic whereas someone else might feel victimized, even guilty for driving poorly? Why would one parent chastise her three year-old for his paint mess while another parent sees a budding artist?" asks Lu.

Or why would one person forgive infidelity while another seeks revenge?

Lu says our stories grow out of:

- past experiences that shaped our sense of self, security, and perceived power
- long-standing family messages about love, fear, power, and loss
- internal conflicts and early unmet needs
- unhealed emotional wounds
- fears of those painful feelings resurfacing
- defenses we build to avoid experiencing those feelings
- (mis)perceptions of ourselves and others that we develop as a result of those fears and defenses

Lu emphasizes, "If we want to change our behavior, habits, or thinking, it helps to realize that our stories—or *interpretations of events, circumstances, people's actions, and our own motivations are rarely anchored in reality.*"

When we begin to "connect the dots," as Lu says, we realize how we've held ourselves back from our full potential—out of fear, self-doubt, or a concern for what others might think.

The way we see ourselves and the world around us, relates directly to our stories. For us to live authentic lives as our true selves, we must know what these stories are about and *recognize the hold they have on us*. Only then can we begin to release their power and truly make way for change.

My Own Internal Process

Sometimes a painful story might have had such a profound effect on us that making peace with it is a release on the inside.

When I was five my brother Robert died from complications during birth. As you can image, this was a tremendously traumatic experience for the entire family. I remember waking up at home and going into the living room to find my aunt Virginia on the sofa sleeping because mom and dad went to the hospital to have the baby. Although I didn't quite understand what was happening, I remember going to the hospital to see him and the baptism before he died, and then the funeral home and services at church. I was devastated, I cried and cried.

For nine months there was anticipation that I would have a little brother or sister to play with, that I was the big brother and who would have to help take care of this new addition to our family. There was much excitement.

Growing up in the country, I didn't have a lot of kids to play with, and with the loss of my brother, although I didn't know it at the time, I felt alone and abandoned.

It wasn't until I was well in my 30s that I realized how this experience from my childhood was affecting my relationships. I was constantly looking for a relationship that would rescue me from these subconscious feelings. And, my own insecurity kept playing out in behaviors of neediness (I needed a relationship) and of self-sabotage because internally I always felt that the relationship would end—*I would be abandoned*.

What I came to realize is that I was living in my "story" and not my "truth." The story I created when my brother died was that I was abandoned and was left alone—that everyone would abandon me and that I would always be alone.

These limiting beliefs, negative self-talk, and *perceived fears* literally controlled my life for decades.

But what was my "truth?"

The truth was, yes, my brother died; however, I was never abandoned or alone. I was surrounded by loving parents and our family. And, although I did play by myself a lot, I actually enjoyed it and had cousins and friends that I played with too. However, because I was living out my story and not grounded in my truth, my *story scenario* played out in every relationship I had.

How to Make Sense of Our Stories

Alright, so we can't just press the delete button and move on, free of our stories. Nor would it be a good idea to do so. Lu and I addressed how valuable our stories are to us; each one offers important messages and lessons. How do we make sense of our stories?

We hear a great deal about *overcoming* self-limiting beliefs, but Lu offers unique insight into what exactly these beliefs are trying to limit and whether or not those limits are self-impeding or self-preserving.

"Self-limiting beliefs act as a form of control, an expression of our fear, like riding the brakes when we don't have to. We've long believed we *need* these brakes. Our thoughts and beliefs aren't simply a way of maintaining control, but they're part of *who we think we are*—even if we're dissatisfied with ourselves."

Our self-impeding beliefs are those beliefs that tend to hinder us in our lives, in ways that aren't very obvious to us or less apparent over time.

STORY GUIDELINES

Lu offers a number of ways that stories show up in our lives. Here are her "story guidelines," the most common kinds of stories that perpetuate our pain:

- **The Recurring Conflict:** You may discover this by looking for patterns in your life—recurring conflicts in relationships, recurring types of painful relationships, repeated problems with debt, health, weight, marriage, kids, jobs/bosses, and so on. The pattern has a story behind it.

- **The Roadblock:** This kind of story blocks your path, potential, and purpose. It tells you what you *can't* have and why—although the reasons aren't rational. It tells you to stay where you are. It says you *can't do* what your heart longs for or you *don't deserve* it.

- **The Label:** You acquire many of your labels as a child, a process that continues into adulthood through your experiences. For example, you may have been labeled a *fighter,* a *black sheep,* a *control freak.* Such labels constitute signals of stories at work on your psyche, creating more of the same in your life and current circumstances.

- **The Contradiction:** For example, let's say you're a successful business person who can't find love, a physician who smokes, an educated person who doesn't follow proper nutrition, a professional leader whose spouse treats you like a child at home, or a professional athlete who chokes on the winning shot. Any of these conflicts point to a chasm between your demonstrated story and your true self.

- **The Pretty Book Cover:** You may have an unconscious story *behind* the conscious one that you created as a "book cover" to disguise the incongruent pages inside. If so, you're not alone. Many people want to create the illusion of perfect lives and families, but within the cheery exterior, they hide deep rifts and problems—and shame.

- **The Rationalization:** To avoid reality, **you might create** illusions, or even *delusions, I could've been a doctor if I'd wanted to.* Fantasies often feel safer than the hard work of persevering.

- **The ShouldaCouldaWoulda.** You might create a story to punish yourself repeatedly. *If I'd only chosen this over that, or done this rather than that.* Regret becomes sludge in the engine that stalls you if you fixate on the imaginary idea that your life could have been different except for this one incident, person, wrong turn, or mistake. This story creates a *self-imposed roadblock.*

KNOW YOUR TRUTH | 51

Self-limiting beliefs can be deeply ingrained. Even if they don't totally destroy our relationships, our finances, or our health, they can erode our joy, our purpose, our dreams—our very reason for getting up in the morning and making the most of our time.

Don't Wait to Discover the Whole Truth

Lu believes choosing isn't the *final* step but rather the *first* one—the one that sets the tone for a journey of choosing throughout life.

"The key to living inside-out," she says, "lies in discovering how much of our lives we actually live consciously and how much we don't. No judgments. No regrets. At the heart of everything is choosing whether we want to make the unconscious part conscious. And then, what do we do with that? There's a distinction between *wanting* and *choosing*. And there is also a myth that once we choose, everything swiftly clicks into position."

How much do we live embracing perceived reality and our flaws versus speaking and living our truth? It dawned on me that without the awareness to live from the core of our truth, we *can't* make the kind of change Chris Waddell so bravely made in the days after his accident. He became acutely aware of how much he wanted to live. And in that awareness, he decided to live fully and not become a bystander in his own life. This message was pivotal for me—one I had to explore if I was to share my Inside-Out Philosophy™ with people in search of their own ultimate truth.

So I asked Lu how we can ever discern our *truth* if our story is all we've ever known.

"It's difficult to become aware of the very things we *don't want* to be aware of," Lu admits. "Such as how much a particular sore spot in our past prevents us from feeling truly loved and valued. *Our stories become our filters through which we perceive the world.*"

The question is not why we ever had to feel pain or get hurt in the first place (when the story was created)—that's part of being human—but, she says, "whether we choose to let ourselves *stay in that state* of being guarded, angry, resentful, or worried." Do we have the power to transcend those hurts in order to fully live our lives? Absolutely.

Are we willing to tap into that power where our story lives? Sometimes, we are not. As long as we are aware of that," Lu says, "we can make an honest choice and live with it. That's another way to know our truth. It's not always about lifting the veil and making a 180 shift."

Becoming Aware of Our Dreams

Yes, it's possible to live our entire lives without ever becoming aware of these beliefs, and, therefore, without ever taking steps to change them. That's how we unknowingly limit the vitality, the happiness, the peace, the success we can experience and, in turn, share with others.

Lu shared an example of a frustrated, weary, 40-something woman whose mother had never lived her dreams. When she recalled as a teenager witnessing her mother's emotional crisis in her mid-40s, the woman had a stunning realization. The way her mother had placed a ceiling and lived with regret had made a profound impression on this woman. To her amazement, she realized she'd created the same scenario for herself—at the same time of her life.

"It's not uncommon to feel guilty about surpassing our own parents' comfort zones," says Lu. "Many of us hold ourselves back from all that we can be in an unconscious identification with a parent who was afraid to be too happy, too peaceful, too successful."

When we're at odds with ourselves, we're effectively stuck—with limiting beliefs being only part of the problem.

Shining a Light on Where We Get Stuck

Lu points out a powerful clue to discerning our own limiting beliefs: *Our own judgments and criticisms of others are a mirror of what we dislike and reject in ourselves.* The more negative our reaction, the deeper the wound in us.

In psychological terms, it's called projection. Carl Jung referred to our shadow self. In really visual terms, Lu says it's "like playing hot potato with the stuff we don't like in ourselves." This is fantastic clue, she says, because we now have something on which to shine a light. But she goes further to say—and I think this is a huge revelation—the *limiting* we do to ourselves is *more t*han simply holding ourselves back or down.

"I think of self-limiting beliefs as self-*rejecting* beliefs," says Lu. "If you think of it, *what is the effect* of limiting ourselves from love, from joy, from living with heart, purpose, and vitality? The effect of it is not just that we are shut down, but that we are shut *out*. A limiting belief is not an invitation; it's a rejection slip. By carrying these beliefs with us, we are, in effect, rejecting our own growth. Rejecting our own well-being. Rejecting our own truth."

Every once in awhile, you hear something that makes you want to write it on the walls and shout in from the rooftops. This is one of those *a-ha!* moments for me.

This is exactly what I had experienced with my dad. For the years that focused all of my attention on what I perceived my dad was doing wrong, I was stuck. I was stuck in making him wrong. In reality, I was so unhappy with myself and I had no outlet but to project it on my dad.

As much as we wish it were, life isn't perfect. Especially during our teenage years, many of us blame our parents (for everything). I can recall the times that I was so nasty towards my dad, so desperate for my life to change I was blinded of the truth.

But the truth is, in retrospect, I was very fortunate. Yes, the fact was that the lack of money was the constant drum beat in our family and it just seemed to get louder and louder. It drowned out most everything else, and from it I created stories that I played out for decades. However, like many parents do, mine made sacrifices and went without many times to provide for me. My dad would work to find other loads to haul with his eighteen wheeler and my mom would pick-up extra shifts as a waitress. They did the best that they could.

My parents are very loving people, and over the years, I can't tell you the countless times I've experienced people falling in love with my dad and mom. They are so down to earth and have an open heart for everyone they meet.

My dad and I have learned to create some safe boundaries—we don't talk about politics, religion, and couple of other topics that will quickly head us in the wrong direction. And he still drives me crazy, because I'm a planner and he has no idea how the day will unfold. However, I've discovered the many ways in which we are alike.

The little guy in cowboy boots grew up with a relentless determination to achieve his goals, hard headed at times, a persistent attitude to do whatever it takes, a heart as big as Texas ... just like my dad.

This is the truth—my truth—that I was missing for so many years.

Make a Shift to Empathic Thinking

Isn't it amazing the number of insidious ways in which self-limiting beliefs can be transmitted over time? The question is, what can we do with this information once we realize what's occurring? Lu suggests making a shift from "defensive thinking to empathic thinking." Getting to know ourselves from the inside-out, she asserts, takes "great empathy." We can't nurture positive feelings when we berate ourselves for our perceived weaknesses and inadequacies. Rather we should embrace *forgiveness* for ourselves and those who we feel betrayed us.

As a regular self-empathy practice, Lu offers the following suggestions:

- **Get to know your themes**, your hot buttons, your sore spots, and old wounds. "This knowledge isn't a red flag; it's an open door," says Lu.

- **Notice your reactivity traits** *in times of stress*. Do you fight or run—or freeze? Do you turn inward or lash out? Do you overeat, overexert, overwork? Ask good questions of yourself that don't judge, but rather inquire.

- **Listen for the "*yes, but*" in your mind**. Understand this is your *story* talking loud and clear, trying to keep the truth out of reach.

- **Look for patterns**. Notice how certain negative reactions and beliefs repeatedly show up in your partnerships, your work, your parenting.

- **Follow the circuitry of your belief.** Become an *observer* of yourself from the inside-out. Trace your internal judgments to their origins.

Once we can understand how our stories have shaped our perceptions and choices, we start to feel less tied to them, less defined by them. "They begin to loosen their grip on us. We get used to reaching within ourselves for answers instead of rejecting ourselves as our own expert witness," she assures.

Turning Wounds into Wisdom

We're generally *not* taught to see the value of mistakes. Instead, we learn to cover them up, to pretend we have it all together when we don't. So, we may feel ashamed and guilty about our shortcomings and perceived failures. But there's profound value to be found in our mistakes and a purpose for our flaws, as Lu explains. "When we pretend we're not flawed, we easily slip into blame. We can't be tolerant of other people's flaws if we recoil from our own."

Blame often pushes up between the weeds of our flaws—our limiting beliefs. We tend to feel guilty on some level for not being stronger, wiser, richer, thinner, happier, and so on. But contrary to what society tells us and what we'd like to believe, we can't blame anyone for our limiting beliefs. They're nobody's fault.

Lu explains, "Our obvious cultural perception is that limiting beliefs stem from bad parenting, but they can arise equally out of loving parenting. Our parents' own fears and self-limiting beliefs can unintentionally become ours. The good news is that if we frame struggles, mistakes, and conflicts in a *learning light*, we can turn our wounds into wisdom. We can stop perpetuating our own fears and preempt negative story-making for our kids."

Embracing Our Truth

As mentioned in chapter 3, I've always believed that we must *look for the gift*. And a gift lives inside every story. If we unravel our story, we can rewrite it. The whole premise behind the Inside-Out Philosophy™ is to discover our true-self buried underneath all of our self-limiting and self-rejecting beliefs and deep-seated fears.

"The gift to ourselves and those around us," states Lu, "is to turn that rejection into a profound inside-out acceptance of who we truly are, and then to free ourselves to transcend the limits we've placed on our dreams."

Of all the things that we are or aren't, could be, or will be, nothing galvanizes us more than the desire to leave a legacy. Even those who aren't parents have the desire to carry forward a legacy of giving, a positive message of purpose, hope, and life-affirming energy.

By discovering our truth and living inside-out, we don't just change our own lives; we affect the lives of every person we touch—especially our children, whether we can measure it or not, by leaving a legacy of knowing our own truth.

As you reflect your own truth, prepare to meet Byron Katie in the next chapter. Her story of near self-destruction and eventual renewal and redemption helps you realize you can find your way out of the worst of circumstances—simply by asking the right questions.

"If we frame struggles, mistakes, and conflicts in a learning light, we can turn our wounds into wisdom."

— Lu Hanessian

Living Inside-Out Lessons from Chapter 4

- The way you see yourself and the world depends upon your "lens."

- Your stories originate from what we experienced or witnessed in our early lives and the self-limiting beliefs we developed as a result.

- Parents often unwittingly pass their stories on to their children.

- To live an authentic life, discover how your stories hinder you, and recognize the effect on you and your choices.

- When you begin to question and change your beliefs and perceptions, you intuitively begin to make different choices that reflect your *truth*, not your story.

5

The Questions are the Answers

"When I argue with reality, I lose, but only one hundred percent of the time."

— Byron Katie

As we make a conscious decision to live from the inside-out, know our truth is a foundational component. Another component is accepting reality. And what I've discovered is that the questions we ask ourselves provide the answers to our reality.

However, many of us go through our lives searching for answers from people we're sure know us better than we know ourselves. Even more amazing, we often look for these answers without first choosing the questions. We mistakenly assume these questions are either too complex for us to formulate, or we ask questions that have no simple answers because of the way we ask them.

Why don't I have enough?

Why can't I lose weight?

Why can't I find someone to love me?

Why do I have such lousy luck?

When will I ever learn my lesson and stop choosing bad partners?

We tend to search futilely for a magic formula that will reduce the answer down to a quick reminder we can apply in a crisis—and *poof!*—everything changes for the better.

But life just doesn't work that way. You know that. I know that.

So that's why I was stunned to find four questions that *do* produce results.

Yes—four questions. Only four. No gimmick. Through a process Byron Katie calls *The Work.*

Arguing with Reality

Katie (as she likes to be called) tells her story of struggling through life, living on the edge of madness and depression, alienated from herself to the point of self-destruction, when she had an epiphany. It was an awakening so profound, she suddenly saw the meaning that had eluded her for a long time. Literally in an instant.

"In my early thirties," she explains, "I became severely depressed. For almost ten years, I spiraled down into this depression with bouts of rage, self-loathing, and constant thoughts of suicide. I felt worthless and unlovable. For the last two years, I rarely left my bedroom and wallowed in those negative emotions."

I've never experienced that kind of nightmare, so I couldn't imagine her darkness. But I felt compelled to find out how she survived and learned how to transcend regret and fear. In February, 1986, Katie experienced her "life-changing realization."

"It's as if I woke up to reality, and not only did it change my life, it saved my life. *I discovered that when I believed my thoughts, I suffered, but when I didn't believe them or rejected them, I didn't suffer. I discovered that suffering is optional.* I found a joy within me that's never disappeared. That joy is in everyone—always."

I know what you're thinking.

What? How is that possible?!

I'm telling you, this is the real deal. When I met her, I realized Katie was put on this earth to do the work she does. She's the best-selling author of five books: *Loving What Is; I Need Your Love—Is That True?; A Thousand Names for Joy; Question Your Thinking, Change the World*; and *Who Would You Be Without Your Story?* She not only walks the walk in her own life and in her workshops, but she's the embodiment of living inside-out. She puts on no airs. She's learned how to do the one thing most of us haven't yet figured out—*accept reality.*

Before meeting Katie, such a concept rarely occurred to me. And when it did, it seemed like too monumental a task. Luckily, Katie breaks it down into doable parts. Her mission has become to teach others how to end their suffering by understanding how they argue with and deny their own truth.

I'm not talking about the little irritations of life. I mean suffering on a *life* scale. The burdens we bear. The negative internal chatter we propagate. The conflicts we create and play into with others that never seem to get resolved. The kind of struggles that hold us back and throw a wrench into our machinery. The kind of pain we bury, let fester, and end up fighting in deteriorating health, divorce, exhaustion, debt, or the deep regret of a dashed hope or dream.

What do we tend to do with our suffering? We numb out. We run harder. We self-soothe in ways that are far from soothing and further damage us. Ultimately, all the anxiety and fear we stuff down comes out in other ways. It catches up with us somewhere, somehow. It always does. Always!

Where the Questions Come From

Because the fifth inside-out principle states *The Questions are the Answers*, I thought it fitting that the questions, in this case, come from the process Katie created called *The Work.*

It's based on taking a belief or thought and answering these questions:

1. Is it true?
2. Can you absolutely know that it's true?
3. How do you react when you believe that thought?
4. Who would you be without that thought?

After you answer these questions, you do what Katie calls "the turnaround," where you apply the reverse of these questions to yourself. (You'll see how later in this chapter.)

Naturally, you likely have a hundred of your own questions, but start with these four as the foundation and build from there. The answers will spring up from places you never thought to look.

Whose Business is It, Really?

I suspect you've had *aha!* moments when a light flashes on in your mind and illuminates a truth or understanding. Katie says, "I love when we understand it (an *aha!* moment) because it's the biggest wake-up call. Even though it's just a beginning, it's huge, just huge. Why? Because we begin to work on ourselves, and we stop focusing so much on other people when it comes to what we can change."

In pointing out the three types of business in the Universe—"mine, yours, and God's"—Katie says that much of our stress comes from mentally living in other people's business instead of our own. "I realized," she says, "that every time I felt hurt or lonely, I was in someone else's business.

"So the next time you're feeling stress or discomfort, ask yourself whose business you're in mentally, and you may burst out laughing! You may come to see that you've never really been present, that *you've been mentally living in other people's business* all your life."

It may be hard for us to accept this, let alone understand it. We've gotten used to blaming others for our problems and thinking that if only other people would change, we'd breathe easier or our problems would be solved. However, *suffering is optional*.

Yet, if it's optional, how can we crawl out of our own suffering once we've invested in it? Katie says, "By examining your own thoughts and perceptions." That comes from when she realized what had caused her depression was not the world around her, but *the beliefs she had* about the world around her.

"I was projecting my own suffering onto the world instead of dealing with reality," she says. "Rather than hopelessly trying to change the world to match my thoughts about how it *should* be, I questioned these thoughts by meeting reality as it is."

That means the only time we suffer is when we *believe a thought that argues with what is.*

As Katie puts it, "When we want reality to be different than it is, there's no way we're going to be anything but unhappy and disappointed. It's hopeless. We cause all the stress we feel in our daily lives by arguing with *what is.*"

No, she *isn't* saying we *shouldn't* be angry, fearful, anxious, or sad, but rather, we can discover the truth about our judgments by asking those questions of ourselves. "Any time you're depressed, angry, or resentful, get excited! These emotions are fertile ground. Identify your thoughts. Put them on paper. Do *The Work*," she offers.

Listening to Judgments

People judge others constantly—friends, family members, coworkers, strangers. Listening to our judgments might sound like this:

- People should be more considerate.
- Children should be well-behaved.
- My partner should be more communicative.
- I should have accomplished more by this age.

All *shoulds*. All judgments that stem from our wish for reality to be different than it is. Not only do we make endless judgments in our present, we also do it constantly with the past. "We use the past to project a future that doesn't look any brighter than the way we see our past," explains Katie.

Lies We Live By

And it's all bogus. Lies we live by that we *think* are true.

"I invite people to go back into their past and judge every interaction or event as critically as they can," Katie says. "Not to be spiritual, not to be wise. But to make a list of all of the stressful thoughts around situations, their bodies, their lives, themselves and others, their children, parents, jobs, bosses, financial status—and to include their fears around money and health. I invite them to put all of those stressful thoughts on paper and then to do *The Work*."

You don't have to write your autobiography to respond! Katie suggests you can start by choosing *one area* of your life you're feeling pretty lousy about.

Go ahead. Think your nastiest thought. The more critical, judgmental, angry, and painful the better. Don't hold back. Your pain will be your compass.

For example …

Judge Your Neighbor

Fill out Katie's *Judge Your Neighbor Worksheet* here and you'll see how much of your struggling has to do with your own perceptions and judgments. Think about a partner, friend, neighbor, or relative (dead or alive) you judge in some way—someone you haven't totally forgiven.

Then fill in the blanks on the worksheet using short, simple sentences. Don't censor yourself. Take this opportunity to express your negative feelings on paper.

JUDGE YOUR NEIGHBOR WORKSHEET

Who angers, irritates, saddens or frustrates you, and why?

I am _____ at _____because

_____

*Example: I am **angry** at **Jason** because **he doesn't listen to me, he doesn't appreciate me, and he argues with everything I say.***

How do you want the person to change?

What do you want the person to do?

I want _____ to _____

_____

*Example: I want **Jason** to **see that he is wrong and apologize.***

What is it that the person should or shouldn't do, be, think or feel?

What advice could you offer?

_____ should/shouldn't _____

_____

*Example: **Jason** should **take better care of himself. He** shouldn't **argue with me.***

What does this person need to do in order for you to be happy?

I need _____ to _____

_____

*Example: I need **Jason** to **hear me and respect me.***

What do you think of this person? Make a list.

_____ is _____

_____

*Example: **Jason** is **unfair, arrogant, loud, dishonest, way out of line, and unconscious.***

What is it that you don't want to experience with that person again?

I don't ever want to _____

_____

*Example: I don't ever want to **feel unappreciated by Jason again.** I don't ever want to **see him smoking and ruining his health again.***

Now, once you've filled out the worksheet, Katie invites you to investigate each statement and ask yourself the four mind expanding questions:

1. **Is it true?**

2. **Can you absolutely know that it's true?**

3. **How do you react when you believe that thought?**

4. **Who would you be without that thought?**

During my time with Katie, I thought of how I judge myself and still struggle with feeling "overworked and overwhelmed." I think I worry "too much." To address this, I asked her to walk me through her process. Here's how I answered the questions:

1. *Is it true?*

I certainly feel like it is! It seems that I always have too much on my plate, and as soon as I get one project completed, I'm on to the next, with five more waiting for me. Completion dates get pushed back, and it's a never-ending vicious cycle.

2. *Can you absolutely know that it's true?*

Well, no, I can't. I mean I don't *always* feel overworked. I do actually have peaceful moments when I feel a quiet calm within me. I do have times when I can have fun with family and friends. So I guess it's not always true.

3. *How do you react when you believe that thought?*

Ha! Easy! I get short-tempered and irritable! At times I feel like any additional request someone makes of me is just too much to ask. But I temper my temper. I mean, I don't lash out at people. I try hard to stuff it all down. I try to go *faster* and accomplish *more* and squeeze every minute out of my day. I lash out at myself by beating myself up. Then I feel drained and exhausted.

4. *Who would you be without that thought?*

WOW! Who would I be without that thought? I'd be free from the feeling that I have to prove myself to others. That I have to make an impact on the world. As a result, I'd be calmer, more peaceful, more relaxed, and a much more pleasant person to be around. I'd feel as if I could take time for small pleasures or an evening out instead of feeling so guilty because I have so much to do. I'd feel like I'm living my life fully and freely.

Honestly, the lights went on for me by the time I hit the third question. I was shaking my head in disbelief at how simple this was as I wrote out the answer to the last questions: Who would I be *without* that thought?

I want to be *that* person. Not the worried, angry, limited, deluded person I tolerated on a daily basis. It's not that I consciously chose to be that way, of course. It's that, like most of us, I fell into an alternate mindset, a pattern of thinking and living so insidious that I didn't even realize I'd veered so far off my intended path. That's why *The Work* is so powerful. It allows us to become aware and take responsibility for letting go of the thoughts that are causing us pain.

Turn it Around

"When we question those thoughts and we turn the issue around, it's really about us. In fact, it's *totally about us*," says Katie. This isn't a guilt-inducing statement (unless, of course, you make it one!). Rather, it's a starting point for accountability and feeling empowered enough to make change happen.

At this pivotal point, many of us fall off the path because we buy into the guilt. We think, "Okay, it's all about me, so I'm bad, I'm worthless, I'm guilty of my own misery." And then we shut down. Remember those self-rejecting beliefs Lu spoke about in chapter 4? That's when we stop trying to look inside; we don't like what we see.

The *turnaround* that Katie has devised is a brilliant, practical, and simple way of looking in the mirror. So, how does it work?

Take the belief you're questioning, and then turn it around, giving at least three examples of the turnaround. Here's what I did with mine:

My belief: "I'm overworked."

My turnaround:

- "I'm *not* overworked—I have plenty of time."
- "I *do* have time to spend with others."
- "I *do* have time to enjoy myself."

This process seems so simple, but it reveals that I'm not *really* overworked; I just allow myself to think and feel that way. I choose to be annoyed and irritated with others when I'm really frustrated with *myself*. And even my frustration with myself is *an active choice*. Does the frustration make me work harder or faster, or accomplish more? No. It just makes me feel irritated that I have so much to do. But *who* chose to do so much?

Um ... that would be me again.

Looking at Objective Reality

One of the biggest *aha!* moments I gleaned from Katie was about accepting responsibility for looking at objective reality—*what is*—as opposed to what was, what isn't, should be, would be, or could be. After all, our problems lie in our emotions that surround reality, and *we choose* those emotions.

Let's take the example on Katie's worksheet. Perhaps you and your partner aren't getting along and you can relate. You might start with the idea, "Jason should understand me." Now fill out the worksheet and deeply examine what you feel. Go ahead and ask yourself the four questions. When you complete that task, offer at least three turnarounds. They might be statements such as:

- "Jason *shouldn't* understand me." (Isn't that reality sometimes?)
- "*I* should understand me." (It's my job, not his.)
- "*I* should understand *Jason*." (Can I understand that he doesn't always understand me?)

In doing the turnaround, we quickly learn that our judgments of others *directly reflect our judgments of ourselves*. That is, if we judge someone else to be critical, we, ourselves, are being critical of them being critical. If we think of someone as being selfish, deep down, we believe we are selfish, too. If we see someone as dishonest, we're fighting with our own integrity as well.

It's never easy to see in ourselves the negative traits we point out in others. But this truth goes back thousands of years for a reason. It's a Universal Law.

Katie offers a few more examples of turnarounds for common problems. Do you see yourself in any of these?

"I need her to be kind to me."

- I don't need her to be kind to me.
- I need me to be kind to her. (Can I live it?)
- I need me to be kind to myself.

"He is unloving to me."

- He is loving to me. (To the best of his ability.)
- I am unloving to him. (Can I be?)
- I am unloving to me. (When I don't inquire.)

"Gina shouldn't shout at me."

- Gina should shout at me. (In reality, Gina does sometimes. Am I listening?)
- I shouldn't shout at Gina.
- I shouldn't shout at me. (In my head, am I playing over and over again Gina is shouting? Who's more merciful—Gina who shouted once, or me who replayed it a 100 times?)

Accepting Reality

The last step in *The Work* is to embrace reality as our ticket to peace and freedom. Once we accept what's happening *externally* is a reflection of what's happening *internally,* we have the awareness to make the change we want.

Katie explains, "If I have the thought 'I'm overworked' or 'I'm overweight' or 'I'm unloved' or 'I'm not good enough,' I immediately notice how I react physically. My shoulders tense up and I heave a sigh of dread. I've already begun to live out the identity of that thought or emotion. But I can choose to reject that idea and *not let myself* live it out."

That resolve bears emphasis.

"We often use our negativity as a crutch for interacting with others. We complain and moan, making others feel bad and ourselves feel worse—and all of that is a choice, in fact, it's a habit for many. When we think we're overworked, overweight, unloved, or not good enough, our mind and body react *as if we actually are*. We live out that idea even if it's not reality."

For example, I don't want to feel overwhelmed and overworked, but I'm choosing to think I am. I can just as easily choose the opposite emotion and think, "I'm *not* overwhelmed; there *is* enough time."

Isn't this just denial? Katie says no. *It's the beginning of change.*

When we think of ourselves differently, we feel differently, and our thoughts lead to different behaviors, actions, and choices. This is the pathway to changing our stories. When she talks about accepting reality, she isn't saying we ought to settle for status quo and compromise our dreams, nor is she advocating we take a back seat in our lives. The powerful message I get is that *accepting reality is the antidote to suffering*. Once we can wrap our heads and hearts around that—let go of fantasy and regret—we can begin to claim our own true power.

There's no power in being "in control." In fact, there's no such thing as being in control. We created that hoax to make ourselves feel less vulnerable. The real power lies in accepting reality—what *is* versus what *might be*.

That's a gold nugget. Hold on to it.

What If We Invest in "I Can't Change" Thinking

I frequently talk with people who think they can't possibly change. They protest, saying, "I've been like this for years. That's just the way I am." These thoughts actually build walls higher and stronger instead of scaling them or knocking them down altogether. I asked Katie to describe the emotional roller coaster ride we impose on ourselves when we invest in this kind of thinking.

"When people believe they can't change, they remove all their options and become resigned to their fate. They embrace a victim mentality and often become depressed," she explains. "They often compare themselves to others, which makes them even more depressed, and they frequently take on various addictions, such as alcohol, drugs, gambling, overeating, under eating, compulsive shopping, obsessive compulsive disorders—you name it.

"They might resent people who appear to be changing and growing. As the emotions and feelings escalate, so does the addictive or compulsive behavior. This is why people who lose a lot of weight gain it back. It's why they smoke that fateful cigarette after quitting for ten years. And it's why addicts go from cigarettes to heroin. People emotionally react like this when they believe the thought 'I can't change.'

"It's not unusual for someone to believe they can't change because they've been told that, or one event repeated itself and convinced them of their hopelessness. But it's important to understand that *we all change all the time*."

What often works for people—and what worked for me—is to spend time becoming very quiet and think through these questions:

- What would it be like for me to *not* have this problem in my life?
- What would it be like for me *not* to think that I'm not smart enough?
- What would it be like for me *not* to think I'm not good enough?
- What would it be like for me to feel happy?

Think about the turnaround questions that are most relevant to your life, and ask them.

"This questioning process allows your mind to actually practice a specific emotion *as if that turnaround were happening*. Just this small step can get people who are totally convinced they're hopeless to see that no one is hopeless—unless and until they give up."

Answering Katie's four questions and the turnaround for ourselves may seem like a small step, but it can be a tremendously significant turning point. To be willing and open enough to examine our lives, sometimes we have to reach a sense of despair, even disgust, with the way things are. A willingness to honestly answer these questions can lead us to life-changing answers. Without that willingness and openness, we could be blocking the ultimate life we desire and not even notice. Accepting reality can provide the fuel; arguing with it only drains us.

What floors me about Katie's questions is their simplicity in approaching something as complex as the tangled webs of belief that people weave. We pay such a price for maintaining our lives the way we do—without rest or reflection, desperate for other people's feedback and approval, always feeling like we come up short. Yet it's so simple to untangle the web if we make that choice.

Quit Fighting Ourselves

To live inside-out and become reacquainted with our true selves, we have to quit arguing with what's going on—even if we don't like what we see and *especially* if we don't like what we see.

After waging an exhausting war inside ourselves for years, we have to decide to quit fighting ourselves. Yes, it's time to recognize the destructive nature of our beliefs and choose otherwise. Then we can discover the truth beyond our story, be present to our possibilities, and willingly embrace the changes we need to make to create the life we want. This is our *real* power.

Where does that power come from? In the next chapter, you'll meet a fascinating man named Paul Scheele who will uncover our source of power and guide us to awaken to our *natural abundance*.

"When a person begins to do The Work, they actually open the door to an internal life, and the outside life ceases to be able to compete with it because of the realization that the inside life is so exciting. That's why I encourage people to live from the inside-out, not the outside-in."

— Byron Katie

Living Inside-Out Lessons from Chapter 5

- Suffering is optional.

- When you believe your thoughts, you act on those beliefs.

- Stay focused on your own business.

- When you accept reality, you free yourself from pain.

- Real change comes from accepting what is.

Awaken to Your Natural Abundance

"Awaken to the abundance and power that is your natural state."

— Paul Scheele

Living from the inside-out is about becoming *aware*—awakening to our natural state of being and who we really are. Yet too often, we invest tremendous energy, time, and resources camouflaging the essence of our being.

We become experts at wearing masks. Masks of control. Masks of confidence. Masks of indifference. Masks of money. Mask of happy marriages. Masks of looking good.

We pretend we're perfect—happy or together or whatever—when we're not. Sometimes, our masks can be a stance we take with the world, like pretending we've got it together, with a mask of authority and confidence, when, really, we wonder if we measure up.

We also create masks of being overwhelmed, overworked, over-committed, and others for protection.

I've worn my share of masks. One that continues to challenge me is the mask of introversion, which for me stems from the feeling of not being good enough while at the same time wanting others to like me. This just happened again this week; I was at a conference with nearly a thousand attendees. Upon reflection I realized that I didn't speak to anyone I didn't know previously or that I wasn't personally introduced. During breaks I was secretly frozen while I watched others meet and talk with one another.

As I reflect back, I realized that this kind of "turning inward" originated from childhood, as a kid riding the school bus. The senior high kids would always sit in the back and I became a target of name calling, teasing, and bullying. Thirty years later, I can still re-live the scenario that, although I want others to like me, I fear that I'm not good enough to like. As a grown man, I found myself hiding behind the mask of introversion (my story), frozen in my tracks, instead of extending myself to meet those around me.

Most of us tend to *exist in a trance*, living our entire lives thinking we're awake or present, when in fact, we often live in a state of distraction, preoccupation, worry, regret, even numbness. We've figured out a million ways to avoid our authentic selves and not address our true needs, let alone our life's purpose. And we wonder why self-improvement courses don't work.

Okay, we feel great in that moment, maybe even for the whole course weekend. But in short order the honeymoon ends. We're left thinking we're just not capable of improving at all, so we pull out our old reliable masks again. While deluding others, especially ourselves, we continue to play the "if only" game. *If only I had a lot of money, I'd be content. If only my partner loved me more, I'd feel secure. If only …* And the more we grovel, grasp, and groan, that abundance of wealth, health, happiness, and love continues to elude us.

The truth is we don't have to live behind masks or the "if only" game.

To help unlock Principle #6, *Awaken to Your Natural Abundance*, I called on the remarkable expertise of Paul Sheele, co-founder and creative program designer of Learning Strategies Corporation. His unique blend of expertise includes degrees in biology as well as learning and human development, plus a rich background in neuro-linguistic programming (NLP), accelerated learning, preconscious processing, and universal energy. Paul has written two best-selling books, *Photo Reading* and *Natural Brilliance*. His work has been translated into more than 18 languages and purchased by enthusiastic readers in 185 countries.

As Paul points out, "We get self-improvement all wrong, thinking we have to work on *ourselves*. However, we have to recognize the fullness we have within and begin to create from that place. How? By relearning how to educate ourselves beginning with the word *educare,* which means to *draw forth,* or draw out."

"We're not born as empty vessels; we're born quite full," Paul says. "The mind is a tool we can use to illuminate this magnificence that's within us. So, rather than thinking we have to improve what's not very good, we're awakening more and appreciating the fullness that already exists within us."

As spiritual beings, we live in an unlimited Universe; however, the human experience has profound limitations. We're born unable to take care of ourselves or communicate, and we're typically raised and influenced by well-intended parents, family members, teachers, friends, and other kids who are caught in their own webs of limiting beliefs. As a result, we take on these beliefs developing our own feelings of not being good enough and live with a tremendous amount of fear that can permeate our entire lives.

Abundance is Our Natural State

Dr. Buckminster Fuller, the great inventor and developer of the geodesic dome (among many other things), wrote in Mario Montessori Jr.'s book, "All children are born geniuses. 9,999 out of every 10,000 are swiftly, inadvertently, 'de-geniused' by grown-ups." [Source: Foreword by Dr. Buckminster Fuller in the book *Education for Human Development,* Mario Montessori, Jr., Schocken Books, 1976]

To explain that, Paul says in addition to projecting to us their limiting beliefs, well-intentioned adults also instruct us on how to succeed which actually *prevents* us from exploring the world. We're stuck in right and wrong, multiple choices, testing and assignments, homework—a worksheet wasteland, as some have called it.

"We're taught to follow a model that's culturally prescribed," notes Paul. "And if we don't fit in, we get marginalized or pushed to the side. Much of my work is about awakening that genius potential that's been on hold as a result of early education."

What stops us from successfully developing our brains? We've gotten into the habit of thinking that *this is as good as it gets*. Instead of accepting that, Paul suggests we consider such development from an energetic standpoint. "If we look at the molecular bonds inside the chemical components of our physical bodies, we have enough electricity, power, and energy contained within one body to power an entire metropolitan area for a year. We have literally trillions of molecules within our physical bodies. And every one of those molecules possesses an amazing intelligence.

"But once you accept the negative or self-limiting belief that you can't do something, you will live and die with that being the case. Byron Katie says that any thought or story you tell yourself—and think of trance as another way of *imagining* a story—your mind becomes devoted to proving, fulfilling, testifying to, or demonstrating the essence of it.

"This shows that whether you believe 'I can't do math,' or 'I'm not good at relationships,' or 'I can't remember names,' your mind sets out to prove it. But the mind can also be used to prove you *can*. The key is to harness this understanding of how the unlimited potential within you can be either accessed or shut out by your ongoing thinking. Then you can discover your ability to tap into great abundance. It's a natural part of who you are and your existence in the world."

Paul refers to abundance not in terms of how much sits in our bank accounts, but how much we have in our internal spiritual and emotional accounts. This kind of abundance few ever realize we have, and yet we could tap it daily for an extraordinary shift in our lives—from our moods to our energy levels, to our relationships and careers. Discovering the abundance that's our own birthright affects every aspect of our lives.

He says, "The key here is not that we begin to improve ourselves, but we start to awaken to the fact that there's a lot more going on than we've been led to believe. With awakening, we experience wonderful coincidences and synchronicities. The guidance we need shows up for us. We run into the right people at the right time, and we find ourselves in perfect places to further ourselves, to challenge our fears, and discover what we're made of.

"We've had amnesia for who we really are, and begin to discover *our tremendous power is hidden behind the thing we fear the most*, the place we dare not go.

"Right inside what we fear most, we tap into an amazing amount of power. It was always there, and we reveal it. We discover it."

We Hide Our Power in What We Fear the Most

Each of us has what Paul calls a "Reactive Robot, or r2." Our r2 learns to take care of us so we can survive in the physical world. But beyond this robotic, preprogrammed, cause-and-effect, survival mechanism shines an *intelligence that's the consciousness of the high-self.*

"On the day I began to perceive my fears as something exciting, as my own excitement," reflects Paul, "everything turned around for me. This ability to frame our experience and to *reframe* it allows us to always have our resources where they will serve us best.

"So we realize it isn't about fixing our r2, but rather playing full out. We're spiritual beings here to play in the human experience. However, *we hide our power in what we fear the most,* and our r2 is perfectly programmed to make sure we never go there. So every time we get close to our power, our r2 throw us off track. It causes distractions to protect us. But the fact is we don't need to be protected."

Rewind!

Did that finally sink in? I've mentioned it three times already in this chapter ... Understanding that *our power is hidden behind the thing we fear the most* was one of the most powerful life-changing inside-out *aha!* moments I had while writing this book.

When fear presents itself, this is the exact place we need to dig into to uncover our strength, our abundance, our true essence.

Ironically, our r2 will show us where we've been hiding our power. The r2 *communicates through feelings*. Every time we feel fear, pain, anger, or discomfort—when our r2 is telling us to stay away—it's also showing us *the exact place to reclaim our true selves.*

We're entering new territory to explore, and when we first try to wrap our minds around these concepts, we might feel uncomfortable. But when we confront our fears head-on we tap into our power, and we grow.

Paul emphasizes "I'm offering the idea that when you have a feeling experience—whatever it is—embrace it. Step into the feeling of it without any thoughts, judgments, considerations, or labels that say it's good or bad. You discover that the energy in your feelings is the creative energy you can use to make your life what you choose."

Focus Your Feelings

When you acknowledge that energy and the power in the moment, you're reclaiming it as your own. You're acknowledging yourself as the creator of it. Paul suggests that we use the "Feeling Exercise," originally introduced by Arnold Patent in his book *You Can Have It All*, to directly confront your limiting beliefs and fears.

THE FEELING EXERCISE

Pick one of your core limiting feelings that has juice to it—power and energy. Then *go into the feeling—the vibrational energy—of this core belief.* For example, "I'm not good enough." Go into the feeling of this false identity.

"Close your eyes and scan your body. Notice how you are feeling. Then:

1. Feel the feeling free of any thoughts you have about it. Feel the energy, the power, in the feeling.

2. Feel love for the feeling just the way it is. Feel love for the power in the feeling.

3. Feel love for yourself feeling the feeling and feeling the power in the feeling."

[Source: Based on "The Feeling Exercise" in Arnold Patent's book, *You Can Have It All*, Beyond Words Publishing, 1995, p. 50]

This exercise helps us to identify the emotions—the energy, the vibration—behind our feelings without blame or judgment and reclaim the power that our negative emotions control. We can then redirect the power from those feelings to create what we want. It's like discovering a gold mine of energy! The exercise also helps us empathize our own struggles and challenges instead of rejecting ourselves. It's soothing self-care.

Shifting Negative Emotions

Here's an example of how Paul helped me face one of my own challenge using this idea.

"Paul, I know this material," I told him. "Everyday I focus on living my life from the inside-out. But a couple months ago, fear came up around a great new product we launched. We were really excited and received tons of positive feedback about it. But even so, in doing the tasks for the launch, the fear came up as I called radio stations and affiliate partners and such. The fear (my story) took over.

The voice in my head went on and on, 'This won't be successful. I'm going to fail. What happens if the money runs out?" A tsunami of fears, negative emotions, and limiting energies. How do I reframe this situation and use the Feeling Exercise to take back my inner power?

Here's Paul's reply: "You have the right idea, Eddie. Normally when people have a sense of anxiety, they want to stress-manage and make the anxiety go away. But I don't advocate making the feeling go away. I suggest leveraging the energy and power that's in the feeling by utilizing the three steps of the Feeling Exercise. By doing so, we shift from a negative emotional state to a positive one. Then we harness this new positive energy by focusing on the present.

"Often when we're faced with that big gap between our vision of what's possible and our present reality, we project anxiety, apprehension, because we're holding an image of an imagined future state—one of failure. We don't realize that, in this moment, right now, we're fine. Everything's okay right now.

"The only way to feel anxiety is to project an image of some imagined future failure or lack. If you ask someone who's anxious, *how are you right now?,* they'll say 'I'm really anxious.' *No, I mean right now, in this moment, right here, talking with me.* 'Oh, I'm fine. What you don't understand is blah, blah, blah.'

"No, stop. How are you now? 'Well right now, I'm okay. It's just that I'm not going to be ...' *Stop. How are you right now?*

"Keep bringing yourself back to the now. Breathe into this moment. Become aware of the moment, right now, and realize that *everything is okay in this moment.*

"You can use your imagination to take that energy residing within your fear beyond the time when you've successfully achieved the result. Then you can look back on the steps that took place to bring you there. Like stepping stones. You can't always discern the steps, but if you take that next step, you'll discover you actually have some place to put your foot. The next step always appears. If you do that, the anxiety instantly dissipates.

"So let go of your *thoughts about* your fear. Let go of any judgments. Just be here in it now. Sense the energy and power within your fear. Feel it and love it—and love yourself for creating it.

"Now project that energy beyond the time when you've attained your goal. When you do that, your mind builds a bridge between your present state and your imagined future state of success. This process enables you to harness the power and energy in your fear—or any negative emotion—to fuel your success."

Paul is right as this created a big shift for me. By becoming aware of our feelings, connecting to the present moment, and redirecting our fear-based energy to a powerful focused intention, we "wake up" and tap into our natural abundance.

Tap into Your Abundance

Paul offers these three objectives regarding tapping into your abundance:

1. Open access to your infinite intelligence;
2. Manifest the abundant life you choose; and
3. Step into your power.

TAP INTO YOUR ABUNDANCE

1. *Open access to your infinite intelligence* within you. It's already guiding your life, and you can increase its effectiveness exponentially. "Knock, and the door will be opened unto you." When you tap into your deeper resources, you open your mind and allow infinite intelligence to flow through it. You can do this through meditation, imagery, visualization, and/or prayer.

2. *Choose the abundant life you desire.* Recognize that you're always in a position to choose the life you desire. Whatever you choose, you can create. By saying *yes, I now choose to create this*, you're setting your focused intention to bring it into the present and change your vibration to match that of what you desire. As you begin doing this, you'll confront a limiting belief that might say, 'Hold it! You're going to do *that?* How do you know you can succeed? What if you fail?' So it's natural to start questioning whether you *really* can have what you want to create. It is at this point your natural abundance is waiting to be revealed.

3. *Step into your power* every time you confront fear. Take your doubt not as a reason to turn around and run or a stop sign that says you can't go any further, but as an opportunity to ask good questions of yourself. Not doubting ones, but honest inquiries of what you *really* believe, desire, and fear. Question the doubt that confronts you. Fully engage the presence that's on the other side of the stop sign.

These are important nuggets of wisdom to digest. You have just awakened to the fact that there is enormous power behind your fears. What a life-changing revelation. Throughout the day as your negative self-talk, limiting beliefs, and perceived fears show up, simply lean in to discover the enormous abundance that awaits you.

Let's review the six principles of the Inside-Out Philosophy™ —*Focus Your Intention, Embrace Change from Within, Be Present to Possibilities, Know Your Truth, The Questions are the Answers,* and *Awaken to Your Natural Abundance*.

As we move to the next section of the book, you'll discover how these principles can be practically used in our daily life. We'll start with the new revelations as to how the brain works, and then explore our happiness level, health, finances, relationships, and spirituality.

"You are infinite abundance. Recognize who you are from the inside and create from that sense of fullness. Go into your abundance, into your power, and choose what you want to create."

— Paul Scheele

Living Inside-Out Lessons from Chapter 6

- **Our power is hidden behind the thing we fear the most.**

- **Abundance is your natural state. By awakening to this truth, you can start to live it.**

- **Most people live their entire lives thinking they're awake or present, when they're living in a "trance" state of distraction, preoccupation, worry, regret, even numbness.**

- **From this trance state, perceived limitations arise.**

- **As you awaken from the trance and discover you are the creator of your life, not a victim, you gain access to the energy, power, and possibility of living your fullest potential.**

LIVING INSIDE-OUT
PRACTICAL GUIDE

7

MINDING YOUR BRAIN FROM THE INSIDE-OUT

Unleashing the Power of Our Mind

"Change your brain. Change your thinking. Change your life."

— Doug Bench

Now, that I've laid out the foundation for why living from the inside-out is so crucial to experiencing our potential on a daily basis, let's look at 'how' the Living Inside-Out Principles can be applied. This section of the book covers specific areas of our daily lives starting with *Unleashing the Power of Our Mind*.

When I started my own journey of personal growth, I yearned for something concrete that would explain why we are the way we are. How do we learn? Or more specifically, how can our beliefs change and alter our *perceptions* of the world and of ourselves?

Is there a tangible reason behind why we allow fears, negative self-talk, and limiting beliefs to hold us back, some physiological part of us that actually prevents us from doing what we wish we could do differently?

The answer is, Yes! And, more importantly this same part of our makeup is also what facilitates internal change. It involves both our intangible thought: our mind, as well as our physical body: our brain.

To help us understand not only the psychology, but the physiology of how our brains work, I enlisted the expertise of Doug Bench MS, JD,

AAAS. His knowledge is nothing short of revolutionary in understanding how we think, feel, and ultimately create an ability to change.

A retired lawyer and former applied physiology researcher, Doug sought out studies and waded through more than 100,000 pages of brain research to create his *Mind Your Brain* course. In it, he provides a practical approach to understanding how the brain works and how we can change our behavioral patterns.

Doug has written two books on the subject, *Revolutionize Your Brain!* and *Do It Yourself Brain Surgery!*, and has presented this exciting brain-science research to over 240,000 people. Due to advances in the last ten years and outreach like his, we're beginning to understand the capabilities of our brain. "Once we learn how the brain works, there isn't anything we can't do," Doug states.

How Our Brains Work

A new scientific brain technology discovery sheds revealing light on a part of the brain called the Reticular Activating System (RAS). According to Doug, the RAS is a set of neurons that fire together, work together, and analyze impulses coming into the brain. Every impulse passes through the RAS—the limbic system (what some call the "reptilian brain") controlling the non-cognitive thinking portion of the brain. It works automatically, which means it doesn't require conscious cognitive input.

Hang in here with me, I promise we won't get too technical!

The RAS analyzes each impulse as it comes into your brain—whether it's something we see, hear, smell, or touch. Even a thought that comes up to the cognitive level from the non-conscious level passes through the RAS. It then sends it to the part of the brain that perceives and gives meaning to patterns or images. In the process of analyzing the impulses, the RAS separates the impulses coming to the brain that are vitally important from those that aren't so important. The major function of 97% of the brain's non-thinking portion—the limbic system—is to keep us safe, keep us alive.

So if an impulse comes in that's not all that important, the RAS sends it to what Doug calls the *basement*, meaning the non-conscious level of thinking. But if the RAS recognizes it as important, it automatically sends it to the conscious level, like knocking on the door of the conscious brain and saying, "Hey, pay attention to this. It's important!

"Now, how do things get on this Important List? They stem from our most dominant thoughts at a conscious level. Our brain, at the limbic system level, isn't as smart as our conscious level. It simply reacts to what we tell it. If we keep sending impulses through our brain, then our limbic system or RAS assumes it's important. So anytime my eyes see something I'm focused on, whether it's with the conscious or non-conscious portion of the brain, it calls attention to it. I don't have an option. It's automatic."

How is it useful to know this? It directly relates to focusing on our goals. If we can intensify our focused intention on our goals so that our RAS recognizes them as crucial and places them on our Important List, from that point forward, our brain knocks on the door at the conscious level when any impulses related to our goals come into our field of seeing, hearing, smelling, or touching. We have no choice but to react to them.

So how do we do this? Through inner-states.

As Doug says, "Many people call them affirmations; I call them *inner-states*. They're a pattern of neurons that fire together to create new roads of patterns called neurodes or inner-states. These inner-states reflect phrases we say over and over to ourselves, not to memorize them but to burn them onto our Important List in our RAS. Then the RAS kicks in automatically and we start noticing things around us that relate to our goals."

Some people believe that, by sending thoughts out into the Universe, the Universe will deliver what's requested. But what happens in the brain? *We begin to see what was there all the time*; it simply didn't get sent to the conscious level because it wasn't on the Important List—yet.

Until we start shifting our focused intention by imagining what we desire and setting affirmations for it in order to transfer our vibrational energy, we won't experience it. Because we won't become aware of what is already accessible to use. The RAS function of the mind is designed to knock on our conscious door with everything related to it. Then suddenly we *see* it and can eventually *achieve* it.

The Brain's Capacity to Change

As Doug points out, our brains are capable of greater change than anyone formerly anticipated. "The previously held idea about the brain being hard-wired and unchangeable is totally wrong. New research indicates that we can change our brains by increasing the number of connections in our brain, which also increases our brain's capacity for achievement." This is called *brain plasticity*.

So what does the brain's RAS have to do with you?

Let's say you're feeling overwhelmed, living a lifestyle that has become overcommitted and overscheduled—a professional, a parent, a caregiver in your 30s, 40s, 50s, or 60s and you're barely managing to handle life's daily grind. You rationalize and reason, "How do these new scientific discoveries make any difference to me and my life?"

Think of your brain as a thick jungle. When you create a new pathway in the brain—you begin thinking in a different way; it's like cutting a path through the jungle for the first time. You first cut the new path and continue to re-cut it until the path becomes natural.

How do we create new pathways in the brain? Through conscious practice over a short period of time. Doug says *twenty-one days is the least amount of time we need to wire a new neural pathway—make new connections—and create a new "habit"*—break an old habit.

Less than a month!

"It's because thoughts are physical, physiological things. Modern brain science tells us that we are no longer bound by our past habits. In twenty-one to thirty days, we can generate new pathways in our brain, new habits," he says.

So, we can practice being on time for three solid weeks, and find that we are rarely late again. We can practice creating a budget and balancing our checkbook for a month—daily, consciously, with intention—and by month two, three, and six, money management will begin to feel like second nature. You would look back on your painful period of overdraft notices and shake your head in disbelief thinking "Who *was* that person?"

Yes, it takes some serious effort. But the more you walk down that path, the easier it gets—like taking the path of least resistance. That's what also occurs in the brain. *Neurons fired in the brain go down the path of least resistance.*

Why not help yourself by picking the path of least resistance?

Ironically, the ease of walking down the RAS path becomes our biggest obstacle when we want to change. That's because we're used to seeing the same boulders and trees blocking our way on that old familiar path. We don't seem to say, "Wait a minute. I can go down a different path and bypass the barriers."

This shows a lack of information and understanding about how the human brain works. "It's almost a Catch-22," says Doug. "We keep going down the path we've been on before, even while what we say to ourselves is negative."

Negative Self-Talk Once Vital

So we know now that about 83% of the brain falls into the reptilian limbic system reactive-responsive brain. In our ancestors' day, to stay safe, our brains had to always be alert to surrounding danger and on guard for possible food shortages in the hunter-gatherer phase of our evolutionary development. A time of constant fear-based emotions.

In this way, it's evolutionary for us to think of the negative because responding to negative self-talk was once vital, the difference between life or death. Culturally, we've evolved beyond that point, but the brain, as hard as it may be to believe, simply hasn't caught up.

We have to stop beating ourselves up for our inherent negative self-talk. People often say to themselves, 'I can't help it; it's just the way I am.' Well, knowing about brain plasticity has changed all of that.

We *can* change the brain's pathways; however, the RAS resists that change.

Why? Because this non-thinking, non-cognitive thinking portion is designed to keep us safe. It also controls our heart rate, our breathing, our heart muscle, our digestive system, our reaction time, even the dilation and constriction of our eyes. All of these are automatically controlled by the brain through a powerful portion of the limbic system called the *amygdala*. It is what Paul referred to in the last chapter as our Reactive Robot, r2.

Doug agrees, "The amygdala keeps us from changing because it senses our efforts to change as danger. This, of course, creates discomfort. Therefore, it will do anything it can to keep us from making that change as if it were doing us a favor. As a result, we fall back into the same old ruts. With changing becoming uncomfortable, we quit any effort to change when our amygdala tells us to."

This isn't a chance for us to begin blaming our amygdala! It's a chance to see choice and change in a whole new way. An inside-out view of how we want to live our lives.

New Discoveries in Brain Research

What is the difference between our conscious and non-conscious thought process? And how does that impact our ability to change our brains? Doug explained this by citing experiments using a PET scan with people performing math problems. They discovered that not only did the left side of the brain become active, but five other areas of the brain also became active—areas that were not conscious.

"Those other five areas of thought in the *non-conscious* level of the brain are firing all the time. *We're not aware of those thoughts, yet that's five-sixths of our brain's thinking.*

"Compare that to the *conscious* level of thought only being *one-sixth* of our brain's power. Let's look at it this way: all thoughts are images or patterns of pictures in the brain. We see and think in pictures. We're not even aware of the characteristics of these non-conscious thoughts. The brain can't distinguish whether they're real or imagined, whether they're truthful or a lie. It interprets them as happening in real time, whether they are or not.

"This explains why a sad movie appears to be sad, even though at the conscious level in *one-sixth* of our brain, we know it's a picture being projected onto a screen and we're watching actors in a movie. But *five-sixths* of our brain reacts to those pictures and patterns as if they were real—

especially in a scary movie. We know it was a fake shark in the classic movie *Jaws,* but our bodies responded in fear because five-sixths of the brain thought the shark was real. How powerful!"

Tame the 500-Pound Gorilla

When I asked Doug about the power of this non-conscious part, he had a memorable metaphor for it: *a 500-pound gorilla.* Doug says the gorilla controls five-sixths of our behavior because *it controls five-sixths of our thinking.*

"To influence the thoughts that are firing at our non-conscious level — and to get our goals onto our RAS's Important List — we've got to be exact in what we say. After all, five-sixths of the brain, the gorilla, won't see situations the same way the conscious brain does."

Here's an example: If you pour a child a glass of milk and say, "Oh, Jimmy, I poured that glass too full so don't spill the milk when you drink it," you've just created a picture in Jimmy's brain and five-sixths of it "sees" spilling the milk. In contrast, only one-sixth of his brain consciously gives meaning to *not* spilling the milk. So you've just generated an 83% chance that Jimmy will spill the milk when you told him not to.

If you don't want Jimmy's RAS to take in your message as a negative picture, you could say, "Jimmy, I want you to enjoy that milk right down to the bottom of the glass by holding it with two hands."

Now you've generated a positive picture — what Doug calls a *positive-positive* — in all six parts of the brain. As a result, the likelihood of Jimmy spilling the milk goes down dramatically.

Applied to Our Goals

We can apply this important principle to our own goals. If our goal is to lose weight, it won't work if we say, "Don't overeat. Don't overeat. Don't overeat." Why? Because five-sixths of the brain "hears" the overeat, overeat, overeat part! Instead, we need to say, "I'm fit and thin and eat healthy foods." It doesn't matter whether we consciously believe that goal is possible; if five-sixths of the brain accepts it as real, then it will manifest.

Here's an example that one of Doug's students in his *Mind Your Brain* course experienced. He weighed 340 pounds. Every morning, he stood in front of the mirror and said, "I'm fit and thin, and I eat healthy foods." Consciously, he knew this was an absolute lie, but five-sixths of his brain believed him. So he stood in front of his mirror everyday looking at a fat body and said, "I'm fit and thin, and eat healthy foods." A year later after no dieting, he weighed 205 pounds.

Positive thinking affected his metabolism. Pure and simple. OK, not so simple. But, research has been compelling in its exploration of how our thoughts affect our bodies. If science tells us that *hugs* can boost our immune system and speed up our metabolism, we can see why thinking positively and favorably about ourselves can change our physiology from the inside-out—including our brains, hormones, neurotransmitters.

So, if in a certain aspect of your life, like your weight or your relationship or your job situation, you believe you're consciously telling yourself positive things and setting yourself up for positive results, but you're not getting them, what is going on?

What's the disconnect?

"Perhaps it's an indication that, *on an unconscious level, you're absolutely not agreeing with yourself*. Given that things aren't changing, the unconscious part of your brain must be holding onto negative thoughts."

That's why Doug encourages us to *practice* responding differently to a given stimulus for 21 to 30 days. Let's say you feel compelled to grab the ice cream every time you open the fridge door, and each time, you can't seem to stop yourself.

"Go to the refrigerator, open the freezer door, and see the pint of ice cream. For twenty-one to thirty days, *refuse* to take that ice cream out of the freezer. Go in there for the purpose of *not* taking it out. *Most people don't stay with it long enough*. When a change in thinking doesn't happen soon enough, they quit trying to make it work."

In the process of practicing a change for a month, we'll likely feel fearful or uncomfortable. Doug advises us to embrace the discomfort—"step into the fear," as Paul Scheele says—and understand that this is a short-term process that empowers us to achieve exactly what we want.

Amplify Success by Adding Emotion

When beginning our positive thinking about the changes we want to create, Doug says we can amplify our success and create longer-lasting change by adding high levels of emotion to our affirmations.

"The more I read about brain research, the more I realize that, for motivation to last, it has to be generated *intrinsically*."

Why? Because when we experience self-generated emotion from within—high levels of joy or trauma—more proteins in the brain are released, creating new connections, more connections, and stronger connections.

In addition to emotions, journaling is also vitally important for reasons based on brain science. He says, "The more tactile we are, the more senses we're involving, the stronger the neuron connections are. Something that we only *think* doesn't have neuron connections that are as strong as something we both *think and say out loud*. That won't be as good as something we *think and say out loud and write down*. Attaching emotion and a visual picture to all of these is best of all."

Another reason to write things down is based on what scientists have learned about short-term memory. Doug says, "We live in a culture of clutter, and the older we get, the more mental clutter we experience." Research states a thought that comes into *the brain fires from seven seconds to twelve minutes*, with the average time being *forty seconds*. Because many of us are in a constant overwhelmed multi-task state of mental clutter, our mind shifts focus every *ten to fourteen seconds*—well short of the forty seconds average. *By writing our goals and journaling, we are more effectively igniting our RAS, and getting these intentions on our Important List.*

If you are a person who already does this, no doubt you are nodding right now. I know that I have seen this outcome firsthand many times in my life. In the middle of chaos and discouragement, I have journaled, said aloud what I needed, wanted and believed in, and focused calmly and regularly on it, and witnessed how it unfolded—in ways I couldn't have imagined.

That's a really important point I realized too: it's one thing to change your thinking, but it's another to feel humbled by it and let the consequences of that change surprise you for the better. We are not puppet masters of our lives. We aren't here to manipulate circumstances as much as we are here to do the most with what we've been given. With a phenomenal brain in our heads, we have the power to create so much good in our lives and the lives of others without even realizing it.

When you want to create *conscious sustainable change* from the inside-out, remember these points:

THE MIND'S POWER TO CHANGE

- The brain is capable of changing and science has proven it.

- The RAS or Reticular Activating System processes all information going into the brain. So to achieve your goals, you need to get them onto your RAS's Important List through saying affirmations and writing them down.

- The amygdala is a primitive part of the brain designed to keep you safe. When making changes that are uncomfortable, it attempts to keep you the same by stopping you when you begin to feel uncomfortable. So allow yourself to feel uncomfortable and you'll make progress.

- To make lasting change, it takes 21 to 30 days of consistent repetition through conscious choices and affirmations that evoke feelings. If you miss a day, you need to start the process over to effectively make the desired change. Use the *Clarity & Focus Journal* (visit www.EddieMiller.com) to track your progress and even an accountability partner.

Repaving the Pathways of Our Inner States

What's the fastest way to circumvent a negative thought process?

Simply by interrupting your own thoughts.

As Lu Hanessian explained in chapter 4, our thoughts keep our story on a loop. A recurring narrative. Everybody's *story* is a series of neural connections that keep replaying until we stop them.

So if, in your inner-states, you say to yourself, "I can't lose weight and I can't control my anger," then five-sixths of your brain accepts that *as a direct order*. Consequently, you can't achieve your goals related to weight loss, anger management, or anything.

Remember the path of least resistance? To change your story and actions to ultimately create conscious sustainable changes, you need to create new neural pathways that replace the ones that no longer serves you. Doug's "ANTs" is a good starting place for recognizing any negative self-talk that's going on and then developing a way to stop it.

His ANTs technique refers to stomping on your ANTs—*Automatic Negative Thoughts*. As he says, "Once we recognize those negative thoughts, we stomp them out by transferring them into the *positive-positive*. I have people put a rubber band around their wrist and write 'stomp the ANTs' on it. So each time they say something negative, they snap their wrist with that rubber band and then change the sentence to be a positive-positive."

For example, instead of saying to ourselves "I'm not smart enough to really excel at the level I want to in my career" say, visualize, and journal "I'm a strong and intelligent person with unlimited resources available to me to excel in my career."

Try saying this out loud.

"I'm a strong and intelligent person with unlimited resources available to me to excel in my career."

Feel the immediate shift in your vibration energy—you're lighter, more confident, empowered? You can use this technique to tackle every self-limiting belief you have. With this simple change to an emotionally charged positive-positive statement we properly align our focus intentions and open ourselves to endless possibilities.

After about 21 to 30 days of doing this, negative thoughts aren't eliminated forever but their incidence will fall below 50%.

"That's when people start achieving like crazy," Doug affirms.

Visualization Creates Reality

Mastering how to change negative thought patterns into positive-positive ones can lead to creating a happy, healthy, and prosperous life—using what Doug calls a VCR, which stands for *Visualization Creates Reality*.

He tells a wonderful story about a golfer who used to shoot a round of golf right around par—a phenomenal achievement in the golf world. During the Vietnam War when he was a soldier, he was captured. To mentally survive the ordeal of the prison camps, he visualized himself playing a round of golf at several of his favorite golf courses back home.

He "practiced" in detail down to how much wind was blowing. He'd vary the conditions daily, imagining it being rainy or hot or chilly. In his mind, he'd dress accordingly. And he'd even smell the grass. Everyday for seven years, he'd step up on the tee box, put his tee in the ground, take his practice swings, and hit the golf ball in his mind.

Three days after returning to the United States (and having never touched a golf club since his capture), he shot one over par—just like he normally scored before he left.

Like this soldier did, we have to actively engage the brain, stimulating it to form new pathways. Visualizing our goals and doing exercises for twenty-one to thirty days will help you form new pathways in your brain. High-level performers like Olympic athletes are taught to consistently visualize the effort, visualize the movement, and visualize the steps over and over.

What about you? What would you like to see change in your life?

In the following chapters we will look at each component of our lives—our happiness, physical and spiritual health, finances, and relationships—as we do, I invite you to take an inventory …

1. Write down all the things you wish were different in your life.

2. Picture what you *want*, not what you don't want, so five-sixths of your brain will work to bring that exact desire to you.

3. Start by being aware of negative thoughts and limiting beliefs resounding in the brain.

4. Generate the awareness of the proven techniques revealed in these chapters.

5. Use your awareness to make intentional and positive change in your life.

As Doug concludes, "Pay attention to your brain. Your brain controls you. Learn how to change what's occurring in your brain and you can reach whatever goal you want to reach."

We can't change our life by *trying* to change our life. That doesn't work. We have to change our thinking habits—for they control our behavior.

———————————

"Once you understand how the brain works and learn techniques based on that—regardless of how cluttered, negative, and underachieving your life is—there's no one who can't turn that for the better. You can totally change your life from the inside-out."

— Doug Bench

———————————

Living Inside-Out Lessons from Chapter 7

- You can "re-wire" brain pathways at any time in your life by changing your thoughts and actions. This is called brain plasticity.

- Making new pathways of connections in the brain requires 21 to 30 days of repetition.

- Realize that 5/6 of your brain's thinking is unconscious; the conscious part is only 1/6 of your brain's power.

- Create positive-positive affirmations in all six parts of the brain so the RAS creates a positive picture, rather than a negative one.

- For motivation to last, it has to be generated intrinsically. The most effective method for creating change is by creating a desired change that you think, say out loud, write down, and attach with emotion and a visual picture.

8

HAPPINESS FROM THE INSIDE-OUT

The Power to Embrace Our Own Happiness

"What would it take to make you happy—a fulfilling career, a big bank account, or the perfect mate? What if it didn't take anything to make you happy? What if you could experience happiness from the inside-out, no matter what's going on in your life?"

— Marci Shimoff

So, if you didn't already know it, most people who write non-fiction books do so for their own growth and development—and I'm no exception.

In each of these chapters, a part of me moves into a deeper exploration and discovery mode by asking question after question in search of authentically living my life from the inside-out. I want to unlock the "knowing" that exists within me, and I assume you do too.

Having uncovered the fundamental principles of living inside-out and realizing the power we have to *mind our brain*, let's go a step further and address our happiness, health, finances, relationships, and spiritual essence.

The Essence of Happiness

When you think of happiness, what comes to mind? The birth of a child? The feeling of elation that comes over you the moment something exciting happens? The thought of a person you once knew who exuded happiness from every fiber of his or her being?

For many people who are struggling with life's issues, experiencing happiness is rare. And for many others—those who enjoy their relationships, careers, families, and home life, but know something is still missing—the ability to fully enjoy life can be challenging.

We may not realize that we *can* and *should* experience happiness everyday. Although the very idea may seem unrealistic, I discovered that it's actually unrealistic to live fully otherwise.

To explore the topic of *happiness*, I reached out to happiness expert Marci Shimoff, whose latest book *Happy for No Reason* is a *New York Times* bestseller.

Indeed, one of the best-selling female nonfiction authors of all time, Marci has seven best-selling titles, including *Chicken Soup for the Woman's Soul* and *Chicken Soup for the Mother's Soul*. She has sold more than 14 million copies worldwide in 33 languages; her books have appeared on the *New York Times* bestseller list for a total of 108 weeks.

Marci is also a featured teacher in the international film and book phenomenon, *The Secret*. Through her books and presentations, her message has touched the hearts and rekindled the spirits of millions of people worldwide. She is dedicated to fulfilling her life's purpose of helping people live more empowered and joy-filled lives.

Wondering why the idea of happiness seems foreign to so many adults these days, I asked Marci for her insights.

"It's interesting that we catch the emotions of the people around us just like we catch their colds. It's called 'emotional contagion.' As a result, we become the average of the five people we associate with the most. In fact, if we are happy, *we are helping the people around us much more than if we are not*. If we're not happy—if we're staying unhappy just to 'please' them—it certainly doesn't serve anybody. The best thing we can do to affect the happiness environment around us is by living at a higher vibration, a higher frequency. This is this state I call *happy for no reason*," she explains.

"This means we carry a back draft of peace and well-being so that no matter what's going on around us, we maintain a state of peace and well-being. That state influences everyone around us."

Who's Responsible for Being Happy?

In the past, I've thought—and have even heard others say—that it's naïve to be happy in the midst of a world so full of suffering. How can we expect to be happy when so many others aren't? We've heard from Byron Katie that suffering is optional. I've learned to ask this question instead: *How does my being unhappy serve those around me?* In truth, it doesn't.

I believe people have a right and even an obligation to choose to be happy. Nothing you do can force others to be happy. Their happiness is 100% their responsibility, just as is your own. Nobody can *make* me happy; nobody can *make* me unhappy. This is another one of those *aha!* inside-out moments. Said another way, what we do or don't do doesn't make others feel a particular emotion; they *choose* their own emotions and so do we.

Yet our culture implies that our moods depend on the people around us.

Everyday, we hear conversations such as, "You make me feel angry" or "You make me so sad" or "You make me happy." But that's not reality. They may feel a certain way *in response* to us, but it's still *their* responsibility to take ownership of their happiness—or unhappiness.

The Myth of Happiness

Many fall into the trap of projecting happiness out to a future date in the form of what Marci calls the myth of "I'll be happy when."

"I'll be happy when I buy a bigger house."

"I'll be happy when I lose 20 pounds."

"I'll be happy when I get out of this relationship."

"I'll be happy when I get a higher paying job."

Look at these statements. They're either about gaining something in the future or getting rid of something we don't like, not about being okay with *what is*. That distinction is important because happiness is *not* about something we want to acquire. Rather, it's about accepting what we already are and then opening ourselves to creating the conscious, sustainable changes we desire.

Habitual Thoughts and Behaviors

Marci discovered happy people *let love lead* in their daily lives.

"Although they have the same kind of fears, pains, and disappointments as the rest of us, happy people simply have different habits that allow them to keep their hearts open."

It's no secret that we humans are habitual creatures, both in thought and behavior. We can change many things directly, and we can adopt behaviors and habits that will influence those things we can't change directly. It's mainly our habitual thoughts and behaviors that influence our happiness.

Therein lies the clue: through these thoughts and behaviors, we have the power to choose our own level of happiness.

So rather than scrambling around seeking happiness from the outside by trying to change our circumstances, it's more effective to work on changing our habits of thought and behavior from the inside. As Marci points out, "People who are happy don't believe everything they think; *they question their thoughts.* In contrast, people who are unhappy don't even question their thoughts. They believe whatever thoughts come into their consciousness and hang on to them.

"So their thoughts might be 'I'm a bad person. I can't do this. I'll never be any good at this. I'll never be able to lose weight.' But those are old, repetitive thoughts that they've had since they were young. Ninety-five percent of our thoughts were the same as we had yesterday and the day before. And eight-five to ninety percent of these thoughts are negative.

"So unhappy people believe all these negative thoughts, while happy people don't. Indeed, they *reject* the ideas that don't follow their choices for happiness," Marci concludes.

Creating Our Own Happiness

Success will make us happy, right?

In reality, *happiness brings us success*. Why? Because when we're vibrating at a high level, we are more keenly aware of the resources that are readily available to us.

In her book *The Secret*, Rhonda Byrne writes, "I want to let you in on a secret to *The Secret*. The shortcut to anything that you want in your life is to *be and feel happy now*. It's the fastest way to bring money and anything else you want into your life." [Source: *The Secret* by Rhonda Byrne, Atria Books & Beyond World Publishing, 2006, p. 100]

Set your thoughts and frequency on happiness.

So how do we learn to vibrate at a higher level? The answer is simple: we already have that ability! Observe healthy newborn babies and how happy they are. Notice the innate spark in their eyes and their overwhelming sense of happiness and joy—the essence of their souls, of who they are.

Unfortunately, over the years, one's essence can get buried because of negative messages and limiting beliefs instilled from parents and family, society, and the media. Advertising is designed to convince us that we'll be happy if we purchase a particular product. We're constantly bombarded with messages linked to unhappiness! Telling us we can't be happy without their product or service.

The only way to bring back your true and natural state of happiness is through focused intention and practice. Take an honest look at your life and take full responsibility for everything in it. You can also do these things:

- Stop blaming others if you feel like a hamster on a wheel.
- Stop complaining about how tough life is.
- Stop feeling ashamed you're not spending more time with your family.
- Resist the urge of blaming your boss, the economy, or your loved ones.
- Don't fall into the victim mode.

Stated in a positive way, realize that you chose your life and you can choose your own happiness level.

Marci advises, "*Say yes! I'm responsible for my happiness and I'm able to make changes in my life*. That is the very first step. Yet most people don't even get that far. They just settle into thinking that life is about just getting by, surviving. 'Maybe someday if I'm lucky I'll feel better."

We know it won't happen that way. Rather, it will happen when we become more aware of our thoughts and behaviors, and then actively choose different ones. And that shift need not take years.

Our Happiness Set-Point

Scientists have made a revolutionary discovery that each of us has a happiness set-point. That means no matter what happens to us—good or bad—we tend to hover around the same predisposed range of happiness *unless we deliberately do something to change it.*

Marci offers this example: "Take people who've won the lottery. Within a year of winning—which we think is the golden ticket to happiness— they've returned to their original state. The same is true, shockingly, for people who've become paraplegic. Within a year of a sudden physical change, they've also returned to their original happiness level or set-point range."

Yes, our happiness *set-point*—not the circumstances of our lives— determines how happy we feel. But what forces determine that happiness set-point?

Consider these facts:

- 50% of our happiness set-point is determined by genetics—that is, we were born with it; it's in our DNA.

- 10% is determined by circumstances, so saying, "Oh, if I just changed my circumstances, then I'd be happier" is only 10% of the equation.

- 40% is determined by our habitual thoughts, feelings, and behaviors—and fortunately we can change them.

Marci says, "In my research of people who are happy—unconditionally happy and experiencing lasting happiness—I found the major difference between them and everybody else is they have empowering habits and experience more joy, spontaneity, and fulfillment in their lives." People who are unconditionally happy embrace what they can change—the 40% of their happiness set-point.

Silent Inner Practice

So making a change in our outer world comes by changing our inner world. We have the power within us to bring our own happiness into being. Yet what changes can we really expect to make in our lives?

To illustrate, Marci shares this incredible story: "A woman had been diagnosed with Lupus for fifteen years. She got very depressed as the disease progressed. She was confined to a wheelchair and became overweight. Still, she wanted to change her life and experience happiness, so she made the decision to practice wishing others well—a silent inner practice, not something she expressed out loud.

"Everyday, she made the habit of silently sending a wish of happiness, health, and well-being to the people around her. As she passed people on the sidewalk or highway, she said silently, *I wish you health. I wish you happiness. I wish you well-being.*

"Within a year of doing this, her happiness level soared. Amazing! Today, she's out of the wheelchair and exercising three times a week. She's become symptom-free and the doctor says it's a medical miracle. Yet the only thing that changed was what she chose to do within herself. It created a huge shift in her mental, emotional, and physical well-being."

The best thing about this story is knowing that this technique of sending positive wishes to others can be practiced by anybody anytime. It doesn't matter if you're getting angry at the guy who cuts you off in traffic, you can stop raging and start sending positive thoughts that mirror what you want in life.

These thoughts can actually change your heart rate pattern as you feel connection, love, gratitude, and appreciation. In contrast, angry thoughts can raise your heart rate and release stress hormones as you watch your happiness go out the window.

The Heart of Happiness

Scientific research has discovered that the heart is the epicenter of life. The Institute of HeartMath—the world's leading researchers dedicated to transforming stress, improving regulation of emotional responses, and harnessing the power of heart/brain communication—found that from the heart emanates an electromagnetic field several feet in diameter.

In fact, this heart-generated field is *5,000 times more powerful* than the electromagnetic field generated by the brain. As Marci explains, "We have been trained in our society to honor the mind, but I think that the mind isn't the great master. It's a great servant, yes, but the *heart* is a greater master.

"Every spiritual tradition talks about the heart being the truth, the center, the essence of who one is. In fact, right now, if you were asked to point at your own essence, it's ninety-nine percent likely you would point to your heart. Nobody points to the head or belly button or kneecap. Why? Because instinctively you feel the heart is at the core of who you are," Marci says.

While sending positive thoughts to those around you takes little effort, doing so can shift your awareness and attention. In the beginning, you may find that can be challenging, but its payoff is huge in happiness and ultimately getting what you want. Being happy is the goal of all goals—why you believe you want a nicer house, more money, better relationships. By creating happiness first—from the inside-out—all else will follow.

"Happiness is like building your muscles; it takes daily practice," Marci emphasizes. "It's a process that requires surrounding yourself with support. Because of so much negativity out there, having others help you focus on your deepest desires keeps you on track." The result? Raising your happiness set-point.

Happiness practice is another example of building neural pathways in the brain. Practice makes … joy. (Not perfection!)

Here are the three guiding principles Marci teaches that can renew our happiness in life.

THREE GUIDING PRINCIPLES OF HAPPINESS

1. **What expands makes you happier.** When your body is in a state of contraction, you roll into a ball and feel tight. Its opposite is the feeling of expansion when you put your arms out and take in a deep breath. Everything in life is either moving you toward contraction or expansion, so know that you can move toward that feeling of expansion on a moment-to-moment basis.

2. **The Universe is out to support you.** It's what Jack Canfield calls being "reverse paranoid." Do you feel the world is out to get you? Reverse that assumption and live by the belief that this is a friendly universe and that everything happens to support your greatest good. Even when bad events occur, look for the lesson, the gift, by asking, *"If this were happening for a higher purpose, what would that be?"*

3. **What you put your attention on grows stronger.** If you want more good in your life, become more aware of the goodness you already have. By focusing on what you want and how you want to be, you can make that your norm through daily practice—and in the process, you'll build your happiness muscles and raise your happiness set-point.

Unexpected Gratitude

I would say that generally my happiness set-point is set on 'life is good.' But that doesn't mean that my life doesn't have its ups and downs.

Several years ago I started a new company, which actually lead to the idea of writing this book. However after about six months, the company wasn't taking off and I realized I need to get a job to keep moving forward with my dream. After trying several avenues, I reach out to my friend Michael who worked for one of the top interior commercial construction companies in Miami.

My background was non-profit operational management, and I knew nothing about construction; however, the owners gave me a shot. The company was amazing, and the job paid me very well. Although getting up early each morning and dealing with the so-called daily grind was challenging, I was grateful for the job as it was continuing to fuel my ability to write this book.

After a little over two years, I decided to take off for three months to focus on this book and other projects. When I was ready to go back to work, the economic took a downturn and the construction company was laying off instead of being able to hire me back.

I had no idea what I was going to do. Three months later, I was up late one night and saw an infomercial about investing in real estate, so my partner, Alekxey, and I began doing some research and found Ron LeGrand. This lead to a prosperous new opportunity, and we began buying and selling properties. In the first year, we became one of the fastest growing private investors in Miami, and made more money than we ever made in our lives.

A major focus of our business is renovating distressed properties; without the two years working for the construction company I *wouldn't have had the knowhow* to build the business so quickly.

You never know when unexpected gifts will appear in your life or why you are being guided in a certain way instead of another. This is why focusing on happiness habits—the 40% we control—is critical; when we do, the Universe responses in our favor ... even if you don't realize it at the time.

High Intention, Low Attachment

Jack Canfield also talks about a concept called *high intention, low attachment*, which asserts that it's wonderful to have a grand vision, but recognize that your state of well-being doesn't depend on that vision coming through. Having a low attachment to achieving your loftiest vision is where the issue of expectation comes in—a concept Marci explains through her phrase *intention, attention, no tension*.

INTENTION, ATTENTION, NO TENSION

- **Intention:** Be clear about what you want—in this case, greater happiness.
- **Attention:** What you put your attention on grows, so put your attention on the happiness you desire to create.
- **No Tension:** Let go and relax. No doubt every time you've had a major breakthrough, you've been about to "let go" in a state of no tension.

When you have high expectations and attachments—the opposite of *high intention, low attachment*—they can create suffering. When you have intention or vision while keeping an underlying state of peace and well-being, you'll experience great freedom.

In fact, anyone in sales knows that the person who makes the sale is the one willing to walk away from it. Same principle at play here. Why? Because when you're willing to walk away, you aren't hanging on to your anxiety, fear, and desperation. You enjoy a sense of freedom without tension. And that state of freedom allows for the good to come in. Conversely, it's hanging on to a particular outcome that can create problems.

As we struggle to overcome the negativity and pressure of everyday life, we must be aware they exist. From there, we have the option of going through everyday either with dread and drudgery or with happiness and gratitude. We can choose.

So echoing back to Byron Katie's questions in chapter 5, we can confront the voice that says "I can't do better" or whatever your limiting thought may be. Ask, "Is that really true? Can I absolutely know that it's true? How do I react when I believe that thought? Who would I be without that thought?"

I believe we're on this planet to experience the happiness and joy that life can offer. To achieve our greatest good. If you aren't experiencing these feelings right now, you likely weren't aware of them being *options*. Don't just take what life hands you. Instead, choose the set-point of happiness you want and make that your focused intention.

"When we are happy from the inside-out, we bring that state of happiness with us to our life experiences rather than trying to extract our happiness from our life experiences."

— Marci Shimoff

Living Inside-Out Lessons from Chapter 8

- Happiness is only 10% based on our current circumstances.

- Nobody can make you happy; nobody can make you unhappy.

- Happiness is about accepting what you already have and are, and opening yourself to creating conscious sustainable change.

- Adopt the silent inner practice of wishing others well.

- Have "high intention, low attachment" to the outcomes desired.

- You're here; experience happiness and joy everyday of your life.

9

NUTRITION FROM THE INSIDE-OUT

Skillfulness is the Path to Conscious Eating

"To pursue health is the pursuit of happiness.
It is the golden opportunity all of us have and we should take advantage of it."
— David Katz, MD

And now, we delve into what many consider to be one of the most challenging, possibly life-threatening, areas of our lives. According to current statistics in the United States, the majority of us struggle with weight and weight-related health issues. I'm the first one to raise my hand as one who is challenged. But why do we struggle?

We need food, of course. We love our food. Food often represents comfort, security, and a love affair in our lives. As well, with hectic schedules and the convenience of buying fast foods, the basis of our survival—eating well—becomes the last priority on our long list of things to do.

We attempt diets and exercise programs; however, many of us fail to stay committed.

The result? We end up heavier and unhealthier. Our state of health directly affects how we feel physically and mentally as well as what chronic diseases we might experience due to poor nutrition, overeating, and other lifestyle choices.

This chapter addresses eating foods that fuel our bodies, not those that feed our emotions or the stories that our mind leads us to believe. Remember

113

the old saying about our body being our temple? Well, the foods we eat are what provide fuel to keep the structure of our temple strong.

Ripple Effect of Health

When we eat healthy and exercise often, we reduce stress and gain more confidence as the way we feel about ourselves improves. This core principle has a ripple effect into every area of life—relationship, career, finances … well, everything.

I have to confess. I have a sweet tooth bigger than the entire state of Florida, and having grown up on a Midwest farm, I know all about comfort food. When I get stressed and overworked, I quickly supplement my feelings of lack or insecurity and emotions of overwhelm and frustration with my favorite foods—like roast beef, mashed potatoes, and any kind of dessert, especially chocolate. I followed this pattern for years until I became aware of what I was doing.

As my self-esteem dropped, I ate more. I watched my waistline expand and my self-confidence plummet in a self-perpetuating cycle. Like millions of others, I know first-hand how hard it is to get off the unhealthy track.

Yet, from a health standpoint, I knew better. I mean, I knew I was creating the potential for many chronic diseases that have run in my family for generations. If I didn't change my poor food choices, I was on a path to internal self-destruction.

I decided to take 100% responsibility for my health and my actions. I started by becoming acutely aware of answering this powerful question for myself: *As my life unfolded on the outside, how was I responding on the inside?*

I learned to realize that, internally, when my mind triggered feelings of discomfort, which led me to crave foods that weren't necessarily healthy for me. And, believe me, I'd eat them in large quantities. Can you put two and two together with me? I was stressed and unhappy, and I wasn't dealing with the source of my painful feelings. I tried to eat them away, like millions of us in this country, which, of course, got me more stressed and unhappy.

What We're Really Eating

In addition to understanding what's going on mentally, I really wanted to learn exactly what is or isn't good for a healthy body. With so many fad diets and crazy eating habits, it's hard to know the truth about what helps our temple function at its best—and what hinders us from reaching our ultimate health goals.

To clarify this dilemma, I reached out to renowned doctor David Katz, M.D., a physician and nationally renowned authority on nutrition, weight control, and chronic disease prevention. An associate clinical professor of epidemiology and public health, he is also director of medical studies in public health at Yale University School of Medicine and author of *Flavor-Full Diet, Way to Eat,* and *Stealth Health* to name a few.

Perhaps you've seen Dr. Katz on the *Dr. Oz Show*; a blogger for *Prevention Magazine*, or as a medical contributor for ABC News, and from his regular television appearances on *Good Morning America*, *20/20*, and *World News Tonight*. He's also a health contributor to *Huffington Post* and has been a regular columnists for the *New York Times* and *O—The Oprah Magazine*. He is the principal inventor of the Overall Nutritional Quality Index (ONQI) algorithm used in the NuVal System—www.NuVal.com

When you meet David, you can tell from his trim physique, bright smile, and incredible energy that he walks his talk about leading a healthy lifestyle—despite his hectic schedule and making time for his family, including his wife Catherine and their five children.

What is David's "take" on America's epidemic of unhealthiness?

"I think we see so much obesity and related chronic disease because eating is one area in which people simply say enough is enough. 'I'm working too hard. Given the complications of modern living, my crazy schedule, my kids' activities—I've had enough. On top of all that, at the end of a crazy day when I'm exhausted, it's challenging to figure out when and how to exercise; and avoid eating the tasty temptations that at least give me immediate gratification. It's just too hard.' It seems being *healthy* is the toughest route, so being *unhealthy* has defaulted to the path of least resistance. And having a bit of convenience, a bit of comfort in a crazy world, is good."

So how do we get out of this unhealthy cycle? Wouldn't going on a diet work if we're serious about losing weight and becoming healthy?

David contends that, when it comes to dieting, one fundamental myth prevails—*that going on means coming off.* "There's no real advantage to going on a diet in the first place. Why? Because if we go on a diet, at some point we'll go off the diet. Then we'll gain back the weight (usually plus interest) as fast as we took it off. We wind up driving ourselves mad by being totally fixated on our weight rather than living an invigorating life.

"What's true is the flip side of the myth. For lasting weight control, we must focus on health first and foremost. We have to recognize some things that cause us to lose weight are just bad for our health." He believes it's better to think about how to lose weight over time and recognizes the strength in taking a unified approach to changing both the way we live *and* the way we eat. "We can support one another in that change by turning to the people who are intimate in our lives," he adds.

Why We Tend to Eat Way Too Much

We know the basic reason we gain weight—that is, we ingest more calories than we burn off. So why do we still eat way too much of primarily unhealthy foods? To our ancestors food was simple. Reliable food sources not only meant survival, but also wealth and social status.

As David indicates, "We have equated food with currency. We speak about making dough, being the bread winner, bringing home the bacon. Those are expressions that equate food with stature and success—and money."

Yet, in our modern world of plenty, our relationship with food has become complicated. Instead of feeding our bodies, we try to "nourish our souls" with high fat, high salt, and high sugar food that once comforted our ancestors in the name of survival. Today, these foods give us a false sense of comfort in the presence of emotional discomfort or pain.

Add to that our tendency to beat ourselves up when we fail to sustain an exercise routine or eating regime. I'm no stranger to beating myself up, either, but why do we do it?

"A lack of understanding," David explains. "Eating is often an emotional shield for things we don't want to deal with. If we're eating to soothe troubled emotions, those emotions won't go away no matter the state of our weight or health."

So we need to first accept this reality and then understand we can stop beating ourselves up by *focusing our intentions* and *expanding our knowledge*. That requires taking responsibility for creating change in how we live—a consistent message through this book!

"It's easy to fall into a victim mentality," David emphasizes. "There's such a profoundness of self-blame around eating and weight, but it's rarely what we let go of." That's why many of us who lose a great deal of weight gain it right back—because *we never deal with the underlying emotional reasons*.

David continues, "No aspect of one's life is lived on an island independent of the rest. We can't address overeating if we don't address our emotional needs at their origin." We can address that by discussing emotional issues with a good friend, a significant other, or a healthcare provider. That confidant can help us look inside, discover our stories, the emotional needs we've created based on them, and figure out why we knowingly eat what we shouldn't.

"Whatever issues come—boredom, stress, abandonment, loneliness—first let's define what our needs are, then take the opportunity to figure out how to address them." He adds, "That said, I never tell people to just stop using food to address an emotional need. *I want to know what the emotional need is*. Then I want to figure out other ways to address it. This applies to any kind of dependency, not just food."

Our Bodies Designed for Stone Age Survival

Yet beyond the complexities of why we eat, isn't eating to support our bodies' maximum functioning instinctive? Doesn't it override any emotional or mental influences? David says, "We often don't understand why we're overeating and under exercising in the first place. We are creatures; we have physiology; we are not responsible for these aspects—we inherited them."

In previous eras—even as recent as a hundred years ago—people spent their lives being in fear due to the scarcity of food. They experienced only intermittent periods of comfort and security when their bellies were full.

David points out, "We used to suffer from scarcity of calories; we now overproduce food. It was hard to get salt; we now have food supply that's highly over salted. It was once hard to find sugar; we now have an excess of sugar, and so on. On the physical activity side, it was impossible to avoid physical activity in previous times. It wasn't called exercise; it was called survival."

The fundamental functioning of our bodies is still designed for a Stone Age environment, a concept that may seem hard to grasp. Similarly, our brains haven't caught up to our cultural changes. Survival traits like binging on food (especially fat, salt, and sugar) when available once was natural for our ancestors in "their nutritional environment." But today, they represent a detriment in our modern nutritional environment of abundance.

As David explains, "In essence, when we look at the chronic diseases plaguing modern society, they are mostly diseases of excess. We have epidemic obesity from an excess of calories. We have coronary artery disease from an excess of the wrong kind of fat and calories. We have an excess of labor-saving technologies that allows us to be sedentary. Clearly, we live in an environment that's fundamentally at odds with our native traits and tendencies.

"If we are here today, it's because generations before us managed to survive in a world where calories were relatively scarce and physical activity demands were high. It stands to reason that, in our native environment, we too are adapted to a world of high physical activity and relatively scarce calories.

"But put us in a world where physical activity is scarce and calories are abundant. That environment conspires against us. I use the analogy of a polar bear living in the Sahara Desert to describe this. We have no native defenses against caloric excess or the lure of the couch because we never needed them before.

"But we *are* smarter than the average bear. We have the capacity to change that environment. We do, in fact, have one native defense: our *homo sapien* brain power."

Skill Power vs. Will Power

As we learned in chapter 7, once we're aware of a certain trigger and pattern we're experiencing, we have the capacity to create new brain pathways. New ideas or actions usually cause discomfort at the neural level of our brain, leading to possible physical discomfort.

When we become conscious of this process, we can change the outcome to the point where, eventually, this new pathway becomes natural to our brain. Thus, we replace the discomfort with a new way of being.

For me, I had to *catch myself* as I was falling into old patterns; to become *consciously aware* of the food choices I was making and why I was making them.

Was I tired, stressed, upset?

By being consciously aware of my feelings and emotions, I could more easily *change my behavior* to make new, healthier choices.

The conscious choices I made produced a positive result. By bringing only healthy foods into the house, ordering balanced meals (with moderate portions of protein, fresh vegetables, and whole grain carbohydrates), and joining a gym (with a workout partner to keep me accountable), I have decreased my waist size. Better yet, I feel more energetic than ever and have a stronger sense of self-esteem.

I also know I need balance in my life, so I include one or two personal indulgences each week. That means I *consciously* select a time each week to eat my favorite foods without guilt or shame. I'm no longer *unconsciously* eating these foods based on my emotions.

I've also done what David says is the first priority: I've stopped beating myself up when I slipped off track and simply keep in mind my focused intention of eating healthy.

In addition David emphasizes that "Previous generations had a better consumption/exercise ratio than us because they had fewer choices, not more will power. We have to learn the skills necessary to eat what's good for us as quickly as other options like fast food become available on every corner."

To determine the right types of food for our bodies, let's move from "*will power* to *skill power*." As he says, "First *do an inventory on what prevents you from eating well*. The common ones are 'I'm too busy, it's too difficult, I don't know what to do … Try this: think of being healthy as a challenge that requires new skills and these skills can be acquired."

For example, you can learn to read through the deceptive language on food packages and make more nutritious choices. You can also practice preparing nutritious food to take with you, thus insulating yourself against hazardous exposures to vending machines and fast food. Be sure to hang in there and give these new skills 21 to 30 days to become habits. "Doing this need not be a burden but an opportunity to acquire skills that will enhance the rest of your life. Yes, it takes effort, but everything worthwhile does," David emphasizes.

To create a new habit, appreciate these two facts:

1. You can do it, and
2. You likely need to develop new skills.

Not having adopted better eating habits is nothing to be ashamed of or feel guilty about. "If you have the right kind of skill power, if you know how to choose nutritious food, you actually can get the food to love you back. Your body will respond and your energy level will soar. That result is closer at hand than you realize," advises David.

Healthy Eating Tips

Everything we eat—including highly processed foods with detrimental additives and little nutrients—affects our blood sugar and insulin levels, so eating foods that work *with* our bodies rather than *against* them helps stabilize moods and manage stress effectively.

As David emphasizes, "It's important to eat closer to nature, preparing meals that are minimally processed and include a high percentage of fruits, vegetables, nuts, peas, and whole grains. You can combine that with a protein source and use healthy oils. Don't get overwhelmed by adopting a complicated program. Just focus on a few simple ideas and stay close to nature with your choices."

Remember these few basic truths when making your eating choices:

TEN BASIC TRUTHS

1. **Don't diet; create a lifestyle of healthy eating.** When on a diet, it's common to feel deprived that's why you gain the weight right back when you go off them. Remember, having long-term good health is a *lifestyle*. (Yes, you can have your 1 or 2 weekly indulgence meals—just not all the time.)

2. **Eat Vegetables and Fruits.** In most cases, *vegetables and fruits don't have a lot of calories*. This means you can eat as many as you want, feel full, and know you're not ingesting a huge number of calories.

3. **Don't Eat Large Quantities**. Eat in moderation in smaller meals throughout the day. For the majority of your nutritional strategy, select foods high in nutrients, and low in calories, such as vegetables, fruits, and whole grains. These foods should be accompanied with a smaller portion of higher calorie foods like nuts, seeds olives, avocados, and some lean meat and fish.

4. **Eat High-Volume Foods.** Foods high in volume, such as vegetables, fruits, and broth-based soups, fill you with a low number of calories. These foods are also generally rich in nutrients. This is especially important if you are trying to lose weight.

5. **Take in Fiber Content**. Eating high-fiber food reduces your risk of chronic diseases, including heart disease, diabetes, and cancer. It also aids in controlling your appetite. Fiber is found in whole cereal grains, fruits, vegetables, nuts seeds, beans, and lentils. (Note: Most Americans eat less than half the recommended amount of about 30 milligrams of fiber a day.)

6. **Watch Fat Content.** Fat is less filling, calorie for calorie, than either proteins or carbohydrates. However, fat is more energy dense, which means it packs in lots of calories into a small volume. Select foods that are naturally low in fat. Make a particular effort to minimize saturated and trans fat; be sure to include healthful mono- and polyunsaturated fats.

7. **Eat Organic and 100% Natural Foods.** This choice may not always be available; however, read the labels and know what's included. Organic produce tends to be higher in nutritional value than non-organic. When buying more processed foods, organic is better because it doesn't have chemical components, genetically modified substances, and preservatives. Always a win-win. Again be a savvy shopper, labels can be misleading.

8. **Choose Processed and Fast Food Wisely**. Obviously we know eating fruits and veggies are the goal; however, that isn't always feasible in the realm of our overwhelming lives. Many processed foods in a bag, box, bottle, or can—and most meals from fast food restaurants—tend to be higher in calories and loaded with fat, salt, and sugars, often causing electrolyte and insulin imbalances. Not all processed and fast food is created equally. There are healthier options. Choose healthier items by reading labels watching for hidden fat, sodium, and sugars. David has helped to create a new way of determining the most beneficial and nutritious foods when shopping and helpful tips. Go to **www.NuVal. com** for more information.

9. **When to Eat and How Much.** Eating three moderate meals and three snacks each day with two to three hours between your meals and snacks helps keeping your insulin levels steady and your energy consistent throughout the day. Your first meal should be eaten within the first hour of waking up and your last snack right before going to bed to ensure that consistency.

10. **Drink Plenty of Water.** A good rule to follow is to drink eight to ten 8-ounce glasses of water a day. Organic green tea is a great option, too. Avoid drinking soda, energy drinks, and most juices as they contain high levels of sugar.

These ten keys continue to help me embrace my healthy eating lifestyle everyday. It isn't a surprise to announce that health is directly related to happiness. We feel good; we feel happy. But, health is an inside-out lifestyle choice, not the result of a fad diet that worked.

I agree with David's words of wisdom and his encouragement to take the opportunity to feel vital and alive. We only have one body and taking care of it is a priority for thriving and preventing chronic disease. With our children getting many of the chronic illnesses once slated for aging adults, like diabetes for example, our society's survival is becoming contingent on learning those skills.

Give yourself permission to embrace eating choices that fuel your vitality. Reinforce this by using the positive-positive affirmations Doug discussed in chapter 7 like, "I'm fit and thin, and I eat healthy foods." By applying the ideas outlined in this chapter, healthy eating will begin to come naturally to you, and you will see the benefits in your body, mind, and life as a result. You'll evaluate your healthy eating lifestyle honestly and accurately, and become motivated to eat well.

"Living inside-out is a golden opportunity to shift the way we think about our health, our eating habits, and our activity. There is nothing more important to one's enjoyment of life and health vitality. We simply have to acquire the right skills and apply the right focus."

— David Katz, MD

Living Inside-Out Lessons from Chapter 9

- When you eat healthy and exercise, you reduce stress and gain more confidence as your body image improves.

- High fat, high salt, and high sugar foods gave our ancestors comfort in the name of survival, but today they can give you a false sense of comfort in the presence of emotional discomfort or pain.

- The reason many people lose a great deal of weight and gain it right back is because they never deal with the underlying emotional causes.

- Focus on eating closer to nature. This means eating foods that are minimally processed and include a high percentage of plant foods such as fruits, vegetables, nuts, peas, and whole grain. Combine that with a protein source and use only healthy oils.

10

FITNESS FROM THE INSIDE-OUT

Emotional & Physical Fitness for Life

"Exercise can improve creativity, productivity, improve your total overall health, and boost energy levels. Every ounce of data proves we will live longer and be healthier, less stressed and more productive if we embrace exercise. Exercise trumps genetics every time."

— Jim Karas

Do you have energy that lasts throughout the day? Do you walk into meetings with confidence knowing you're at your absolute best? No, these are not trick questions. And yes, I know they're rhetorical.

Let me guess. You answered "no" and "no"—right? I'm with you.

As we learned in the last chapter, when we talk about living a happy, healthy, and prosperous life from the inside-out, our health is at the very core. But, we tend to race through our days, becoming easily overwhelmed, overworked, overcommitted, and then what's the first thing that falls through the cracks? Taking care of ourselves by eating well and exercising! We procrastinate on our health while scrambling to meet work deadlines or family obligations.

Surprise, surprise. I know this routine well. Yes, me, the living inside-out guy who gets up every morning with the focused intention to live my best life and inspire you to do the same.

See, my office is in my home, and although it is a great luxury, if I don't stay focused on getting to the gym I can easily be drawn to my computer and then it's all over. Before I know it my assistant rolls in and I haven't even taken a shower. The gym get's pushed aside.

Guess what? I'm human! Like you, I can get so caught up in life that I lose sight of what's good for me.

That's why living from the inside-out means being *consciously aware* of the decisions we make every moment, *getting real with ourselves*. You can make today the day to choose to put your health and vitality first. Everything else flows from there.

Model for a Fit Lifestyle

When I think of fitness role models—those who lead by example—one person comes to mind: Jim Karas.

A nationally recognized fitness and weight-loss expert, Jim provides practical solutions for managing energy levels, weight loss, and stress reduction. He is the author of three *New York Times* bestsellers including *The Business Plan for the Body, The Cardio Free Diet,* and his latest, *The 7-Day Energy Surge.* He also wrote *Flip the Switch: Discover the Weight Loss Solution and the Secret to Getting Started.*

Jim has been the Fitness Contributor for ABC's *Good Morning America,* is frequently seen on *The View* and *FOX News* and has been profiled in countless publications such as *O—The Oprah Magazine, Vogue, Time,* and *Glamour.* He helps people from all walks of life incorporate fitness into their day and make it a lasting part of their lives.

Jim says, "People simply don't realize that if you invest in your mind and your body by reducing those flaming hormones and being calmer, less stressed, you will be infinitely more productive."

Jumping the First Hurdle

As I have stressed throughout this book, it's important to take 100% responsibility for the choices we're making. In our efforts to lose weight and exercise, if we say we *can't,* then we play the victim; if we say we *won't,* then we have to confront the choice we've made about our health and fitness levels.

I know all of the excuses. Remember, I've used them myself. But, as Jim says, few people make it past those first two critical weeks of a new exercise routine.

"Two weeks is the honeymoon period," he says, "and then the programs hit the fan. Most of the time within the two weeks, one thing happens to derail us. One dinner we attend when we eat more than we should. One day in that second week we skip our exercise after promising to exercise three times a week. As Americans, we tend to have an all-or-nothing mentality, so the minute we miss one part of our expectations, we throw in the towel. It's because of our desire to get it all done fast."

What's the major hurdle we need to jump when beginning a new exercise routine?

Setting realistic goals. I always thought it was about setting the goal, period. But, many of us have a little issue with keeping them attainable.

Jim gives this analogy: "When most doctors prescribe medication, they start with a low dose, determine if it's effective in their follow-up appointments, and then ascertain whether they need to increase or decrease the amount.

"Do most people act like that with exercise? No. They haven't exercised in years, so they put on an ancient pair of running shoes that have absolutely no support left and horrible old sweats, then attempt an exercise program that's far above their current fitness level. Consequently, it feels terrible. They hurt. And they become completely discouraged. It's frightening."

What didn't happen? Setting a *realistic* goal and progressing from there. "We didn't set a benchmark that could be adhered to—one of the biggest problems we can create! We make the exact same mistake with an eating plan. We're eating horribly, then decide in one day to do a one-eighty in our eating. Suddenly, we expect to eat perfectly.

"You and I know that won't happen. It's best to set small goals for the week—like not drinking soda or juice, or limiting our fast food dining to twice a week. "If we do this, then at the end of that week, we can pat ourselves on the back. We say, 'Good work; let's set more goals for the coming week.' Before we know it, we're doing beautifully!"

Because of our ever-present all-or-nothing mentality, it's *essential* to set realistic goals and stop creating a vicious circle of beating ourselves up for missing a workout or eating poorly. That negative voice kicks in and says, "I'm a loser. I can't stick with anything, so I might as well live, look, and feel like a loser.

Consequently Jim adds, "At the end of the night, you look at yourself, you feel awful, and you've eaten awful foods. You don't feel good about your health, possibly your job, your relationship, your sex life, you name it. And then you eye the pint in the freezer and think, 'That will taste good going down.' You've just made matters worse."

At this point, I'm wondering if maybe Jim has had a spy cam in my house.

Get an Accountability Partner

Avoiding issues of getting fit and eating well has become an unconscious way of punishing ourselves, of holding us back. What does Jim suggest? "The most important tool I teach *is making a commitment to accountability*. If people can afford it, they can pay someone who can hold them accountable, a trainer, a nutritionist, a doctor, whatever. But for most people, that's a luxury."

So how do we hold ourselves accountable? It can be as simple as finding someone — a friend, family member, or even someone at the gym who is as committed to a workout program as you are. Select someone who will help keep you motivated. Why? Because some days, you may not be energized to go to the gym or eat healthy. However, your partner will insist you keep going on the path *you* chose. Likewise, your partner will have days when motivation is missing. That's when it's your job to provide it.

Need expertise to set up the right program? If hiring a trainer strains your budget, the two of you could share the investment. You can schedule a regular one or two times a month check-in with the trainer to review your progress and create your next workout plan.

Your Emotional Epicenter

Accountability starts with taking a lifestyle inventory of your life. From the Inside-Out Principle #4 *Know Your Truth*, you learned that having an account of your life means understanding the stories you play out. That requires an openness and willingess to examine your stories. It doesn't take time or money—just willingess. When it comes to fitness, if you feel you've "let yourself go," the reason behind it is likely found in your stories!

Jim agrees with Dr. Katz and says, "To begin the process of living inside-out, we first figure out what's been going on before we can determine an action plan. When you renovate a house, you don't start knocking down walls and ripping out toilets. You first do a structural assessment to determine where the weak and strong spots are, and what needs attention first. Similarly, with your fitness, weight loss, and health issues determine what needs to be dealt with first."

Jim calls this assessment process your *Emotional Epicenter,* which is about digging deep to know why you make the choices you do. You process internally to determine who and what you want to be and, most important, what keeps you from getting there. Then it's about erasing the mental graffiti—all of your shoulds, shouldn'ts, and can'ts. "A huge component of setting and maintaining a healthy lifestyle is *knowing you can live the way you want,*" he states.

When Jim starts working with someone, he first asks this question: When was a time in your life you felt better about your health, your body weight, your fitness, your energy level, and all that? "Everyone instantly comes up with a time like, '*Oh, when I was in college*' or '*Oh, before I got married*' or '*Oh, when I was turning thirty and I really wanted to get in great shape.*'

"So I ask that person to reach back into the exact moment, and I say, 'You're still that person. You're not opening a magazine to a photo of Elle McPherson and saying 'I want to look like her?' Instead, I try to get that person back into some of those habits that once worked so they can be duplicated today.

"Yes, the habits require modification. But I ask, 'What can we do now that can prove to you that you were a success at one point?' The person can't look at me, declare 'I can't do it,' and be truthful. After all, he or she has already achieved that success!"_

Setting Yourself Up for Success

Jim suggests starting small and *ask for one thing you will do differently this week* in your eating and exercise regime—like drinking more water or getting more sleep or working out twice instead of once.

"All the research shows if you pick one thing to accomplish, odds are it will set you on the correct path of feeling good about yourself. Then you build on that good feeling. That good behavior. That positive improvement," he emphasizes.

Remember the brain research says it takes *at least* 21 to 30 days to create a new habit? We need to keep that in mind as when setting fitness and nutrition goals.

When it comes to making healthy changes, setting up the right environment is also crucial. As Marci said in chapter 7, "You are the average of the five people you spend the most time with." When I first heard that, I had to sit down and really consider the reality of that kind of social math. Like, were the people I spent the most time with TV-loving couchers, brownie-scarfing dessert addicts, people who were allergic to fresh air?

Jim also agrees, he says, "If the five key people around you have no interest in exercising or eating healthy foods or getting sleep or minimizing alcohol consumption or drinking more water, you won't be able to do these things. A University of Pittsburgh School of Medicine study showed that sixty-six percent of those who had kept their weight off had a weight-loss buddy versus twenty-four percent who didn't. That's why I urge my clients, readers, and listeners to get a buddy; it makes a huge, huge difference."

Setting an environment for success includes *making time to exercise and eat well*. Jim says, "Not having time is an excuse. We have one hundred and nineteen hours in one week. That's seven thousand one hundred forty minutes. Surely we can find twenty minutes on two or three different days to do strength training!"

It requires pulling out your day planner for the next week and penciling in three 20-minute exercise sessions. When you do this, you'll instantly find it easier to exercise than you thought because you're managing your expectations.

Of course, part of managing your expectations is anticipating a slip up. That's not to cast a dark cloud of doubt over ourselves, but to essentially know our weak spots and plan for them.

"We all slip up from time to time. We'll have a week without exercise or eating well because we're at a convention or on a vacation. The key is having the structure to get back on our program when we're back in our environment," Jim advises.

Setting an environment for success also includes *establishing realistic weight loss goals*. "We are barraged with promises such as *Lose 30 Pounds in 30 Days*. Impossible! We're set up to be overachievers, yet no one can hit an unrealistic goal like that. Still, I've had clients who dutifully stick to such a plan. When I ask how they're doing, they say, 'Oh, I *only* lost six pounds.' I go ballistic. They're disappointed with *only* a six-pound loss while I think it's fantastic. But because they only lost six pounds, they quit their lifestyle of healthy eating. And what happens? They go back to their previous weight. That's something you absolutely don't want to do."

Planning intelligently is what Jim calls being the masters of our schedules. "With our i-Phones, Blackberries, and other technologies, we're wired up the wazzoo. Yet these tools help us be more organized, but paradoxically, we tend to feel more out of control and disorganized. "I recommend you turn off these type of electronics. They divert your attention, making you less productive than you could be."

Setting an environment for success also includes getting your rest.

"The research on sleep deprivation is staggering," Jim states. "As a population, we're down more than one-and-a-half hours a night compared with the 1970s. This kills one's energy level!

"We tend to think of the heart from a physiological perspective. But, what about a *heavy heart*—how does stress, insomnia, depression, pessimism, worry, and all of the other ways our hearts get weighed down, affect our energy and our health? Our stress levels and our expectations just don't synch up with our abilities. That's one reason we tend to overload our agendas and our plates—juggling way more than we can do, only to feel lousy about what we *haven't* done.

"Consider the man who tries to make tons of money. Every time he steps onto a train or into a restaurant or store or party, he'll bump into others making more money than he is. It's impossible to meet expectations that have been set unrealistically high. And we experience poor life balance as a function of that.

"Are super moms—and super dads, too—likely to have great relationships with their spouses? Probably not, because they have no time or energy left after a high-energy day. This has to do with work, life, love, friendship, and a sense of self-worth. All these things working in tandem can put us in a better life balance. So can losing weight and getting in shape. We've got to pull things back and get into balance."

Progressive Strength Training is Key

Jim says the most effective way to work your heart, reshape your body, decrease stress, and boost your energy is through *interval* strength training.

"When you perform my 'controlled load compound' using many muscles at the same time in exercise movements, you elevate your heart rate a great deal. But you elevate it in intervals, which means, you perform ten repetitions of an exercise. Then you follow it with a fifteen-to-twenty-second period of rest to prepare yourself for the next exercise."

Doing this improves your heart rate variability, which is a superior indicator of heart health. "If you're shaped like a pear and you do a little cardio and lose a couple of pounds, what do you ultimately look like? A smaller pear." By contrast, Jim's method focuses to firm and tone your body while reducing body fat to redefine the shape of your body.

"Many women are fearful of strength training because they don't want to have bulky muscles. In twenty years in this industry, I have never met a woman who became bulky as a result of strength-training exercises. To avoid that, they're told to tone up doing multiple repetitions with light, light weights. That couldn't be more wrong!"

Instead, Jim advocates doing what's called *progression*.

"Progression is accomplished by continually challenging and stimulating one's muscles to the point of confusion. The confusion facilitates change, unlike performing ten reps with ease. The body responds to that by saying, 'I can already do that, so I'm not changing in any way.'"

Here are Jim's six essential steps to get dramatic strength-training results:

SIX ESSENTIALS TO STRENGTH-TRAINING

1. **Increase the tension by the smallest increment.** If you're using dumbbells, go from eight to ten pounds, or ten to twelve, or twelve to fifteen. If you're using weight machines found in most gyms, increase by a two-and-a-half-pound weight (e.g., go from 20 pounds to 22 ½ pounds). If you use exercise bands (which work well in a home setting or when traveling), the tension increases based on the color of the band selected. Using any of these three methods noted here challenges your body. (You can order a set of these exercise bands at www.EddieMiller.com)

2. **Change the angle.** If, for example, you're doing a back row using dumbbells, your palms are facing each other, and you're lying on a bench, you can change your palms to face down or up. That way, you change the angle on the muscle fiber, which is an element of progression.

3. **Slow down the speed.** This is absolutely one of my favorite techniques. I cringe when I go to any strength training room and see how the majority of the people are training. It should be two counts on the way up, and double that to four on the way down or, from time to time, increase to three up and six down. In performing ten reps, each set should take you approximately 60 seconds.

4. **Progression is instability.** Think about the difference between walking on the pavement and walking on the soft part of the sand. Soft sand is more difficult because you're walking on an unstable surface. Similarly, when you perform an exercise use a staggered stance by placing the right foot forward and the left foot back with the heel of the right foot approximately one to one-and-a-half feet in front of the toes of the left. Perform the first five reps with the right foot forward, then shift to the left foot forward for the last five reps.

5. **Failure is key.** When working with people, especially seniors in their seventies and eighties, I've seen a phenomenal amount of benefit from strength training—when done correctly. Reaching a point of failure is the only thing that builds lean, calorie-burning muscle tissue. Based on research, once you increase the weight and gradually go from one to two and ultimately three sets, you're increasing your endurance and making it possible to go to the next level. You would go through these three stages to reach the point of failure:

   - Working Repetitions. These are the first five to six repetitions where you're maintaining good form and working a full range of motion by contracting the muscle on the way up and slowly lowering on the way down.

   - Fatigue. This is when you start to feel the muscle straining and each repetition gets harder. You may feel tempted to cheat, but maintain good form. The fatigue stage should last three to four repetitions, and you will begin to feel it at reps six to eight or nine.

   - Failure. Suddenly you can no longer move the weight, band, or machine. You just hit the final and most important stage— muscular failure. That's when you're no longer physically capable of performing one more rep. This should happen on rep nine or ten. Reaching this point of failure is the most critical, results-oriented step to your workout.

6. **Count calories.** You must count calories to succeed at weight loss; if you don't, you have no idea what you are consuming. For example, the Centers for Disease Control and Prevention state that women are consuming 335 more calories per day than they did in 1971. To lose weight, count calories for all the balanced meals and snacks you eat. They should start low and increase gradually. The following are suggestions you may want to consider.

	Calories for Women	Calories for Men
First Two Weeks	1,200	1,500
Weeks Three & Four	1,300	1,600
Weeks Five & Six	1,400	1,700
Until Attain Weight Goal	1,500	1,800

1,500 for women and 1,800 for men will likely be the range of calories you will need to maintain your ideal weight.

When you exercise, you want to maintain and/or increase your body's lean muscle tissue. Muscle burns between 20 and 36 calories per pound per day while fat burns between two and three calories per pound per day. After age 20, the average person loses 5/10 to 7/10 of a pound of muscle a year, which translates to five to seven pounds every decade.

"Upon entering menopause, the rate at which women lose muscle doubles. This is why women in their forties and fifties come to me asking 'what's happening; my body's taken on a life of its own? All of my dieting doesn't work. My waistline is gone. My clothes don't fit. Help!'"

What's happening?

Jim explains, "As you lose muscle and your rate of metabolism diminishes, so you start to gain body fat with those extra calories you burned when you had more muscle. Starting at age seventy, the average senior loses three pounds of muscle in a year. That health factor could spell the difference between dependence and independence in a senior's life."

Jim's 7 keys to creating a strong exercise plan:

SEVEN KEYS TO YOUR EXERCISE PLAN

1. Short, Intense Workouts > Saves Time

2. Interval Training > Promotes Heart Health

3. Always Going to Failure > Builds Muscle

4. Progressing Your Plan > Ensures Continued Success/Results

5. Compound Movements > Burns Calories

6. Emphasis on Back > Improves Posture and Alignment

7. Slow Movement > Recruits More Muscle Fiber

Geared for Success

Jim stresses the importance of *keeping track of your accomplishments*. If, for example, after two weeks of weight training you've increased from five-pound to eight-pound weights, document that success in your *Clarity & Focus Journal* and celebrate. "When you exercise six times in two weeks, say to yourself 'I'll reward myself with a pedicure or a massage or something you usually wouldn't do. At a minimum, pat yourself on the back. Even though it may seem superficial, it's self-soothing and a way to say 'good for you.' You've got to be your own cheering section."

In addition, Jim advises getting help. "Although living from the inside-out is powerful, every now and then, *allow yourself help from the outside in.* Avoid wearing old, tattered exercise clothes. Buy yourself something new that makes you feel good, not like you're punishing yourself. Exercise in an inviting place, not a dingy basement. If you do, you're setting yourself up to feel turned off. Go to the nicest room in your house to do your strength training, perhaps the living room where you probably don't go often."

It also helps to *do two things at the same time* like exercise to music. "Research says exercising and listening to music can make you smarter, that listening to music is motivating, and it soothes the mind and body. So enjoy your time exercising!"

Connecting With Our Core

An important insight I've gained from working out is connecting with my core being, where I've discovered enormous power. I've found that once I've tapped into this internal strength and power that my ability to go beyond and endure what I originally thought was impossible … is possible.

It's really a shift in your mindset. Like when I'm lifting weights and begin to feel fatigue, by connecting with my core I shift into overdrive and knock out two or three more reps till I hit failure — victory. Or it's when I'm on the elliptical and I've be going for thirty minutes, and I think, how can I go another fifteen minutes? However, by shifting my focus to a positive-positive statements and having fun the fifteen minutes speeds by.

I will literally say to myself, "You're a rock star!" "You can do this without a problem." "You only have a few reps/minutes left, this is a breeze." "You're in the home stretch; let's give it all you got." By connecting with my core, I become my own coach and cheerleader. I tap into my natural abundance to go beyond the fear that 'I can't lift the weight' to access the tremendous power that is always present within me.

As you begin to incorporate these skills and techniques into your own life, know that you have tremendous power and strength within you. Simply go to the point that you think this is all you can do, tap in, and go beyond. You will discover amazing results and achieve your desired goals.

"If you are not physically fit on the inside, it's going to be hard to fake it on the outside. Trust me, looking good and feeling good go hand in hand."

— Jim Karas

Living Inside-Out Lessons from Chapter 10

- Don't take an all-or-nothing approach to health and fitness. Rather set realistic goals and progress from where you are at now.

- Make a commitment to accountability. Find a partner, paid or otherwise, who will keep you motivated.

- Find your Emotional Epicenter; dig deep to know why you do what you do and make the choices you do.

- Remember a time in your life you felt better about your health, your body weight, your fitness, your energy level. Know you are still that person and you *can* do it again.

- Set your environment up for success. Plan, plan, plan. Schedule exercise times and plan meals well so you can manage your expectations.

- Know you're going to flub up. The key is having the structure in our life to get back on your program.

- Tap into your core, your inner strength.

11

VITALITY FROM THE INSIDE-OUT

Health & Vitality for Life

"Our bodies are miraculous machines that are naturally programmed for healing. We just need to get out of our own way and begin to honor the tremendous power of Nature's foods to heal."

— Susan Silberstein, PhD

Chapters 9 and 10 dealt with the importance of healthy eating, weight management, and exercise to help us tune up our bodies and reduce stress to create the ultimate lives we desire.

In this chapter, I want to take our game plans a step further for long-term health and vitality, which directly correlates to how we feed ourselves on the inside.

Increasingly, more and more research indicates a significant connection between the way we eat and disease prevention. According to the World Health Organization, at least eighty percent of all heart disease, stroke, and type 2 diabetes, and forty percent of cancers are preventable by dietary and lifestyle choices. [Pan American Health Organization, *Regional Strategy on an Integrated Approach to the Prevention and Control of Chronic Diseases Including Diet, Physical Activity, and Health*, CD47/17, 2006]

Americans are suffering from an increasing number of health-related issues, despite the medical advancements made in the last twenty years. As individuals, our body weight, dietary habits, and physical fitness—and to a lesser extent our genes—all determine our state of wellness and whether we're courting chronic disease.

Here are the facts:

- Every year, a million Americans are diagnosed with cancer, and 500,000 die from it. The lifetime risk for cancer is now as high as one in two Americans—that is, one out of every two Americans will be diagnosed with cancer at some point is his or her life! [Source: American Cancer Society, www.cancer.org]

- More than one million Americans suffer heart attacks every year, and of those, half a million die. [Source: American Heart Association, www.americanheart.org]

- In addition, 1.6 million Americans are diagnosed with diabetes every year [Source: American Diabetes Association, www. diabetes.org]

- Obesity correlates with all three of these killer diseases, and 65% of Americans are overweight or obese (body mass index of 25 or over). [Source: Centers for Disease Control, www.cdc.gov]

Seems overwhelming!

Well, let's look at how we can empower ourselves and fuel our bodies to experience health and vitality.

Denial Isn't an Option

Susan Silberstein, PhD, has been a good friend of mine for many years. She's founder and executive director of a remarkable organization called the Center for Advancement in Cancer Education. I first met Dr. Silberstein when I was COO of the National Foundation for Alternative Medicine. Her work impressed me so much, I attended one of her events, joined the board, and was elected to serve as its board chair for five years.

Susan speaks internationally on nutrition, cancer prevention, and complementary medicine and has personally coached more than 25,000 cancer patients. She frequently lectures for medical and nursing schools, hospitals, and other organizations. She has written the acclaimed books

Hungry for Health and *Breast Cancer: Is it What You're Eating or What's Eating You?* She's also the creator of the *Beat Cancer Kit* series and the editor of *Immune Perspectives* magazine.

Many of Susan's patients have told her, "I don't understand how I got sick; I've always eaten in a healthy way." Her answer is two-fold: "First, it may not be so much what you're eating as what's eating you. After all, 'stressed' spelled backwards is 'desserts.' Second, there are probably as many definitions of 'good nutrition' as there are people trying to define it. Good nutrition without a doubt does not include the Standard American Diet.

"The acronym for the Standard American Diet is SAD indeed," says Susan. "We are SADly overfed but undernourished."

Those of us who continue to eat the typical American diet are "playing dietary roulette." I know it sounds strong, but Susan has seen this firsthand and cited enough science to convince me that I had to change my eating habits right away. Denial of the dangers of disease can be our downfall. It's easy for us to think, "It's not going to happen to *me*." But the statistics are daunting. They show that it's either going to happen to us or someone we love. Unfortunately, we ignore the statistics and rack up the junk food debt, not believing we'll have to pay for it later.

This denial, Susan believes, comes partly from the lack of nutrition education provided to and by the current medical culture and partly from our own unwillingness to take personal responsibility for our dietary choices. "Yes, screenings and early detection are important, but they focus on disease from the outside. Our lifestyle choices are inner commitments to prevention, and that is the best route by far to ensure a smooth and healthy ride into our later years."

Forget Fads

Fad diets come and go. They help some people some of the time and most people not at all. As Susan explains, "The *homo sapiens* species has been around for about 40,000 years. Our body chemistry evolved on four fundamental hunter-gatherer society dietary principles that provide a more solid basis for health than fad diets. Our genes were programmed to thrive on these dietary principles."

THE FOUR FUNDAMENTALS OF DIETARY EFFECTIVENESS

1. Eat primitive
2. Eat colorful
3. Eat alkaline
4. Eat organic

"Since the Industrial Revolution and modern food processing techniques came along about 150 years ago, the modern western diet has us consuming refined carbohydrates and dangerous saturated fats but few or no fruits and vegetables," says Susan. "We're not getting the minerals and other phytonutrients that these plant foods offer. And the animal protein we're consuming generally provides poor quality protein with the wrong kinds of fats."

Let's look at these four best ways to obtain nutrition that will enhance our health and vitality for the long haul.

Eat Primitive

In tune with Dr. Katz from chapter 9, Susan adds that "one to two centuries represent a mere drop in the evolutionary bucket—hardly enough time for our genes to adapt to our dramatic departure from long-established dietary patterns. Killer diseases such as cancer, heart disease, and diabetes are nearly unknown in cultures that still follow the fundamentals of a primitive hunter-gatherer."

The primitive way of eating was unadulterated by chemical additives, pesticides, hormones, bioengineering, irradiation, charbroiling, and microwaving. So, what else does it mean to *eat primitive*? Here's an easy way to remember. Primitive's food choices include:

- Roots and fruits
- Greens and beans
- Seeds and weeds
- Wild fish or game

A SAD way of eating, on the other hand, is rife with:

- Meats and sweets
- Pies and fries
- Chips and dips
- Cakes and shakes

"One key difference between the modern and Paleolithic (hunter-gatherer) way of eating," notes Susan, "is the fat in the modern—especially saturated animal fat—which contributes to chronic degenerative diseases. But even unsaturated fats can be dangerous. Unsaturated fats are often combinations of omega 3, 6, or 9 fatty acids." Although all have value, high omega 6 fats tend to turn off the immune system, whereas high omega 3s enhance immune function (the omega 9s are neutral).

In primitive hunter-gatherer lifestyle, the ratio of omega 6 fatty acids to omega 3s was about 1 to 1—a good balance for the human immune system. However, the typical ratio in today's western society is at least 25 to 1, and some researchers say 30 to 1, in favor of omega 6, which keeps our immune systems chronically suppressed.

Susan recommends avoiding vegetable oils like corn, cottonseed, soybean, sunflower, and safflower oils because of their high omega 6 content. "Good sources of omega 3s include wild fish, grass fed animals, wild game, free-range poultry and their eggs, sea vegetables, raw walnuts, pumpkin seeds, ground flaxseeds, and hemp seeds."

Eating wild fish or taking high quality fish oil supplements can help to reduce inflammation, the core cause of chronic illness. In fact, adds Susan, about eighty percent of our immunity lies in our guts, and chronic intestinal inflammation can allow disease to permeate the rest of our bodies as well. One of the best ways to reduce gut inflammation is to avoid the whites!

Eat Colorful

Susan's second rule to prevent and fight disease is to eat colorful. Americans in large numbers consume a great deal of white food—white flour, white sugar, white bread, white pasta, white rice, white potatoes. Susan says, "White flour has one job, and we probably learned about it in first grade when we made paper maché! So if we want to glue our intestines together, we can keep eating the 'glue-ten' in white flour."

Fruits and vegetables tend to be deep in color and high in nutrients. But what two vegetables do Americans consume the most? Iceberg lettuce and French fries. No wonder we have such high rates of illness in this country.

Numerous studies demonstrate the health benefits of eating a variety of fruits and vegetables. For example, researchers at the Loma Linda University School of Public Health, in cooperation with the National Cancer Institute and the National Institutes of Health, studied 600,000 Seventh-Day Adventists. The researchers found that vegetarians raised on a plant-based dietary plan had longer than average life spans and a lower incidence of heart disease and cancer than did their non-vegetarian counterparts in the general population. [Source: Seventh-Day Adventist Dietetic Association, www.sda.org]

Susan states, "The Five-a-Day campaign of the U.S. Department of Agriculture and the American Cancer Society leads us in the right direction. The 'five' refers to five fist-sized servings of fresh fruits and vegetables. People have enough trouble doing that daily, and now the new guidelines are actually 13 servings! Ideally, we should consume about three or four servings of fruit and nine or ten servings of veggies daily (negative points for microwaving!)"

Fruits and vegetables contain fiber and many key phytonutrients (natural plant-based chemicals). Why are they important? Susan gave me four reasons which I now have committed to memory—and my fridge door.

"First, many orange, yellow, red, purple, and green fruits and veggies contain *carotenes*, which can be converted into vitamin A in the body. Carotenes play two enormous roles in our health," says Susan. "They boost immune function and they're powerful antioxidants, essential for quenching free radicals. Free radicals are unstable, dangerous compounds that damage cellular DNA and are responsible for aging, cancer, and other disease processes. They are generated during vigorous exercise, stress, toxic environmental exposures, poor quality dietary choices, medications, and general body metabolism. Anti-oxidants in carotene-rich foods help to neutralize free radicals.

"Second, these natural sources of nutrition also provide a purple, green, red, orange, and gold mine of *fiber*. Ideally, we should be consuming 30 to 50 grams of fiber daily, whereas the typical American consumes less than five grams of fiber. Low fiber has been linked to colon cancer, breast cancer, prostate cancer, and lymphatic cancer, and is likely a factor in other cancers, cardiovascular disease, diabetes, and other chronic health problems.

"Third, *chlorophyll*, found in green produce, is one of the most powerful wound healers and blood builders known. Its molecular structure is nearly identical to that of hemoglobin, the protein in red blood cells that carries oxygen. Dark green vegetables are higher in bio-available calcium than dairy products and contain a perfect ratio of calcium and its co-factor magnesium.

"Fourth, vegetables in the cruciferous family offer many disease-fighting properties. Crucifers include broccoli, cauliflower, cabbage, kale, collards, and Brussels sprouts. They support key liver enzyme functions and detoxify carcinogens."

Many research studies have demonstrated that the more crucifers you eat, the less likely you are to get all kinds of cancers, including breast, prostate, lung and colon disease. [Source: Sigrid Keck, PhD, and John W. Finley, PhD, *Cruciferous Vegetables: Cancer Protective Mechanisms, Annals Integrative Cancer Therapies* 3(1), 2004]

Eat Alkaline

The next fundamental of good health is to *eat alkaline*. The important principle of acid-alkaline balance in the body is often ignored, even by those who habitually eat so-called health foods. Susan points out that "many researchers recommend a dietary ratio of about 80% plant-based foods to 20% animal-based foods, approximating an eighty percent alkaline to twenty percent acid strategy. This produces an ideal blood pH balance of 7.3 — 7.4 slightly alkaline, which is perfect to promote healing, energy, and vitality.

"When our blood becomes extremely acid (acidosis) or alkaline (alkalosis)," continues Susan, "we can't survive; but at the optimal level of 7.3 or 7.4, we thrive. In contrast, most diseases thrive in acidosis."

Unfortunately for our health, most Americans have highly acidic eating habits—cereal, milk, meat, cheese, pasta, bread, and desserts. Even health foods such as whole-grain brown rice and free-range organic chicken constitute a heavily acid meal, unless they are surrounded by veggies. This explains why some diets promoted as 'healthy' don't help much. They leave us prone to disease and chronic inflammation, which manifests as numerous serious medical conditions. (An Alkaline Food Chart can be downloaded at www.EddieMiller.com.)

Eat Organic

Susan's final rule is to *eat organic*. Organic means grown without chemicals, pesticides, or other carcinogenic additives, but, as Susan says, organic means not only what's left out but also what's left in. Because organic farmers rotate crops and plow the minerals back into the soil through composting, these plants contain a wealth of nutrients not found in non-organic produce.

I know a lot of people think organic means expensive, but that's just not the case anymore. In some stores, organic food has become as accessible and affordable as food that is packed with preservatives.

Several years ago, the Rutgers University School of Agriculture issued a report comparing the mineral content of organic vegetables with that of non-organic vegetables. The results provide an effective commercial for eating organic.

- The calcium content of cabbage, for example, was 60 parts per million in the organically-grown cabbage versus only 17.5 parts per million in the non-organic cabbage.

- The magnesium content of organic snap beans measured 60 parts per million compared to 14.8 in the non-organic snap beans.

- Organic lettuce contained 176.5 parts per million of potassium, while non-organic lettuce contained only 53.7.

- And the differences in iron content between organic and non-organic tomatoes were staggering: 1,938 parts per million versus 1 part per million!

[Source: Firman E. Bear, Stephen J. Toth, and Arthur L. Prince, *Variation in Mineral Composition of Vegetables*, www.rce. rutgers.edu/pubs/bearreport]

If you don't have much organic produce available or you're on a tight budget, Susan suggests doing the best you can. "If you can afford some but not all, then choose the organic foods that have skins you eat and don't normally peel off, such as grapes, nectarines, or apples—berries, too.

"If you can't afford an organic avocado or melon, it won't matter as much in terms of chemical residues because you won't eat the skins. With regard to nutritional benefits, however, if you're not buying organic, you'll need to eat much more! An organic plant may have from three to one hundred to a thousand times the nutritional value of a non-organic one."

Empower Yourself

Susan explains the fears and hesitations she's encountered with her clients as she encourages them to change their way of eating. One concern has to do with time. "We're a 'quick fix' culture, and we're used to getting rapid results, so we get impatient. We always have to 'beat the clock,' even to make dinner. That's why we microwave our food. But it's killing us!

"Next there's the issue of responsibility. Eating healthfully is not difficult, but many people are afraid of taking responsibility. Consider the following two definitions of responsibility—one is useless and the other crucial to our health.

"The first type of responsibility asserts that you caused your disease. You caused your obesity. It's your fault if you can't remedy the situation. This kind of responsibility lays blame and produces guilt. It's obviously useless because guilt does nothing but make you feel bad, which can be more carcinogenic than anything you might be eating.

"The other kind of responsibility could be spelled *response-ability*, which is based on awareness of what you need to do for your health. Awareness gives you power. It allows you to make choices and control your way of eating, rather than having your eating control you.

"Then there's fear of failure. People need permission not to be perfect. I've seen that over and over with my cancer patients. They think if they take responsibility for their illness and don't do a perfect job with their dietary plan, they're going to die and it's going to be *their fault*. That's fear of failure. If people are afraid of not being perfect, whatever effort they make isn't going to work."

Even for prevention-seekers there are a lot of "buts." Maybe you've tried a number of weight-loss techniques that didn't work. Maybe you want proof that if you make this change in your way of eating, you'll have protection against disease. Maybe you're afraid that you won't be able to stick with a program, that it's not doable. Maybe you don't believe a dietary change could possibly protect you because of family genes.

"People don't realize that genes *im*pel, they don't *com*pel — that is, genes load the gun but they don't pull the trigger," explains Susan. "And lifestyle choices can stop genes dead in their tracks. All these fears get in the way of people seizing their power and forging ahead."

What about people who eat healthy but jump off the program from time to time?

"There's nothing wrong with that," Susan says. "But it's important to make 19 out of your 21 meals each week good and healthy. The body is forgiving to a point. If you lay a foundation of healthy eating, it's okay to cheat now and then because it's Sunday or it's a holiday or it's your birthday.

Ok, so what I take from Susan's wisdom is we don't have to perceive that we've "broken" our healthy way of eating and lost everything we've done to date. Rather, we can take the perspective that we'll get right back to our healthy eating 19 out of 21 meals a week. Our bodies can clear the soda and brownie quickly, if they're not the norm. Our bodies know what to do with that kind of exception.

"Remember," Susan says, "whether we have a scary diagnosis or no diagnosis, everybody eventually dies, so the only thing we've got going for us is the quality of our lives. No one wants to live *long,* if they can't live *well.* So even though we can't prevent death, we can do a lot to enhance the quality of our lives and prevent disease. And dietary choices lie at the core."

Balance, Not Perfection

Good health is not about perfection, but about balance. I found it easy to make changes to my eating over time, and many people have more success with gradual change rather than going cold turkey. If I was told I had to give up my cookies and sweets and never look back, I would have felt like it was impossible.

I'm not a sugar junkie, but I love dessert. I like the idea of not depriving myself completely, but knowing that I can't incorporate sugar into my daily nutrition if I want to be healthy in the long run. This became a healthy choice, instead of difficult deprivation.

I gave myself a timeline, and kept taking one step here, one step there. Eventually it became a way of life and didn't feel like any form of "diet"— because it really wasn't. Gradually introducing different eating habits also makes it easier for your body to adjust to the transition.

If you change everything all at once, you may experience fatigue, digestive problems, and even flu-like symptoms, as your body eliminates its toxic load. Gradual changes diminish these short-term issues and allow you to feel better and better over time.

The bottom line? Use these four fundamentals as barometers to live by; but also give yourself permission to be a little flexible and enjoy life.

The last three chapters have encouraged you to go within to identify what's keeping you from attaining the ultimate health you desire. They have provided ideas to shift your thinking and apply specific techniques for losing weight, getting in shape, and living with vitality.

Techniques that fundamentally enhance your body's—your temple's— ability to perform as you set out to incorporate the inside-out principles in your life. As you begin applying these insights into your daily life, you'll experience powerful shifts that will catapult you toward achieving your dreams with plenty of energy, balance, and health.

"Living inside-out isn't complicated. It's actually quite simple, and it shouldn't be a struggle. Educate yourself on what foods are best for your long-term health and take the steps necessary to keep chronic disease from taking root in your life."

— Susan Silberstein, PhD

Living Inside-Out Lessons from Chapter 11

- *Eat primitive:* roots and fruits, greens and beans, seeds and weeds, and wild fish or wild game. This type of dietary plan helps improve health and prevent disease.

- Avoid oils high in omega-6 fats such as corn, cottonseed, soybean, sunflower, and safflower oils.

- Consume sources of omega 3s like wild fish, wild game, grass-fed animals, free-range poultry and their eggs, sea vegetables, raw walnuts, pumpkin seeds, ground flaxseeds, and hemp seeds.

- *Eat colorful:* Strive for three or four servings of fruit and nine or ten servings of veggies daily.

- *Eat alkaline:* Many researchers recommend a dietary ratio of about 80% alkalinizing plant-based foods to 20% acidifying animal foods to promote healing.

- *Eat organic:* Organic produce has a wealth of vitamins, minerals, and phytonutrients found only minimally in non-organic produce. At least for vegetables and fruits that you eat their skins—tomatoes, berries, grapes—choose organic.

- Avoid microwaving.

- Good health is about balance. Aim for eating healthfully 19 out of your 21 meals each week.

12

Creating a Lasting Financial Foundation

"If you're not sure what your intentions are, look at your
results—because that's what you're intending."

— Mackey McNeill, CPA

As the world's economic conditions have shifted, we've been given a shocking wakeup call. We now know how critical it is to have a financial plan in place. We tend to create extensive stories around money and what it means or says about us. Many of us also develop self-limiting beliefs around money that are extremely detrimental to our overall lives and lifestyles.

Let's address the topic of money in two chapters from two important standpoints. In this chapter, I call on the expertise of Mackey McNeill, CPA, to present a practical approach to creating a *lasting financial foundation.* (In the next chapter, Bob Proctor will address enjoying financial abundance.)

A rare combination of Wall Street-smart business woman and inspiring speaker, Mackey McNeill is committed to expanding the paradigm of prosperity in her award-winning book, *The Intersection of Joy and Money,* as well as her nationally taught curriculum, *Prosperity in Action,* and her audio book, *The Dynamics of Money.* She is president and CEO of Mackey Advisors, Wealth Advocates who passionately purse their client's prosperity.

Our Financial Decisions

I asked Mackey why we continue to make such poor financial decisions when we seemingly know better. The answer, says Mackey, is twofold.

"First, if someone asks us today if we'd like an orange or chocolate, seventy percent of us would pick chocolate. But if we're asked if we want an orange or chocolate delivered to our office in a week, seventy percent of us would pick the orange."

Why the discrepancy? *The emotional part of the brain makes the quick decisions for today, and the analytical part of the brain makes the decisions for the future.*

"This explains why we frequently make seemingly diverse and often destructive decisions about money. We make short-term decisions with one area of the brain and long-term decisions with another. Yet these two areas are frequently at odds with each other. It's been discovered that when most people spend money (short-term decisions), they experience a release of endorphins and it feels good."

Just as we discussed in chapters 3 and 9, the same is true with our money decisions; we have to be aware of the feeling and emotions behind the decisions we are making. Just because it feels good, doesn't mean it's good for us.

A second influence consists of our many belief systems, or mental structures, around money—what Mackey calls "money fantasies" (our stories vs. our truth). Many of these are learned as children from people in our environment, such as parents, teachers, and others in authority. Some of our beliefs came through personal experience, both good and bad. All contribute to what we *think* is possible or not—to what we *think* is reality.

"Once our beliefs are in place," notes Mackey, "they govern our money lives. Eventually we become aware that our belief structures aren't creating the prosperity we want, so we obtain analytical help. We find an accountant or CPA to run the numbers for us and tell us what we need to do. But even then, our belief structures are stacked against us. So unless we directly address and release them or change them, we don't change our behavior.

"Several years ago, as I was expanding my practice to include personal financial planning, I noticed that many people put roadblocks around their money and prosperity. While they would come in and talk about what they wanted to do in their lives, often they didn't make the necessary changes.

"I became curious and wondered *why do we have blocks to making changes?* These people who said they want to make a change have been given a road map, but they're not following it. So I began to study a personal development program called the Enneagram—a method based on ancient principles outlining nine personality types, which each express a distinctive and habitual pattern of thinking and emotions. This process helped to unfold my own stories and notice my own relationship to money.

"When I was a kid and my grandfather gave me a quarter—a lot of money in the sixties—I'd put it in my passbook savings account. Other kids went to the store and bought candy. As a teenager, when all my friends were buying records, I knew I could get free music on the radio, so why spend money on a record?

"It was actually *difficult* for me to spend my money. People would say, 'Mackey, why don't you take part of that money and enjoy it? Spend it on yourself.' My reply was, 'No, I'm going to save it.' Then I remembered what my mother told me when I was five years old. I was getting ready to go to kindergarten for the first time, and she was helping me prepare for what would happen the next day. She said, 'I don't want you to be surprised tomorrow. You'll have a teacher and meet a lot of new people. One thing I want you to know is that you're our *adopted* daughter.'

"She went on to explain the difference between an adopted daughter and a biological daughter, saying, 'I want you to know in case someone brings it up. I don't want you to be confused. We love you very much.'

"And that was the end of the story—from *her* perspective. But I'm thinking, *Wait a minute! This is really big news. I'm five years old and my whole world has changed!* So I asked my mother, 'Why did my birth parents give me away?' She replied, 'Well, they were young and they didn't have enough money for a baby.'

"That conversation created my whole belief system around money: If my birth parents didn't have enough money for a baby, then I'd better be careful about how much money I ask my parents for now—and I never did ask them for money. I'd also better be sure I have my own money because money equals safety."

Mackey went on to clarify that although saving is a *good* thing and she became successful with money, because of her belief system she didn't have freedom of choice. That is, because money represented security ("I won't be given away again"), she wasn't free to do something for herself or spend money when she wanted to. The belief system Mackey created out of that experience—not what her mother told her, but the story she created in her own mind—became her *money fantasy.*

Mackey says, "We all have a relationship with money—good, bad, or indifferent. It either helps us be successful or contributes to our lack of success, but whatever it is, it is our own version, our own money fantasy."

Our Money Fantasies

"I call these stories money *fantasies,*" she explains, "because they're beliefs we've made up that aren't true. I regard them as roadblocks that keep us from our own prosperity."

Understanding our money fantasies is a core component of living from the inside-out. After all, our relationship with money can affect every aspect of our lives. It can cause stress if we don't have enough in our checking account; it can build tension and create distance in our relationships; it can keep us from living the lives we desire.

So how do we become more aware of our money fantasies and shift our (often unconscious) beliefs around money?

The following worksheet, *Identify Your Money Fantasies,* lists questions that Mackey suggests we ask to gain insights into the money fantasies—the stories—that hold us in their grip. (A copy of this worksheet can be downloaded at www.EddieMiller.com)

IDENTIFY YOUR MONEY FANTASIES

1. **Growing Up.** What was your family's money situation like when you were growing up? Look at your early childhood, your adolescence, and your early adult life.

   - Who controlled the money in your household? How did that person relate to money? What did that person believe about money?

   - What did the parent who did not control the money in your household believe about money? How did he or she view money?

   - Did you admire someone in your family or center of influence because of his or her relationship to money? If so, who and what did you admire?

   - Did your family experience harmony or arguments around money?

   - How did your parents come to agreement about money?

   - Did your family have an abundance of money? How did you know?

   - Did your family experience financial limitations? How did you know?

   - Describe the first time you were aware of the concept of money (your earliest memory of money)?

   - Did you get an allowance? What did you do with your allowance? Save it? Spend it? What did you spend it on? For yourself or others?

   - When did you begin work? Why did you want to work? What was your motivation?

   - How did you use this self-generated money? Did you save it? Spend it? What did you spend it on? For yourself or others?

- Did you relate differently to money you earned versus money given to you?

- As a child, how did you view money?

- What event(s) or conversations about money do you remember vividly from your childhood?

- Do you have a money memory that you find painful to recall?

    Once you've answered these questions, identify the patterns or recurring themes.

- What money fantasies do you see in your answers?

Then, write a sentence of gratitude about each past money fantasy. Follow each gratitude sentence with one releasing this old belief into the Universe. Lastly, complete the work with a statement of acceptance of your new belief.

It might look something like this: *In the past I believed that wealthy people were mean and hurtful. That it was impossible to be both wealthy and good. I appreciate this belief and express gratitude for the many blessings it has manifested in my life. I release this belief and accep t the new belief that a wealthy person can be loving and truly good.*

2. **Present Results.** How do you currently feel about money?

- What emotions do you experience when you have abundance?

- How do you feel when you have limitations?

- How do you feel when you have just enough money, without it being abundant or insufficient?

- The action of spending money gives us something. What is that for you?

- The action of saving money gives us something. What is that for you?

- Accumulating money in the form of assets gives us something. What is that for you?

- What's your favorite activity around money: spending, saving, or reflecting on what you've accumulated?

- What similarities do you see between your childhood money situation and attitudes, and your present money situation and attitudes?

- In what part(s) of your life do you still experience your past money patterns?

- Notice what you've discovered. Write a statement about the present condition of your money life.

- Now that you've looked at your present actions and feelings around money, do you see any fantasies you're holding on to?

- Write a sentence of gratitude and release for these past money fantasies just as you did previously.

- Now that you're complete with your money past and present, sit and write down your intention for your money life in the future. For example, "It is my intention to be conscious and prosperous in my money life."

3. **Symbols.** Before leaving this investigation into your money fantasies, explore what money represents for you. Answer the following questions about your money symbols:

- What emotional need in your life have you used money to fill?

- What desires do you have that you perceive money fulfills?

- What does money symbolize for you? What does it represent in your life? What does it provide?

Answers aren't right or wrong. You're simply uncovering the origins of your belief system around money and determining what it represents for you personally. For example, people often say money represents choices, security, freedom, joy, fun, and safety. What does it symbolize for you?

The Saver and the Spender

As I identified my money fantasies, in comparison to Mackey who was *the saver*, I quickly identified myself as *the spender*.

By answering Mackey's above eye-opening questions and reflected on my own upbringing, the word (the story) that kept coming up for me was resounding *lack*. My parents were always hard working, but money was always tight and there was always a mountain of bills waiting to be paid. So my parents constantly were spending everything they had to pay the bills, which created yet another paradigm: Not learning to save.

This was coupled with the fact I had grandparents who lived in St. Louis, about an hour and a half from us, who had a comfortable lifestyle, lived in a nice house, and traveled. My grandma Claire loved to have parties and entertained to the hilt—china, crystal, silver ...

She introduced me to many of the finer aspects life had to offer, which instilled a desire to have the same. This was topped off with my mom and dad's belief in me that, even though they may not have thought it for themselves, I could accomplish anything I set my mind to. In short, the money fantasy I created was a feeling of lack, not knowing how to save, desperately wanting the good life, topped off with an aggressive inspiration to have it all.

It was a set up for me to feel strapped and guilty—and undeserving of more.

When it was time to go to college what I created for myself in addition to the scholarships and Pell Grants, were tons of student loans and credit card debt. Then, I got to the real world and my job didn't pay enough, and I continued to spend my "plastic" money—creating a painful credit card debt that took nearly twenty years to pay off.

The emotional void I was attempting to fill was that I wanted people to like me because of the lifestyle I was living. All because the money fantasies I created were based on *fantasies* and not my truth.

The Five Money Truths

To make long-term, sustainable changes in our money life, it's important to first inventory our belief systems around money as suggested. Then consider the *five money truths* that Mackey says impact our relationship with money and can help unravel our money fantasies.

The first truth asserts that *you are responsible for your money life.*

"In our culture, many of us were raised with a victim consciousness, and we take the perspective that says, 'Well, I can't do anything about that.' However, until we accept responsibility for creating, or co-creating, the money situation in our own lives, we can't shift it. So before we do anything else, we need to understand that *we* are the ones responsible for our own prosperity."

The second truth claims that *your consciousness is required for money health.*

"Consciousness means being in the present. Our belief systems keep us out of the present. They create habitual ways of thinking, feeling, behaving, and interacting. We act from those old habits instead of making present-moment choices that are always available and enable us to transform our money lives."

The third truth states that *each piece of your money life gives you the whole.*

It's important to understand that our money lives are not just about what we have in our checking accounts or about creating a budget. Mackey has created an excellent tool called the *14 Points of Your Money Life Assessment*, which can be downloaded at www.EddieMiller.com.

The 14 Points include:

- money habits of mind,
- goals and strategies,
- current cash flow,
- future cash flow,
- planning for big ticket items,

- current net worth,
- liquidity,
- risk management,
- financial independence,
- estate planning,
- income tax planning,
- college funding,
- investment planning and management, and
- aligning work with your essence and passion.

Referring to the 14-point assessment, Mackey notes, "It's a simple system. You give yourself a one to ten, and I provide clues as to what might be a one and what might be a ten. This assessment can help to identify which area of your money life you want to focus your attention on. Money is a big conversation—not only about investing or cash flow or money fantasies. It's about *all* of those things. At any one point in time, we give certain areas our attention.

"People can't focus on everything or they'll become overwhelmed. This assessment helps them establish a priority system. I ask clients to fill out the 14 points and then pick the three they're the weakest in—that they want to work on. Then we work on those over three to six months. Little by little, they gain insight into their whole money life."

The fourth truth asserts that *choice is the ultimate power*.

"If we're effectively going to change, we need to recognize *we* are the ones choosing what we're experiencing. How do we put together new choices for ourselves? Let's start with a budget. I find most people resistant to the whole idea of a budget. However, I say *a budget is just a way of choosing* in advance, so we're more empowered by that choice. If we look at it that way, we'll look at it more positively.

"On the other hand, if we look at a budget as something that keeps us from what we want, then we're probably never going to do it or live with it. If we consider it a format for deciding what we want to *choose,* we're more likely to be interested in sitting down and saying, 'This is how much money is coming in for me. How am I going to choose to spend it?'"

The **fifth truth** declares that *money is energy and has value because we all agree it does.*

"Money is a form of energy or power or life force that we can trade. It's a physical form—paper and coins—in exchange for which we give our life force, our labor. We can use this form of life force for the things that we want, or we can store it," says Mackey.

But, money has value because we agree that it does. Investments might have a set value, or a business might have certain value, or some of our assets might have intrinsic worth, but money itself has value because we assign it meaning and value in our lives.

"A lot of people never thought about it that way. We don't have a gold standard anymore. There's not a nugget of gold in Fort Knox that supports the value of your dollar bill. It's simply that we all agree it has a certain value."

Here is the importance of understanding the money truths; we *have freedom and power over money*. Money is just an exchange. It can't define us; however, it takes our insight from within to grasp it.

Money Set-Point

I had to work diligently to transform many of my own money stories. Sometimes, I thought I'd never change them. There were times when I thought my fate was to struggle like I always feared I would.

Many of us hit similar walls. We get to a certain point and our financial progress stalls out. We can't seem to get past a given amount of income or wealth accumulation. As Mackey and I were discussing this, it triggered a correlation with what Marci Shimoff says about our *happiness set-point* in chapter 8. So I asked Mackey if this meant we have a comparable *money set-point*.

"Yes, some of us have a limited set-point, and some an unlimited one. I have a friend who's never been without a great deal of money. It just comes to her because of her unlimited mindset about money. When she was growing up, her parents had a drawer that always had money in it, and she was allowed to take whatever she wanted out of it. So her perspective was—'Hey, there's always lots of money in this little drawer, and all I have to do is go and get it.' That was her frame of reference. And that's exactly what she's created in her adult life—the idea that there's always plenty."

This story makes an important point. *We choose.* It may not be a conscious choice, but we choose how much money we will have and how we will live. It can mean abundance or poverty, but it's all determined by our consciousness.

It isn't about what our parents did or said, but rather how *we interpreted* what they did or said. Our *interpretation* crystallizes our stories, our beliefs, and our money set-point.

Seven Laws of a Prosperous Life

Understanding that we can choose to change our money beliefs starts with awareness—being clear on what we want and not avoiding the issue of our finances. As Mackey reminds us, "If we're not sure what our intentions are, *we can look at our results because the results show us what we're intending.*"

It's important to release all judgment around what we've created—not label it good or bad; then we can embrace the empowerment that comes with awareness.

Also part of the process for change is being grateful for what is, loving and blessing what we've created. This doesn't mean something undesirable will automatically go away, but I firmly believe it won't go away until we find the gift in it. The premise of *Groundhog Day,* the movie, is how we keep creating the same situation over and over until we "get" the lesson.

This chapter has provided three valuable tools to analyze your current relationship with money by: identifying your money fantasies; understanding the five money truths; and the fourteen points to assessing your money life. In addition, Mackey offers the *Seven Laws of a Prosperous Life.*

SEVEN LAWS OF A PROSPEROUS LIFE

1. Spend less than you earn.
2. Be in integrity with money.
3. Insure.
4. Save, save, save.
5. Practice good money habits.
6. Hire a fee-based advisor.
7. Get a plan.

Money is good. Money is your friend. And getting an accurate picture of where you are is the first step. Take inventory of what's going out and what's coming in, and use actual numbers from the past couple of months, not your guesstimate, which is notoriously inaccurate.

The challenge many of us face is the disconnect from what we want and the choices we are making. This refers back to the example Mackey gave of choosing the orange or the chocolate. Without goals and a budget, we always choose chocolate.

Mackey says, "Look at your short and long-term goals and the inconsistency of your daily choices. If you want something long-term you have to change your current habits."

What is your goal?

- Be debt free?

- 20% down to buy a house in 2 or 3 years?

- Retire in 10, 20, 30 years?

In each case, you have to determine what it will take financially to achieve your goal. Then, reflect on your reality. Compare how you're currently doing with the financial goals you have for your life. If you see you're spending $10 going out for lunch five times a week while you're struggling to climb out of debt, you've now become conscious of that. You can make long-term decisions to put more money toward achieving your financial goals rather than short-term decisions that move you further away.

Here are some general rules Mackey suggests:

1. *Plan for unexpected expenses* so that you are prepared. It could be tires for your car, the air conditioning in your home needs replaced, anything unexpected. Work towards getting one month of expenses in savings and work up to three months. Even if all you can do is save $50 or $100 a month for the next year. This way you are never caught off guard.

2. If you have debt, *focus to pay off the smallest debt first.* You will still pay the minimum due on everything else, but this way you will more readily be able to see your progress. Once you pay off the smallest debt, add that payment to what you are paying on the next smallest debt you have.

3. *Plan for retirement.* You are never too young to plan for your future. There are a number of online retirement calculators to plan for when you want to retire and determine how much you would need to invest each month. If your just starting out, even if it is only $20 a month, start saving. If you're over 45, your strategy will be much more aggressive.

4. *Create a "because you want it" fund.* This could be for a vacation, new outfit, furniture, boat, house ... The key is to be realistic with your other financial priorities and plan accordingly.

5. *Celebrate along the way* by realizing the progress you're making. This doesn't necessarily mean that you have to spend money, but decide what would be rewarding for you.

No one can snap their fingers and suddenly know everything about money. Becoming financially prosperous is a process. After we let go of the beliefs and fantasies that have been hindering us, it's important to keep learning about the next steps to take. Now that we've created a lasting financial foundation, let's continue to chapter 13, Enjoying Financial Abundance.

"Living inside-out on our personal financial journey means going within. We often view money as an external circumstance that we don't have much control over. In reality, we have tremendous control over our own money stories and how they affect us. It isn't possible to live in prosperity and maximize our true potential until we understand the internal ideas that are keeping us from achieving our financial dreams."

— Mackey McNeill, CPA

Living Inside-Out Lessons from Chapter 12

- **People subconsciously create "money fantasies"—limiting false stories around money.**

- **You are responsible for your money life.**

- **Your consciousness, or awareness, is required for money health.**

- **Becoming aware of the false belief structures that block your prosperity helps you release or change them so you can consciously change your behavior.**

- **To become aware of your money fantasies, look at your results. What beliefs created them?**

- **Release judgment of what you've created around money to free yourself to choose and change.**

- **Choice is the ultimate power.**

13

Enjoying Financial Abundance

"Always remember money is a servant, you are the master.
Be very careful not to reverse this equation."

— Bob Proctor

Chapter 12 covered the essentials for establishing a practical, lasting foundation for your financial life. Let's go further and strengthen, even stretch, your beliefs about *creating* financial *abundance*. I struggled with this for years until I began to deeply understand the Law of Vibration and the Law of Attraction. When I realized the two were connected, everything changed for me.

To help us zoom into the heart of the matter, I called on one of the best-known leaders in the field of personal development, Bob Proctor. Bob is a featured expert in *The Secret* and the author of two bestsellers, *You Were Born Rich* and *It's Not About the Money*. For more than forty years, Bob has traveled the world teaching people about the concepts of prosperity and wealth and how we either attract them or create a mindset that repels them.

Like nearly everyone I've met who has discovered the power of living inside-out, Bob, too, had known the pain of deprivation, struggle, and living disconnected from his true self-worth and potential. I was stunned when Bob shared his story with me, because I always saw him as this strong, focused guy who just planned out his life and watched the abundance roll in.

167

I was wrong. Way wrong.

Bob, this grounded, centered, wealthy, empowered man was once so lost and broke, he contemplated ending it all in despair. Until he met a man named Ray Stanford who confronted him in a kind and supportive way that resonated through the pain and profoundly spoke to his broken heart. It literally woke him up from his numb state and sparked a new course of action and living.

Bob recalls, "My life started on very rocky ground. At age twenty-six, I was totally lost. I was earning four thousand dollars a year and I owed six thousand. I never had a good job. I only went to high school for two months. I'd been in and out of the Navy and a series of jobs—a couple of which lasted an hour. I was going in the wrong direction and picking up speed.

"I met Ray who convinced me I could do better. I could get out of debt. I could be happy. Inside, I really didn't believe it, but I believed *he* believed I could. And he was there to guide me in changing my thinking.

"Ray got me to look at where I was. He said, 'I'm not talking about how much money you have or what are you working at.' He said, 'What do you do? What are your thoughts? How do you behave?' When we talk about where we are, we have to take a look at how we are living. What are we doing with our day? Then we have to know where we're going. We have to have a target that we're shooting at. Most people decide on the target, but they never take a look at where they are.

"I also started reading *Think and Grow Rich* by Napoleon Hill, and my life changed dramatically within a year. I earned a hundred and seventy-five thousand dollars that year and increased my income to a million a couple of years later. It was a huge shock that earning money was actually *incidental*. That's why I'm in the business I'm in today. I had to understand what had changed."

Everything We Want Is Already Ours

Why did Bob's life change so dramatically?

"I began to realize that the Law of Attraction is always working in our lives, although we've likely been completely unaware of it," Bob says.

"This law states that *everything that comes into our lives is attracted by our thoughts and intentions*.

"Over the past few years, the Law of Attraction has received a great deal of media attention. The movie *The Secret* brought the idea to the masses, but it also caused confusion.

"People often say, 'I'm thinking positively, I'm saying my affirmations, but I still have nothing. Nothing has changed, nothing is better. I don't understand.'

"The Law of Attraction, a sub-law of the Law of Vibration, states that *everything is energy and is constantly moving, or vibrating*. This is true for the physical objects we see, which are vibrating on an atomic level, as well as for the energy created by our thoughts. Every time we think something, we put that energy in motion. Similar energies attract each other—like attracts like—and energy will move to create that which we focus on. Whether this focus is good or bad, we'll attract its existence into our lives."

Although we use the terminology "attract to us," it's not meant to imply that money or wealth exists *outside* of us. Remember in chapter 7, Doug Bench explained how putting our goals on our brain's Reticular Activating System's Important List, we see resources that had been there all the time in support of our goal? Likewise, when we raise our vibrations by shifting our thought processes and retraining our minds, we begin to perceive *what's already there to support us*.

Brain scientists agree that this isn't off the wall stuff but real and quantifiable through the new technology of brain imaging. We can now see what fires in the brain, what wires together, and changes in the brain in practicing new thought patterns and actions over a period of time.

Think of, "I'm broke. I'm broke. I have no money. I'm strapped for cash." translates to in bodily terms: stress hormones, a chemistry of anxiety and fear, depression, anger. And now, think of how these affect our whole brain and nervous system. How can we be "open" literally and conceptually to abundance when we are feeling so closed down?

As Bob further explains, "Scientists say that energy is neither created nor destroyed, and everything in its original state consists of energy. It necessarily follows that everything we'll ever want is already here. It's simply a matter of choosing the thoughts that will put us into harmonious vibration with the good we desire. So we don't have to *get* anything; it's a matter of becoming more aware of what we *already possess*.

"The moment we bring our lives into harmony with the Law and with the current of divine order, we'll find that the negative has taken flight because its cause has been removed. Then we no longer attract what we *don't* want."

To experience the positive results and wealth we *do* want, it's necessary to first understand that our vibrational focus has been on the wrong target and have produced the results we've experienced thus far. *It's not about blame. It's about simply taking responsibility for how our thoughts and beliefs may have blocked abundance and prosperity from the inside-out.* I know it can be painful to accept responsibility for our lives, so we may blame people or circumstances while pushing aside the idea that our own beliefs carry a lot of weight.

So how can we change?

Focus is the Key

Let's say you have a mountain of bills to pay and not nearly enough income to cover them. You're scrambling to find more money to reduce your debt. You feel totally frustrated, just spinning your wheels. How can the Laws of Vibration and Attraction help in this situation?

"The hardest idea for most people to grasp," says Bob, "is that their habitual negativity is attracting more negative situations into their lives. The more you worry and focus on your fear that you won't make enough money, the more likely you'll become insolvent and be unable to pay your bills. The Law of Vibration never switches off, so it can only help if you focus on what you *want* instead of the mess you're currently in.

"By focusing on creating more wealth, you'll attract (become aware of) the solutions and answers that will provide more income. This will take care of expenses without your worrying about them."

No, it's not a snap or an overnight process. It's a whole way of relating to life and to yourself. I didn't understand this for a long time ... and then, one day, it started to click. It's like I finally digested it. And when I did, I could not imagine how my world, my relationships, my health and, yes, my income, changed.

What about people who know about these so-called laws yet continue to get the same results in their lives? Explains Bob, "Often people stop at that first step—looking at their results. This step requires serious introspection, so when they take a good look for the first time, they discover facing responsibility for their lives can be heartbreaking."

I think I know what he's saying without saying it.

Regret.

We can't bear it. The idea of knowing we can't get a do-over, and seeing the mistakes we may have made or how we could have, should have, would have done it differently can produce such anger and self-hate, we often stop right there and turn around.

The idea that our thoughts have such powerful energy and influence is not only key to getting our lives back on track; it also explains why we have such a tough time doing so. First, it can be difficult to accept that we created our negative situation. And second, if our thoughts are so powerful, then so are the thoughts of those around us. That means our environment presents another sizeable factor contributing to success or failure.

Every individual we spend time around—everything we see and hear from the media or pick up in random conversations—has energy. If we continually place ourselves in negative situations and associate with people who have negative vibrations, we make it difficult to consistently choose positive thoughts and ideas.

For example, if your friends or family members constantly spout geysers of negative thoughts—complaining about their jobs, their relationships, their lack of money—it will adversely affect your ability to project the positive.

Have you noticed that, after being with certain people, you feel physically drained? Sure, we can avoid them. But, because we don't always choose our family members and business contacts, avoidance isn't always practical. If you're in this situation, the best way to protect yourself is to develop healthy boundaries. Not commiserating lessens the impact of their negative thoughts and allows your more positive ones to shine through.

Remember, your positive vibrations have the power to uplift those around you. So, why not find people who want to spend more time with you? They become energized.

Understanding Money and Wealth

Once you've faced your own negative thoughts about money and decided what you want, then you can open your mind to understanding exactly *how* money *works*. If you're already a millionaire, you know what I'm talking about. If not, then learn from millionaires. Bob has made tens of millions of dollars, yet he started by earning a mere $4,000 a year.

When wondering how to make money or if a particular business opportunity is right, we tend to ask friends and relatives. Unfortunately, unless they've been successful in the particular field you're considering, they don't know more than we do. So the best way to learn what millionaires know is to listen closely to their insights.

"I often confuse people when I tell them that, in order to accumulate wealth, *money can never be the goal,*" says Bob. "So when I say money isn't the goal, I mean that wealth isn't about accumulation; it's an ongoing journey of *growth and circulation.* Wealthy individuals already understand this, which is why they use money as a commodity of exchange rather than squirreling it away for a rainy day. Many people have a difficult time understanding this concept because they've been taught that the whole point of making money is to accumulate it. The point is to make it grow.

"Think of it in comparison to water. A drop of water by itself has no significant power. Neither does a single dollar. Not much can be done with either one. However, as drops—or dollars—come together, they flow into streams and then into rivers, creating a torrent of abundance. This abundance has the power to carve vast canyons in mountains, but *only as long as it's moving or circulating.* If the flow ceases to circulate, the water stagnates and stops producing abundance. The same is true of money."

One major block to living with an abundance mindset is wrapped up in our misperceptions about money and wealth—and whether we deserve either. Mackey talked about this and Bob takes it to another level by confronting our money vibration, so to speak. What kind of energy do we associate with money?

Is it positive? In other words, a flow? Or is it negative … out of reach or debt-filled?

"A common misperception is that you must have vast amounts of money to accomplish anything. Not true. Just like water, even small amounts of money applied in the right way can be deceptively powerful. Have you ever stood up in the current of a swiftly flowing stream? It takes only a small amount of water to knock you off your feet!

"As small amounts are invested in opportunities that produce cash flow, they come together to form a river that provides a constant stream of wealth. The secret lies not in the amount *but in the motion*. Money works exactly the same way," Bob emphasizes.

According to Bob, only three income-earning strategies exist.

THE THREE INCOME-EARNING STRATEGIES

1. **Trading time for money.** By far the worst of the three income-earning strategies, yet approximately 96% of our population—doctors, lawyers, accountants, laborers, and every hourly employee—trade time for money. The inherent problem with this strategy is *saturation.* We run out of time, and time is our only nonrenewable resource. No matter what we do, we can't make more, buy more, or even steal more.

   When people accumulate any degree of wealth employing this strategy, it's at the expense of the rest of their lives. Though nearly all people follow this strategy, they don't earn much. They may save a little for their golden years, but that means they aren't living to the fullest now. They rarely drive the cars they want, take the vacations they want, live in the houses they'd like to own, or even buy the clothes they'd like to wear.

   Trading time for money doesn't make for a good mindset and creates an even worse lifestyle, yet almost everyone does it.

2. **Investing money to earn money.** This strategy is used by approximately 3% of the population. The percentage is small because few people have much money to invest. Many people who employ this strategy effectively follow the advice of a trusted, knowledgeable advisor.

While an excellent strategy, one of the reasons only a low percentage of people invest money to earn money is that they have higher-paying jobs and money left over than most wage-earners. But they're still earning their income working for a wage and investing part of that income. It's better than strategy #1, but not the best.

3. **Leveraging yourself to earn money.** People who use strategy #3 multiply their time through the efforts of others by setting up Multiple Sources of Income (MSI)—without question, the best way to increase wealth. Unfortunately, only about 1% of our population uses this strategy, yet that 1% earn 96% of all the money!

In contrast to the first two strategies, those who employ this method never run out of time. Instead, they multiply, compound, and leverage it. They continually set up more multiple sources of income while freeing up their time—spend time with their families, travel, or follow other pursuits. This strategy allows them to earn money around the clock.

If you want to adopt strategy #3, work on one source of income at a time. Each one can become exciting as you invest in real estate, internet businesses, joint ventures with other entrepreneurs, and so on.

As we learned from Brian Biro in chapter 3, we first need to shift our focused intention to create an opening for our Window of Opportunity—our WOO. Then we can begin to realize the vastness available to us.

Opening to Financial Abundance

In the fall of 2008, when the U.S. economy shifted; so did my entire life. As mentioned in chapter 8, I was a project manager for one of the largest commercial interior construction companies in Miami. Almost instantly construction came to a standstill, and I was left without a job.

Late one night a few months later there was an infomercial for investing in real estate, which led to researching the top real estate gurus on the internet. The only way to decipher between them all was to pick the one who had the most positive and least negative comments about them, and who had a proven track record. Within two weeks, my partner, Alekxey, and I were sitting in one of Ron LeGrand's real estate investing trainings. This was clearly a WOO opening for us—we stayed positive, we were open to possibilities, and waited for the window of opportunity to appear.

We left that seminar with a determination to make this business work. However, investing in real estate can be somewhat overwhelming, and one of our first challenges was determining where to start.

From previous experience I knew that if we were going to succeed we had to *focus our intention* by determining what area of Ron's training we should really hone in on first, and focus on our intended goals. Once we were clear on our intentions, we had to take action.

With Florida being one of the top foreclosure states, we realized our primary focus needed to be on REOs—Real Estate Owned by the Bank. As a result, we learned to select ideal properties, build a powerhouse team, raised over a million dollars in private funds, and produce great rehabs that sold in days of putting them on the market.

In our first year we made more money than ever before and became one of the fastest growing private real estate investors in Miami.

We learned to leverage ourselves to earn money—Bob's income strategy #3. We assembled the right team in order to duplicate ourselves and create a sustainable business model. In addition, we work with private individuals as our lenders—not banks—to fund our real estate transactions, and, in return, provide them a higher rate of return, safely, securely, and ethically.

Although we primarily focus on REOs, we also buy short sales and properties from individual home owners; we resell these properties or hold them for ongoing cash flow as rentals. While our team handles the day-to-day activities, my focus is on growing the businesses, real estate trends, managing the team, writing, and working with our private investors. The tasks I enjoy.

The key was that we were open to the Window of Opportunity awaiting us. And so can you!

Prioritizing

Sounds great, doesn't it? But how can you fit one more thing into your packed schedule? How will you make time to set up these businesses and get the ball rolling? I used to wonder if all these gurus had a special way to stop the clock so they could get everything done! How do they manage their time to make it happen?

Time management is a hot topic these days. People want to know how they can do more in less time. Because we can never make more of it, though, all we can do is prioritize our activities to accomplish what matters most.

Bob explains that "time management means arranging what you do to fit as neatly as possible into the time you have available. Prioritizing means focusing only on the tasks that really matter and cutting down the rest or eliminating them altogether.

"It's similar," he notes, "to the idea of budgeting. Many people use budgeting to rearrange what they're already doing rather than prioritize what's important and eliminate what isn't. People often use words such as *time management* and *budgeting* to convince themselves they're accomplishing something when they're just shuffling the same old problems.

"Prioritizing involves making choices about every activity you engage in to see if it adds value. Let's look at the activities you're currently involved in and think about what you want to accomplish. I suspect you can carve out an hour or two each week to work toward your goals—maybe not much time, but at least *a start*.

"Now imagine your doctor tells you that you have exactly one year to live. How would knowing this change your priorities? Would you piddle around trying to accomplish your dreams in only a few hours a week? Would you plan to take a vacation for two weeks next June and hope you make it? Would you even sit in front of the TV tonight?

"When you think you have a seemingly unlimited amount of time, it's easy to waste it. However, when that time gets shortened and regarded as finite, it becomes precious indeed. In truth, time is *always* precious. Whether you live to be forty or ninety, you'll have only a limited amount of time — and it will never seem like enough. With this understanding, prioritizing becomes crucial so your life doesn't rush past in a blur of busyness that never accomplishes anything."

Crab fishermen will say you can catch a bucket full of crabs and never worry that they'll escape. Why? Because any crab that tries to climb out will be pulled back into the bucket by the others. You may feel like this climbing crab when you strike out in a new direction that others are unsure about. It may seem as if they're doing all they can to pull you back.

Actually, they're projecting their own fears onto your situation. They may even believe they're helping you avoid disappointment and failure.

So, to accomplish what we want, we must resist this pressure to stay with the crowd. Go ahead and do what others *won't* do. We can believe in the parts they question and commit to staying the course. By moving out of the accepted norms of society, we have an opportunity to investigate a wide range of possibilities rather than accept the same expected outcomes.

Prosperity Consciousness

"Money has a greater influence on our lives than almost any other commodity," Bob remarks. "Indeed, the sudden loss or acquisition of money affects our attitudes to a tremendous extent. Therefore, it would behoove us to have a deep understanding of exactly what money is and the laws governing it.

"Yet, not even one person in ten does. Ninety-five out of one hundred of us settle for whatever we get, wishing we had more all the way from the cradle to the casket and never understanding we could have had all we wanted.

"Instead, most of us let those results dictate the *thoughts* we then use to build our *ideas*. For example, if we see that our accounts are empty (results), we choose to think thoughts of loss, and then use those thoughts to build the idea of poverty," he explains. "However, because the ideas held in our minds manifest into future results, we're actually bringing about a repeat performance of the very thing we say we don't want—namely, an empty bank account."

You might think this is an absurd argument, because if a bank account is empty, well, it's empty! How can you realistically look at an empty bank account and visualize great wealth?

If we sincerely wish to improve our results in the physical world, it's necessary to change our thoughts and *understand* that the present state of our bank accounts, our sales, our health, our social lives, our positions at work are nothing more than the physical manifestation of our *previous* thinking. It's the result of our past thinking! Not our future prosperity. We can become conscious of the difference.

That said, what is *prosperity consciousness?*

Bob unwraps its meaning this way: It's an observable truth that human beings will never enjoy anything they're not yet consciously aware of, as these examples show:

- The Wright Brothers became *consciously* aware of how to fly, so we now enjoy the luxury of traveling in airplanes at tremendous rates of speed.

- Thomas Edison developed the *conscious* awareness of moving pictures and introduced us to a brand new form of entertainment.

- Dr. Jonas Salk became *consciously* aware of a serum that would combat the dreadful disease of infantile-paralysis, and we now enjoy freedom from polio.

- Alexander Graham Bell *consciously* knew how to transmit the human voice over metallic wires and, as a result, we now enjoy using his invention, the telephone.

"I could go on citing example after example," Bob adds, "but my point is that the knowledge that brought about these inventions has always been here. In fact, *all the knowledge there ever was or ever will be is present in all places at all times.* But it took an individual to bring those thought patterns together and develop them into what's called the *consciousness* of an invention before we could benefit from it.

"We humans exist in an ocean of thought-energy and knowledge," Bob reminds us. "We're also surrounded by abundance. Indeed, everywhere we look in nature, we can observe abundance; for nature knows no such thing as 'failure.' Therefore, there never has been and never will be a lack of anything except conscious awareness.

"Yet thousands of honest, good, hard-working people labor diligently for their entire stay on this planet and never become wealthy. For those individuals, life can be a constant grind from sunup until sundown.

"If you wish to penetrate this world of wealth, it's essential that you think differently. Open your mind to the stream of thought-energy that will create an image of prosperity—a *consciousness of prosperity*—in your mind."

Bob suggests the following five steps to shift your thought-energy and help you embrace prosperity consciousness in your daily life.

FIVE STEPS TO EMBRACING PROSPERITY CONSCIOUSNESS

1. Prosperity comes as a result of a decision. Make an irrevocable decision that you will be prosperous.

2. Think of how you can improve the quality and quantity of service you render.

3. Think of how you can help people in a greater way (sowing and reaping).

4. Gratitude keeps you connected to Source. Keep a gratitude journal of all of the abundance in your life.

5. Use the following affirmation daily. "I am so happy and grateful now that money comes to me in increasing quantities through multiple sources of income on a continual basis."

"Begin this new way of thinking right now," urges Bob, "because as you do, every fiber of your being will fill up with this new thought-energy."

How does that work? Your body is composed of millions of cells, and your thought impulses influence the vibration of each one of them. The second you entertain relaxing thoughts, your body becomes relaxed. The instant you entertain worrisome, fearful thoughts, your body becomes rigid and tense.

The moment you hold thoughts of prosperity, your body and mind instantly move into a prosperous vibration. When you begin thinking of yourself as a wealthy, prosperous individual surrounded by an ocean of thought-energy and swimming in a sea of plenty, you will become aware of and attract everything necessary to become wealthy.

Becoming prosperous requires opening our minds to the *possibilities* of achieving our desires. By *knowing* we live in an unlimited Universe and *staying focused* on what we want to experience, we become aware of all the resources already available to us.

It took several years for me to grasp the core of Bob's teaching and make a significant shift in my own thought process and vibrational energy. I had to laser focus my intention to experience the abundance that's always at my fingertips. I now know that abundance is our natural state; we were born prosperous in every area of our lives. And when we're open to receive, whatever we need to take us to the next level is revealed.

"Everything that we see in our material world once began as a thought! If you can see it in your mind, you can hold it in your hands."

— Bob Proctor

Living Inside-Out Lessons from Chapter 13

- To say that you "attract" money or wealth does not mean that these things are outside of you. Rather, you raise your vibration to receive the wealth that's already there by shifting your thought process and becoming open to opportunities that are already present.

- Money is not the goal because money, in itself, has no value. The goal is having the things money can be traded for and the freedom of time to enjoy them in an ongoing journey of growth and circulation.

- First, it's necessary to accept full responsibility for your results and understand you've attracted what's in your life so far.

- Don't let your present results dictate the thoughts you use to build your ideas of life. To improve the results in your physical world, change your thoughts immediately. Build ideas of wealth, not lack.

- Abundance is everywhere. There never has been and never will be a lack of anything except conscious awareness.

- As you hold thoughts of prosperity and think of yourself as wealthy and prosperous, your body and mind instantly moves into a prosperous vibration. Then you will become aware of and attract everything necessary to become wealthy.

- Abundance is your natural state. You were born prosperous in every area of your life.

14

LOVING OURSELVES FROM THE INSIDE-OUT

Loving Ourselves & Empowering Our Children

"The degree to which you love, acknowledge, and celebrate yourself is the degree
to which others will love, acknowledge, and celebrate you."

— Lisa Nichols

One of the universal truths I've learned is that we all want to love and be loved.

However, you've likely heard the saying "you have to love yourself before you can love someone else." Easier said than done, right? Yet, if we don't love ourselves, what happens to our most cherished relationships, especially those with our children?

Some of us would never admit to anyone—especially ourselves—that we don't love and appreciate who we are. I'm no exception, as I was in my twenties before I learned to fully accept and begin to love myself.

We might periodically sink into our dark corners or become so numb to our feelings that we either don't know what's occurring or refuse to address it. Living from the inside-out includes embracing who we are and loving ourselves—all of us.

But, if it were a simple choice, we'd all be reaping the benefits. So, what gets in the way?

When contemplating how to address this topic, I was drawn to a remarkable woman. To this day, every time I hear her story, I tune in with all my senses.

"No Matter What" Mantra

Lisa Nichols lives her life with a "no matter what" mantra—no matter what she is going to make it, there is no other choice. She grew up in south central Los Angeles way below poverty level, living between two gangs. She was considered academically challenged for at least 9 of her 12 years in school. For all 12 years, she qualified for free lunches.

Today, Lisa reaches millions worldwide with her riveting message of empowerment, service, excellence, and gratitude. She's the best-selling author of *No Matter What* and co-author of *Chicken Soup for the African American Soul*. In addition, she's CEO of Motivating the Teen Spirit and a featured expert in the movie *The Secret*.

As a dynamic motivational speaker, Lisa's life testifies to her advocacy of personal empowerment and emotional health. She's worked with more than 110,000 teens and has prevented (on record) more than 3,000 teen suicides. She's appeared on the *Oprah Winfrey Show*, *Extra*, *Larry King Live*, and NBC's Emmy Award-winning show, *Starting Over*.

What I love and appreciate most about Lisa is her transparency. She shared with me how her "no matter what" attitude carried her through her most difficult challenges to experience the high side of self-love. While writing her book *No Matter What*, she was faced with sharing many facts about her life she hadn't told anyone. She was unsure if she still held shame, guilt, blame, or frustration about these aspects of her past, so she had to ask herself, "Am I ready to let the world know that I was molested? That I was suicidal? That I gained nearly a hundred pounds because I was afraid to allow anyone to get close to me?"

Behind Our Secrets

Behind the deepest part of us that we keep hidden—our secrets, the truth we keep running from—is our ultimate power and strength.

Regardless of how deep or dark our secrets are, Lisa and I learned that unless we are willing to come to terms with them and make peace inside ourselves, they stifle us. This doesn't mean that we have to share them with anyone else, but that we have to be aware of the mental and emotional triggers they cause and the ways in which we treat ourselves and others because of their lingering affect.

From the time I was thirteen, until I was twenty, I fought with myself weekly, often, daily. I struggled to accept who I was. That I was gay. I can't tell you how many nights I fell asleep praying to God to take this away from me. That I would do anything if I could be freed from the hell I was in.

No matter how hard I prayed, my frustration grew. At twenty, I had a major breakthrough. Through the process of learning to go within I realized *God loved me for who I was and created me whole and complete.*

It was about really knowing and trusting my own truth. After years of self-limiting conversations beating myself up, thinking that I wasn't good enough and didn't fit in, I *began* to appreciate and even *like* myself. It was the most critical *aha!* moment of self-acceptance I've had in my life.

By leaning into my fear by constantly going within to connect with Source, I gained the clarity I needed to breakthrough to the knowing.

I share my personal struggle with you for two reasons.

First of all, I couldn't imagine sharing my own inside out journey with you and leave out the most defining challenge I faced in my life. It was through this internal battle that I was driven to start my quest within. It has been a pivotal awakening.

Secondly, I thought being gay defined me. What I realized is that it is simply a component of my human experience—a component of who I am.

When I was twenty-three I finally got up the courage to share this with my mom as she has always been one I could easily talk with. She helped me have the courage to tell my dad. It wasn't easy, for at the time, it added fuel to the fire of our ongoing disagreements.

However through the tension, I remember what my dad said to me very clearly. "I don't like it, but you are my son and you are always welcome in this house."

I risked it all and in return received unconditional love.

This was just the beginning of the breakthroughs I had over the twenty years that followed. As I continued to connect at a deeper level with my core being I gained more understanding and clarity as to how to love myself.

Behind our secrets is our power and strength. It could be our orientation; abuse we suffer—mental, emotional, or sexual; the disgust we feel about our body image—too fat, too skinny, our appearance; addiction—of food, alcohol, drugs, sex, work; not feeling we fit in; or any number of other secrets we hide behind.

If we hide we are trapped. If we are willing to confront and accept ourselves, then release our judgments (forgive) and let go, we open to our freedom and power of our authentic selves.

Building the Character Muscles

To take a major leap forward in our lives, we have to be honest with ourselves.

"At the core, many of our actions are based on feelings or thought patterns," Lisa explains. "I go to the core and look at the feeling that's producing the action. *What's the feeling? What's the thought behind it?* Often, the feeling of fear has a strong, negative influence. For example, we fear other people's perceptions of us. We think, 'If I get out of line, if I don't show up as the average or ordinary person, then I'm odd. I'm afraid of being rejected.' So we hold ourselves back.

"Often, we're not grounded in the feeling of *knowingness*—because when we *know* something, we're not looking for acceptance. Not that we want to alienate people, but we do want to stand for *who we know ourselves to be*. Then we're not looking for others to validate who we are.

"*Who we are* includes our character. We go to the gym and build our triceps and biceps, eat protein bars, and do other such things to build up our physical selves. We also need to build the muscles in our character:

our resiliency muscle, our faith-in-ourselves muscle, our honesty muscle. When building character, we feel it evolving not just through wonderful experiences but through trials and tribulations as well.

"We develop it through watching parents or grandparents transition and learning to release them, through watching our children grow into adulthood and letting them go, through releasing our anger at someone who's betrayed us. Challenges like these serve to "grow" our character muscles.

"I'm a culmination—you are a culmination—of every experience we've had and the choices we've made around those experiences. Who we are in the dark of the night has to match who we are in the middle of the day. That's integrity," she adds.

Who we are in the dark of the night.

I hung on these words. We are all familiar with this split between *who we present ourselves to be and how we really feel on the inside.* In between, the chasm holds all of our disappointment, grief, pain, and fear. To close that split, we need to know it's there in the first place. Otherwise, we pass it on.

Lisa says, "We need to help our children understand that, regardless of what they do, they are whole and complete as defined by their character. We justify ourselves by what we have, the clothes we wear, the car we drive, the title on our business cards. When we leave the house not feeling whole and complete, we can feel isolated, self-conscious, and lonely. We may interact all day with others, but we don't truly connect with one another."

Lisa says the number one reason people get depressed is that they feel alone. In her adult workshops, loneliness looms as the main theme. Teens also admit they feel alone, in spite of friends and family. They lack feelings of connection.

Love Them from the Saucer, Not the Cup

Whether we have children or not, someone's child is watching us, so we can think about how we might live and act responsibly. On some level— biological, spiritual, or social—we model our lives to young people. We're examples to children in the world. When we fail to give ourselves what we need, we're modeling a lack of self-love.

"Parents present 'the first example' of how the world will treat us," claims Lisa. "Why? Because *the degree to which we love, acknowledge, and celebrate ourselves is the degree to which others will love, acknowledge, and celebrate us.*

"When we come from a needy perspective relying on others' opinion of us more than our own, we're trying to fill ourselves from outside-in versus inside-out. This never works. Even if others poured love and inspiration into us, if we don't love ourselves first, it would be like pouring them into a sifter with hundreds of holes in the bottom.

"Like most people who come from a service-based mentality, we may serve others at the expense of ourselves, believing 'my children come first.' But our children do *not* come first. *We* come first. If we serve our children from an empty cup, we're doing them a disservice because we tend to be short with them and feel resentful. We become exhausted. Most of all, we're poor examples of what they need to do when they grow up and become parents.

"So it's our job to *fill our cups to overflowing*. It's *not* our job to love and serve people from what's in our *cups,* but from *what's in the saucer.*"

I just love this visual. We give to them from the *overflow*.

As Lisa beautifully illustrates, having unconditional love and acceptance of *ourselves* is critical in how we create our lives and relationships. We live in a culture that often suppresses or denigrates our beliefs, ideas, and expressions of who we are. As we learned from in chapter 4, messages that bombard us from family, society, and workplace both overtly and covertly tout conformity and obedience. They reek of conditionality. Programming that says we don't measure up then manifests in our relationships. We pass that on to our children, our nieces and nephews, and other children in our lives.

To counteract this, Lisa advocates four relationship-changing ways of empowering children that go beyond self-love.

FOUR RELATIONSHIP-CHANGING WAYS TO EMPOWER OUR CHILDREN

1. Create safe spaces.
2. Have possibility-based conversations.
3. Talk less.
4. Risk it all to gain it all.

1. Create Safe Spaces

Lisa says that during her workshops, she facilitates connection between people by creating a safe space. "We set up three agreements designed to create a safe space in any environment. Maintaining this safe space is critical both in my workshops and in relationships in general. The moment I feel someone is violating or challenging the safe space, I stop the process and reestablish our agreements."

The first agreement is *no judgment*.

"I can tell people I've been molested. I can say I had a lot of sex looking for a little love because I believed at one time that the 'room' called love had to be entered through the 'door' called sex. If I said no to sex, I'd be saying no to love. How do I dare tell people that about me? Because I ask them not to judge me and they've agreed. They need to let me know they won't judge me—and be honest about that."

Imagine how relationships would change if every mother and father reading this book told their children that they, as parents, commit to *no judgment* whatsoever regarding what their children say or do. Radical transformation!

The second agreement is to provide *unconditional love*.

"It's easy to love others when they're doing the 'right' thing. My son's a teenager. I have no problem loving him when he's getting A's or when he scores a basket or cleans his room—when he behaves 'in line.' But when he gets poor grades and is 'stuck on cuckoo' as we call it around our house, he needs me to give him unconditional love even more. He got stuck on being a teenager and got a D because he finally realized that girls don't have cooties and he likes talking to them. He talked more than he studied.

"When we choose to demonstrate love consistently and unconditionally—through the highs and the lows, the goods and the bads, the happys and the sads—then our children will become comfortable bringing more to us."

The third agreement is *no repercussions*.

"This is the most difficult one for parents to wrap their minds around. It's allowing our children to tell us anything without ramifications to them. This means not holding anything against them or reacting with punishing consequences.

Yes, it's a stretch, but worth it. We can bring up what they told us later—but *only* to encourage and support them and not, *emphatically not*, to hurt them. Because if we do, our children will stop telling us the intimate things. If we ask, 'How are you doing today?' we'll get 'Fine.' 'How was school today?' 'Good.' 'What did you learn today?' 'Nothing.' So much might have actually happened that day: 'I broke up with my boyfriend.' 'My girlfriend kissed another guy.' 'I failed a test.' 'I found out today that I like girls' (and she's a girl). Any of these emotional events might have happened but they don't feel they can share that information because they don't know if we'll use it against them later.

"So they hold it all in. Then when they go day after day, week after week, month after month holding in those little and not-so-little things, they end up feeling alone. They're around us, they eat dinner with us, but they haven't shared what's on their minds and in their hearts—so they feel alone. That's why agreeing to *no repercussions* is vital to creating a safe space."

To reinforce that, Lisa and her son have a buddy hour when she doesn't talk to him as mom. "I don't give him advice—I just listen to him. I don't do anything with what I hear. I walk away and my tongue hurts because I'm biting it so much.

"During buddy hour, I'm just his friend. I let him know it's okay to not like everything about himself. Sometimes I tell him about times when 'I've been there.' Then he can see me as a woman, a peer, a friend.

"Don't get me wrong; I'm always his parent. I won't forfeit parenthood to be his friend. Being his friend is the cherry on top of the cake; being his parent *is* the cake."

If we keep Lisa's three agreements—no judgment, unconditional love, and no repercussions—we can watch our relationships improve exponentially. Our children, our spouses, or anyone we're with can feel safe sharing themselves on a deep level. This goes a long way toward eliminating loneliness and its partner, depression.

2. Have Possibility-Based Conversations

To have possibility-based and not fear-based conversations with our children, Lisa points out the need to first recognize our own fears. Otherwise, we're in danger of projecting them onto our children.

"We say, 'Don't drink and drive because I don't want you to get killed' or 'Put on your seatbelt because I don't want you to get hurt in an accident' or, 'Honey, I don't want you to get hurt like I was.'

"Of course we think we're saying these things from a space of love, but we're actually coming from fear. How will our children enjoy life if they *live to avoid hurt* versus *live to experience love and joy*? So instead of projecting our hurts and fears, we can say, 'I want you to have safety and love and to enjoy your life.' (What Doug Bench refers to in chapter 7 as *positive-positive* statements.)

"It's important for us to recognize this tendency and monitor ourselves. We can do that by thinking before we open our mouths to have conversations with our children. We can ask ourselves, 'What am I about to say? Does it speak to what I want for my child, or does it speak to what I want my child to avoid?' If we're speaking to avoidance, it's probably a fear-based, hurt-based conversation. If we're speaking to what we want them to have, it's a *possibility-based conversation*. These are empowering."

3. Talk Less

According to Lisa, the third relationship-changing component to empowering our children is to *talk less*. "We talk way too much as parents.

We believe we need to impart to our children all of the valuable wisdom it took us decades to attain. Instead, let's *listen* at least as much as we talk. Let's ask more questions—and not respond with 'oh, I've been there,' to everything we hear. We *haven't* been there, at least not in their timeframe of texting, iPods, nanos, MTV, Pimp My Ride, Pimp My Crib, and other gadgets, programs, and activities our children are exposed to. And when we say 'back in my day ...' we're branding ourselves as dinosaurs. That doesn't help.

"So when we ask our children questions, it's crucial to be still and listen to their answers. I can't say that enough. *Be still and listen*. Otherwise, we tend to react instead of respond. When we react, we're ultimately trying to influence their behavior. Responses, on the other hand, ebb and flow. They breathe. We expand and contract with them in a relay. We co-create the next step. That's a relationship.

"I've had my best moments with my son when I've apologized, confessed something, or surrendered to something. Those times produced diamonds in our relationship. Sometimes I admitted that this is my first time being a mother of a teenage son and asked for his help to co-create what's next. It's my job to lead, but it's not my job to tell him how to feel."

4. Risk It All to Gain It All

Lisa warns that the fourth component to empowering children can be the biggest risk of all—and the most rewarding. Why? Because it can facilitate the next level of relationship if we're willing.

"Are we willing to *risk it all to gain it all?* Are we willing to detach from any particular outcome that we believe we have to have with our children—to become vulnerable at a new level for the sake of what could be created?" Lisa asks.

"When we're vulnerable, people usually connect to us at the core. Yet we're afraid to tell our children about the mistakes we've made. We want to protect them. But when we don't share our mistakes, we've opened the door for them to make the same ones, because no one tells them what it felt like to be there. What did it feel like to have sex before I got married?

What did it feel like to try drugs? Of course, we share with our children appropriately. We don't share with a five year old what we might with a teenager, for example.

"When my son first attended one of my workshops and I shared that I'd been molested, I was shaking in my shoes. My boy was only twelve at the time. But the reality is that I *was* molested, and if I'm willing to share that with other people's children, why on earth wouldn't I be willing to share it with my own child?

"My son came to me later that day and said, 'Mom, have you forgiven that person?' I told him, 'Yes, but it took me about fifteen years.' He responded, 'No one's ever touched me inappropriately, Mom.' (Now I didn't ask for that, although you can imagine how happy I was to hear it!) Then he said, 'But Mom, I hope you don't mind, but if something bad like that ever happens to me, I don't want to wait fifteen years to forgive.' Oh, wow! *I risked it all to gain it all!* And I can tell you, release came immediately. I slept much better that night."

This component requires us to trust our children at a new level but it doesn't mean to project our fears because we think they can handle them. We're trusting in the understanding of young people who are fully developed with all the faculties we have.

It's a delicate balance.

"In a healthy environment, we can take bigger risks with them. We can share more of ourselves with them as a woman or a man rather than a parent. It's good to say that 'I'm not speaking to you as your mother,' or 'I'm not speaking to you as your father.' Rather, say, 'I'd like to speak to you woman to woman' (or man to woman, woman to man, man to man, or whatever the combination is). When we do that, we see the young woman or the young man emerge. We're expanding our children's capacity to handle real-life situations. And they can surprise us. We want to send our children out into the world fully protected.

"Normally, by the time our children are eighteen, we *haven't* helped them expand their capacity to handle tough situations. So, at age twenty-two when someone breaks our daughter's heart, she's depressed because we haven't expanded her capacity to understand that others will do that. She may not realize that people will betray her trust, but that she can choose to forgive them quickly," Lisa adds.

How to Embrace the Gift of Love

What's the key message? To love yourself on a deeper level—from your own cup—and *discover the radiant beauty within you*. To access, listen to, trust, and follow your inner voice and become your own biggest fan, best friend, and unconditional lover.

"Before we can help our children, we have to help ourselves," Lisa stresses. In school, we had to learn English, math, and science to graduate. But chances are at no time were we taught to deal with the betrayal of a parent, an absentee parent, the death of a loved one, or the emotional roller coaster of gaining weight or dating. "No one taught us to manage our feelings related to our life experiences."

As parents or partners in relationship, it's essential for us to let go of shame, blame, and guilt as driving forces—to recognize our own fears and hurts, create a safe space for ourselves, talk less and listen more to ourselves, and become more vulnerable. In this way, we can embrace the gift of loving ourselves. Our cups overflow, and all of that understanding and love in our saucers becomes available to our children and others.

We can then create a safe space for our children to talk about difficult issues, have conversations that are possibility-based, listen to them, be vulnerable, and authentically share with them who we were before we became their parents. By doing this, we increase the depth of our communication, their level of trust, and ultimately, our connection with them.

"When we're vulnerable, people usually connect to us at the core. That takes our relationship to the next level."

— Lisa Nichols

Living Inside-Out Lessons from Chapter 14

- The degree to which you love, acknowledge, and celebrate yourself is the degree to which others will love, acknowledge, and celebrate you.

- Build the muscles in your character—your resiliency, your faith in yourself, your honesty—and you'll feel your character evolving.

- Speak of what you want your children to attain (possibility-based conversation), not what you want them to avoid (fear-based conversation).

- Fill your own cup first, then serve and love your children and others from the overflow in your saucer.

- To facilitate trust and connection, create a safe space where all involved know they will not be judged.

- "Risk it all to gain it all" means to be vulnerable with your children and others. Vulnerability and trust enable a true connection.

- Recognize your own fears and hurts, create a safe space for yourself, talk less and listen more, and embrace the gift of loving yourself as you are.

15

Build Relationships that Last

"The first step is to start thinking in terms of us, ours, and we, as opposed to me, mine."

— Jane Greer, PhD

Relationships. They're the greatest thing on earth when they're going well, but can be the source of our deepest suffering when they're not. When something isn't working in our relationship with our significant other, we don't feel right or good. In fact, we can feel downright unhealthy, even sick. Heart sick. That alone, over time, can make us physically sick too.

What can we do about our relationship struggles? How can we find or develop a relationship that works?

At Wiktionary.com, the word *relationship* has two basic meanings. In definition number one, the first part of the word, *relation*, means "the connection or association between two things," or in this case, people.

The second part of the word, *ship,* means "the state of being." Thus *relationship* means the state of being in connection or association with another. Often we judge what our partner (or the person we're in a relationship with) is *doing to* us instead of how we are *being* in the relationship.

Before addressing that, let's look at the second definition of the word *relationship.*

The second definition concerns the degrees of affinity between keys or chords or tones in music. What does that have to do with human relationships? In earlier chapters, we explored the Law of Vibration and how the type of vibration we put out to the world determines what we receive in return. Like the notes in a piece of music, we either resonate harmoniously with someone, or we don't.

But why do we resonate with some people and not with others? We may feel an intense attraction to someone and let those overpowering emotions open our hearts, only to find out this person is deceptive or lacks integrity. Some of us experience this phenomenon over and over again.

How and why is it happening? Do we ever ask ourselves how *we* may lack integrity, especially with ourselves, instead of seeing ourselves as a victim to the person or situation?

If we're in a long-term relationship, we may find ourselves disconnected, wanting more, and feeling empty and resentful. Perhaps we're trapped in self-perpetuating cycles that became ever more exaggerated with each go-around. As with every other area we've addressed in this book, the way to nurturing a fulfilling, sustainable relationship lies within ourselves.

Relationship Insights

To help us dig deeper, I asked Jane Greer, PhD, to give us her insights on why most of us seem to be so disconnected and how we can create the relationships we truly desire.

Dr. Greer, a nationally renowned marriage and family therapist, has been in private practice for more than 20 years. She's the best-selling author of *Gridlock: Finding the Courage to Move on in Love, Work and Life; How Could You Do This to Me? Learning to Trust After Betrayal;* and *Adult Sibling Rivalry.* A Love Network Expert for *Redbook* magazine, Jane has also appeared regularly as a guest expert on national television programs including *The Today Show, The Early Show, CNN News, Anderson Cooper 360, Dateline NBC, 20/20, The Oprah Winfrey Show, The View, Extra!,* and *Hard Copy.*

Jane explains, "A disconnect occurs when one person feels misunderstood and unsupported by his or her partner. When both people feel misunderstood and unsupported, unappreciated, taken advantage of, or taken for granted, then frustration, anger, and disappointment build force. That second layer of feelings amplifies the first layer. When it kicks in, the majority of us become emotionally overwhelmed because we don't have the skills to cope with that much emotional turmoil. So we disconnect emotionally from ourselves and ultimately from our partner."

Our Relationship with Ourselves

Chapter 14 stated that *you have to love yourself before you can love someone else,* referring to parents and children. This truth is relevant to any relationship, especially one with an intimate partner. So why is it so difficult to accept ourselves and what we need?

Jane says, "Acknowledging our truth to ourselves can be a struggle. We have to confront the myths and messages of our past (our stories) and the way we've lived up to this point. We may be filled with guilt and shame around sex. We may feel guilty about taking care of our own needs or anxious about putting them out there and hoping somebody will fill them. It's difficult to own and speak about our needs. And we're frightened to confront ourselves and what we've held inside for years. It's easier to accept and live the other person's reality of us than our own."

It's also easier to read those words than to apply them to our lives. Right?

Many of us became conditioned to this and witnessed others sacrifice *who they are.* Jane explains that most of us know what we *don't* want or what we're *not* getting, but have no idea what we *do* want. The result? We live with a sense of deficiency and lack.

Instead of developing ourselves as self-sufficient people, Jane explains, "We subconsciously *set ourselves up* to find what we lack in another person."

We don't' set ourselves up to torture ourselves. It's that we are driven largely by our past stories and unresolved hurts from our earliest years, as we learned in chapter 4.

Jane explains, "It's no coincidence that the biggest slob marries a fanatic neat freak, or the person who's always late marries someone who's conscientiously punctual. We hook up with somebody who behaves in ways we both judge and subconsciously long to emulate. And often, we never realize the script we're playing out, living in denial of the pain we experience from not living our truth, not loving ourselves, and thus not being able to give and receive the love we so desperately crave.

"Denial blocks the reality of the severity of the problem," Jane continues. "We buy into the other person's reality. So we continue to live with an alcoholic or a gambler or a cheating spouse.

"Those of us who have these problems minimize them so we can live with ourselves. We create a distorted worldview and say 'It's not that bad' and 'I can stop anytime' and 'I can get another job. It'll happen. You'll see.' Whatever the problem, we always have intentions to change. But the divide between our intentions and reality spans the Grand Canyon. When denial sneaks into the picture, our partners accept our *intentions* rather than their own realities. Once that happens, they get amnesia."

So how can we become aware of something we are not aware of?

"To break through the denial and face the problem from either standpoint, we need to ask, 'How does this make me *feel?*'" she advises. "When we focus on how we feel, pain and distress come to the fore. *This is good.* When we tap into the pain, we can see where it comes from. Is it from being abandoned as a child through death or divorce? Is it from being physically or emotionally abused in a relationship? Is it from being ridiculed and teased by classmates?

"Whatever, wherever, or whomever the pain came from, at some point we bought into someone else's reality about us. We believed their story that we aren't enough, that we're flawed, and not loveable. *Their* story became *our* story—or our made-up reality of who we are.

"We can spend years looking outside of ourselves for someone to confirm that we *are* enough, we *are* perfect as we are, and we *are* loveable. But our story about ourselves doesn't change. We wonder why we keep attracting the same types of people who don't respect us, who tell us we're flawed, and who don't show us love."

To Change Yourself, Question Your Beliefs

What is the bottom line? That we don't respect ourselves, *we* think we're flawed, and we don't love *ourselves?*

Well, truth is, yes.

Look again at the definitions of relationship. Do you see how our beliefs about ourselves attract people who resonate with those beliefs? If you see yourself in these descriptions, how do you change these beliefs about yourself?

Recall that from Principal #4, *Know Your Truth*, you can unearth insights about your story. From these insights, you can get clues to your unconscious beliefs you think are being triggered by your partner, parents, coworkers, or others. Only from conscious awareness can you *choose* what you believe about yourself and how to respond in a situation, and not automatically react the way you always have because of your story.

Understanding Our Relationship with Our Intimate Partners

When we unconditionally love ourselves, it becomes almost effortless to unconditionally love our partners. However, the journey to unconditional love can be a difficult process, especially if you've experienced trauma earlier in your life. We can give unconditional love easily if we had the blessing to have been raised with it.

But, for many people whose parents did the best they knew how, conditional love was more common. Many people feel unaccepted for who they are as old traces of childhood rejection or dismissal stays in the system—until we heal it.

That's why it's necessary to be *absolutely* committed to observing our own thoughts and feelings about ourselves and others. How often might we catch ourselves blaming others for our pain?

Jane says, "Many of us talk to each other about our needs through blame and anger. We feel the other person has disappointed us, frustrated us, or left us feeling deprived. We lack the clarity to say, 'Here's what would be great for me. Could you tell me you love me at least once or twice a week? Could you help out with the kids three times a week?'

"Rather, we picture our ideal and talk to each other in terms of our disappointment and disenchantment. Our fantasy of a mate isn't being realized, so we get angry, distance ourselves, and finally disconnect."

We can ask ourselves what we truly need. Jane points out, "Our present needs derive from our unresolved, unmet needs in our families of origin. Perhaps we felt neglected because of a parent's divorce or illness, or we had a sibling with problematic behavior who sucked the oxygen out of the family environment. Our needs are a manifestation of what we didn't get then and still long for. We often wind up getting involved with a partner who represents a combination of the best and the worst of mother and father or sister and brother."

I know. Yikes, but there's freedom in knowing. So, Jane says we can understand how we hold back, how we get stuck, and gradually unlock that gridlock once and for all.

We tend to get stuck in these relationships, despite the fact we know the relationship needs a major intervention, or no longer (or never did) works for us. Therefore, fear of the unknown presents the biggest obstacle for change in relationships.

"The devil we know is better than the devil we don't know," Jane says. "We're afraid to take responsibility for ourselves. We've lived the other person's truth and reality for so long, we have a difficult time trusting our own judgment and reality. Overwhelming anxiety gets triggered at the idea of leaving somebody—even if it's somebody who's making us miserable."

If we want to enjoy our lives from the inside-out, connecting and relating with someone else is the natural outcome of connecting and relating with ourselves. Jane further explains, "The main challenge is to go within and come up with the answer to 'What can *I* do?' for myself instead of asking what the *other* person is or isn't doing."

Wondering how we can get what we want from our partners when they've never been that way—or when they say they'll do something and don't—makes us feel stuck and hopeless.

"To overcome that, I tell people to look at how they can put what they need in place for *themselves*. I say, 'Forget the other person. Take responsibility for yourself in the areas you need to make the changes. That way, you short-circuit the system between the two of you and the way it's been.

"You're no longer *being* controlled because you've *taken* control. You're no longer waiting or asking the other person to make it better for you because you're making it better for yourself.' That establishes a different balance in the relationship."

No, It's Not Selfishness

Selfish behavior isn't what many of us think it is. In fact, selfish behavior isn't the same as selfishness. Selfishness is about having blatant disregard for the other person.

Instead, we're talking about self-centered behavior, with the emphasis on *centered*—that is, centered around our own needs. We show regard for both ourselves and the other person. We know what we expect from the other person in terms of affection, sex, economic, and emotional support. Also, we have to know our partner. So, are our expectations realistic? If they aren't, do we give up our needs?

"The questions to ask include 'How am I meeting my own core needs?' If we're not meeting our needs but expect our partner to meet them, we'll never be satisfied by or with anyone." Jane shares.

"It helps to talk about our needs and desires and make requests rather than demands. Then our partner feels he or she is making a choice to please us rather than being controlled by us. Asking for what we need is a way of being empowered in our relationships as opposed to trying to overpower each other."

In our hectic, overcommitted lives, many of us tend to become defensive with each other instead of taking time to understand the dynamic of our interactions. Jane clarifies it this way: "The skill is to *respond* to what our partner says to us *instead of reacting to it*. Most of us have a knee-jerk reaction. When someone takes a shot at us, we take a shot back. In five seconds, our adult selves evaporate and we become five year olds. Then it's all about 'no fair.'

"Instead of responding to the comment a partner is making, address what underlies it. Suppose a partner makes a critical remark such as, 'You never do the laundry' or 'You're always leaving that door open.' Would you immediately become defensive and counter with something like, 'Well, *you* don't pick up your clothes!' Instead, you could say this: '*I feel criticized when you say that. Where's that coming from? Are you upset about something?*'

I wish I knew this technique last week. You see, I have a tendency to leave the recycle trash on the floor next to the regular trash can instead of placing it in the canister on the back porch. This drives my partner crazy. For me, I think it is natural.

Well, I did it again, it led to a major blow-up, and I took on child-like behaviors as Jane mentioned. It's so key to shift our communication style, and instead of reacting, saying something like … I feel criticized when you say that. Can we talk about it?

"This tells us to start from the baseline that our partners are *not* out to 'do us in' but rather to take care of themselves. In the process, they're having a difficult time understanding where we're coming from. So instead of attacking and blaming, we can say, '*Let me tell you what's important to me, and you tell me what's important to you.*'

"If we learn the art of problem solving and compromise with both getting our needs met, then getting along with the other person won't require performing sacrificial rites."

Us or We, not I or Me

To develop a mutually beneficial relationship, Jane suggests incorporating the concept of *us or we* rather than *I or me*. Problem solving then involves creating options within the context of a couple that cares about each individual's needs.

Jane emphasizes, "If you want to be living from the inside-out, you have to turn yourself inside out and become part of the unit, part of the couple. That way, you're looking to define things in terms of the two of you, not yourself."

We say we want close relationships, but often when we start developing the necessary skills with our partner, something happens to sabotage that closeness. Jane reports on this phenomenon this way: "The closer we are to someone, the more vulnerable we feel and for many the more frightened we are of losing that person.

"Consequently—and ironically—we can push the other person away. This helps explain infidelity, because being intimately involved with and committed to one person means being real and vulnerable—sharing ourselves and being true to ourselves and our partner.

"We're afraid of the nature of intimacy and the attachment it brings up. We differ in how close we can get to another person without feeling out of control, too attached, dependent, or needy. These fears relate to our early development of separation and individuation. They take us back, on an unconscious level, to when we were younger and trying to forge our way. We wanted to separate from our mom and feel safe away from her, yet we were afraid of being on our own and wanted to maintain our connectedness."

We still want both independence *and* connection, which is good—but we often let fear get in the way. As Jane adds, "People who are afraid of commitment often came from families with divorce, loss, and abandonment. If that's been our experience, we're frightened of attaching, being vulnerable, and needing somebody."

In my case, the feeling of loss and abandonment I felt as a child when my brother died had a major control factor on my life for decades. The story I created played out in each relationship and I was constantly fearful that the relationship would end and I would once again be alone. As a result of my own fear, I push a number of relationships away because of the protective walls I built around me.

Knowing that our fears will come up as part of the process of developing intimacy helps us feel less anxious when we get upset. Jane likens this emotional process to the healing crisis that arises when we detoxify our bodies, releasing what we no longer want in order to become healthier. "We bring up the feelings that would otherwise come out in behaviors that create distance and conflict," she explains. "Therefore, the goal is twofold: to acknowledge the way we're feeling, and to talk about it with our partner."

What are the rewards? If we problem solve together more, we'll feel closer. We'll smile more at each other. We'll feel more affectionate. "While that may feel great, we need to be aware that it might trigger feelings of vulnerability, dependency, neediness, insecurity, and anxiety," Jane warns.

She mentions the myth of having the perfect mate as another way we avoid intimacy and commitment. "The myth of the perfect partner can unfortunately perpetuate and facilitate both our dependency issues and fears of commitment. But we need to ask, 'Do I want companionship or do I want perfection?'

"Love, devotion, and companionship are based on inside-out factors—how our partner makes us feel about ourselves, what we're able to share, if we enjoy the same sense of humor and view life in a similar way. These factors aren't based on the kind of job a person has, the person's income, or the host of other requirements people have on their perfect mate lists.

"The core of the issue is that, for most of us, creating distance reassures us that we don't need the other person that much. The art of being a couple, on the other hand, involves creating a *healthy dependency* in which it's okay to depend on our partners, all the while knowing we can survive without them."

Jane suggests the following 5 keys to create relationships that last.

FIVE FACTORS IN BUILDING A LASTING RELATIONSHIP

1. Focus on how you are *being* in the relationship instead of what the other person is or isn't *doing*.

2. Identify your core needs (such as approval or respect) and recognize which needs you are responsible for.

3. Access the painful feelings (such as disappointment or rejection) behind your anger, or your reactive or defensive stance.

4. Stay "self-centered" when balancing needs, instead of expecting your partner to fill in the blanks. What can you do for yourself?

5. The art of being a couple involves creating a healthy dependency in which it's okay to depend on your partner, while maintaining autonomy and celebrating your individual identity.

The Foundation for All Relationships

The anchor of any relationship—be it with a partner, parents, children, bosses, neighbors, or friends—is in *ourselves*. Thus, when we have problems, we know where to start!

The concept of a fifty-fifty relationship is a myth. Sometimes it's eighty-twenty. Sometimes it's ninety-ten. Sometimes it's forty-sixty or thirty-seventy. But it all comes out in the wash. My parents say they follow the sixty-four rule—the other one is always sixty percent (or more) of the time right. And that has been the key to their forty plus year's marriage.

The notion of compromise means we have to be willing to give one hundred percent of ourselves over the long haul. At times, this means giving in to the other person's needs and putting our own needs aside for a while. For most of us, giving in to compromise feels like giving up. But, once again, it isn't about sacrifice. One hundred percent of ourselves sometimes equals only twenty percent of the share— as we are conscious of our own self-centered needs—we can choose to trust that our eighty percent is around the corner. That's reciprocity.

"Living from the inside-out means living your own truth, being honest with yourself, and finding a way to speak your truth with your partner without blaming or criticizing."

— Jane Greer, PhD

Living Inside-Out Lessons from Chapter 15

- It can be easier to accept and live your partner's reality of you than to live your own truth.

- Most people live in complete denial of the pain they experience from not living their truth, not loving themselves, and thus not being able to give and receive the love they so desperately crave.

- Whatever, wherever, or whomever your emotional pain came from, it means that you bought into someone else's reality about you.

- You can spend years looking outside yourself for someone to confirm that you're enough, you're perfect as you are, and you're loveable. But your story won't change until you look within and change your beliefs about yourself.

- When you begin to unconditionally love yourself, it becomes almost effortless to unconditionally love your partner.

- Rather than express your needs through blame and anger, find the clarity to say, "Here's what would be great for me."

- Make requests, not demands, so your partner feels he or she is making a choice to please you, rather than being controlled by you and having no choice.

16

Ancient Wisdom for Modern Living

"In Chinese medicine, we work with the concept of balance in that
we understand if one is too productive, one becomes destructive.
If one is too ready, one loses the capacity to respond."

— Felice Dunas, PhD

For many years, my idea of balance was that of a circus performer with twenty plates spinning in the air on thin little poles. Making sure all the plates continued to spin, I thought I was being productive—but it was exhausting.

Wait, who am I kidding. It was *impossible!*

I lived holding my breath, stressed out, neck in knots, and mostly oblivious to my world and the people in it, unable to enjoy what was happening around me.

Just as I thought I'd achieved balance, a distraction such as a financial or major issue with one of the plates I was spinning would make me lose my focus, and all my plates would crash to the ground. I'd be left feeling frustrated, wiped out, and bewildered in the rubble, knowing I had to pick up the pieces to start again.

As I changed my focus to living from the inside-out, I began studying ancient principles that helped me understand the concept of *true balance*. Not balance in the form of spinning plates or even getting to an imagined place of balance, but balance from the perspective of opposing forces in our

209

lives that create cycles, like the seasons. The ancient Chinese named these opposing forces *yin* and *yang*.

Yin represents qualities such as receptivity, femaleness, cold, and dark. Yang qualities include creativity, maleness, heat, and light. According to ancient wisdom, all things have both a yin and yang side, just as a coin has a head and a tails side. The creation of yin from yang, and yang from yin occurs with a consistent synergistic force in our daily life. One derives from the other.

How can these ancient principles help us shift from being overwhelmed, overworked, and overcommitted?

To help us better understand these concepts, I turned to Felice Dunas, PhD. She teaches ancient principles that evoke success and explains how principles such as balance, focus, and unity apply to organizations, communities, and families.

Dr. Dunas is the best-selling author of *Passion Play,* now published in five languages. Her work has appeared in many periodicals including *Ladies Home Journal, Brides, Cosmopolitan, Men's Health, Glamour, Prevention, Marie Clair, Women's World, Living Fit, New Age Journal, Los Angeles Times,* and the *Chicago Tribune.* Felice is in demand worldwide as an educator for business executives, the Young Presidents' Organization, and other CEO educational organizations. She addresses such issues as leadership, health, relationships, and life balance.

Our Culture's Concept of Balance

I asked Felice how she thinks the culture of the Western world understands balance. She explains, "The essential forces in life—physical, metaphysical, scientific, spiritual, and intellectual—have as their base the principles of balance.

"We work a great deal during the week and need rest on the weekend so we can continue to work hard the following week to accomplish our goals. Overall, our culture minimizes the concept of balance and doesn't recognize it as being vital. Often, we have to fall apart to understand that we need to regroup. That's when we understand that balance is helpful."

As we work hard to meet the needs of our office, home, kids, spouses, families, and friends, we call it multitasking—or juggling, or spinning plates. But often we feel out of control.

Felice says, "Most people have no idea what balance is. I wasn't raised with the concept or the awareness of balance. I was unaware of a need to recuperate and regenerate. I didn't understand that, when I was tired and wanted to take a nap, this was a *good* thing to do!

"In my early twenties, no one explained to me, nor did I realize, that I could destroy my health by pushing myself too much. Or that having a baby and being a single mother would compound the challenges of earning a living and going to graduate school. It's almost a joke that in grad school whenever I felt like lying down, I took that to mean I should get up and *do* something.

"That ignorance of my need for balance led to my illness. I had finished graduate school and was about a year into medical practice when my body said, 'Okay, you can collapse now.' And that's what I did. I got a cold and couldn't shake it. A friend in my field told me my situation could be serious. And it was. The viral infection hit my nervous system and made me extremely ill for many years. It had started off innocently enough, as many chronic illnesses do, but because I was run down, I couldn't fight it off. It took over.

"Think about our cultural vocabulary of stress. We say, *I'm so burned out, I'm toast*. That's how I felt—like burnt toast—as if life kept pushing me back down into the toaster and burning me to charcoal. But when I finally popped up out of that toaster and stayed up, I was able to touch the world in a much larger way with a more important message than I would have been able to give had I not become ill. My mission since then, in my work as a seminar leader, lecturer, educator, and coach, is based on the burnt toast metaphor. No one wants to be burnt toast—and we can avoid it.

"It's not that we're willing to allow burnout to happen to us; we're raised to believe its normal. Our culture is accomplishment-oriented. Once the ball gets rolling, we simply don't know how to stop it. That kind of life is all we tend to know," she says.

The Stress Response

What happens to us—in us—when we get burned out?

"We experience the stress response: the fight or flight syndrome, the release of specific chemicals into the bloodstream, the body's inflammatory response, and the rise of body temperature. Now we're talking about feeling fried," Felice says. "When the fight or flight syndrome kicks in, our bodies become braced and ready, like racehorses at the gate waiting for the bell.

"The endocrine system sends messages through different hormones to prepare for an event—whether it's the alarm clock going off early in the morning, an argument with our spouse, or 'fighting' traffic to get to work. The body expends a lot of energy and effort to maintain that state of readiness.

"From the Chinese medical perspective, the 'fires' of the body must be lit and burning brightly, meaning we hold 'flames' inside, hence the word *in-flam(e)-ation*. The flames run the engine, burn the fuel, and maintain an elevated level of performance.

"If we aren't aware of the concept of balance, we won't recognize that our systems need a cooling-off period. The body has the ability to ignite that fiery force but, to be healthy, it must also have the capacity to douse those flames, alleviate the chemical process that generates readiness, and gain reprieve from that intensity.

"In Chinese medicine, it's understood that if we're too productive, we become self-destructive and if we're too much on alert, we lose the capacity to respond. We become out of balance."

Out of Balance = Disorder of Body & Mind & Emotions

When we're out of balance, Felice explains, it affects both the outer and the inner—both our bodies and our minds.

Imbalance can result in two primary disorders. "One is termed *metabolic disorder*, which results when our metabolism, or the body's ability to digest and use incoming material, fails to function properly. Digestion breaks down what we *in*gest, so, for example, we go from having a piece of steak on a fork to having useable amino acids, fat, and minerals that the body can use. After digestion, the nutrients are absorbed into the bloodstream from the stomach and intestines, and they're metabolized or used by the body to maintain health," Felice explains.

"This same kind of process can be applied to our emotions. How well do we take the emotions that are coming at us from other people and break them down so we can use them? When we're stressed out, our adrenal glands are running in hyper-drive, and we're 'full of flames.' If someone gives us emotional nourishment, we often can't digest it.

"For example, we don't hear the true meaning of the words when someone says something nice to us. Our spouse might lovingly say, 'I wish you'd slow down and rest.' Being unable to digest the loving nature of the comment, we hear it as a complaint about how we're behaving. Our emotional digestive process is limited by stress. We can't digest the steak, and we can't digest the love. From the Chinese medical point of view, mental, emotional, and nutritional information all go through the same digestive process."

The other disorder is *chronic stress response*. "In some warped way," notes Felice, "stress is tied to our *relationship* to our achievements, not the achievements themselves. *We value 'doingness' far more than 'beingness.'* But when we *overdo*, the stress monster kicks in, affecting our system as a whole. Unless the chemicals involved are stopped, they will cause the body to recreate the experience of stress *even when the stress is gone.*

"We're constantly adapting to stress. And even if the cause of our stress is relieved, the subconscious components of our brain don't necessarily respond. Our digestion remains weak and we don't get the nutrients we need, so we become undernourished and fatigued.

"When we become fatigued, we rely on the extra cortisol secreted by the adrenal cortex (prompted by stress) to raise our blood sugar levels and give us a sense of energy. We turn to coffee and other caffeinated drinks. Through lifestyle choices, we over-stimulate the system to raise blood sugar levels enough to compensate for the lack of absorbed nutrients. Thus the body remains in a self-induced stress response," Felice explains.

Taming the Stress Monster

So how do we stop this self-destructive cycle and tame the stress monster? Felice says, "*Getting more sleep* is critical to counteracting a constant stress response," adding, "If we understood that stress can take years off our lives, we'd make a point of getting a good night's rest."

Another excellent way to counteract stress is to *get out of our environment* where we live with at least low-grade stress all the time. "Although we may not consider vacations to be particularly important, they're *vital* because they help our bodies recognize what it's like to feel relaxed and normal.

"We should also take time to *intensely de-stress*. For example, once every month or two, we might schedule a day to get pampered at a spa. Or on de-stress days, we can turn off the phones, make love with our sweetheart all morning, order takeout food, watch a funny movie, and just hang loose."

But what if the stressor involves an intimate relationship with a spouse or child or parent? "Then," Felice urges, "we have to be highly intentional about creating time in which we counteract the stress we experience with this person. It may mean going for a run, taking a Pilates or yoga class, or even screaming in the car. The greater the counteraction, the better."

These emotion releasing techniques allow us to decompress and move into empowering conversations as we discussed in the last chapter.

It also confirms what Doug Bench asserted in chapter 7 about changing neuronal pathways, Felice emphasizes that "our counteractions *need to be repetitive*. We need to find simple things to do daily that counteract the chemistry of stress in our bodies. Calming, grounding, restorative things. That way, we teach our internal system—our brain and body—to stop reacting and start relaxing from the inside-out, as if that threat or irritation were no longer there."

A need for balance relates to the fact that our bodies remain on hyper alert and our minds maintain a negative emotional state. We need to take definite action to calm them down. We won't come out of this by accident, and we can't expect a miracle. We need to do something either internally—such as changing our self-talk—or externally by shaping our circumstances differently.

Creating Our Own Balance

I'm no exception!

What I enjoyed most was tropical weather and the water, and yet, I didn't live near either. After living 30 years in Missouri—12 of those in Kansas City, and then five in Washington, D.C., I wanted to make a drastic change. It was something inside of me urging me to take the leap, urging me to change my environment. So, in October of 2004, even though I was still living pay check to pay check, I decided to move to Miami.

What an amazing experience; everyday I wake-up thinking I'm in one of the most wonderful places on earth—even in the hot summers. I can go for walks on the beach or sit in the back yard to watch the spectacular cobalt blue sky. I'm grateful I made the move as Miami is an environment that provides me balance and feeds my soul.

However, I've learned *creating balance is a continuous process*.

When our real estate business took off, my workload intensified, and the time to focus on this book and my writing dwindled down to bare bones. Luckily, one day we were at an auction and found an amazing home at a ridiculously low price, two hours from Miami on Lake Okeechobee. Now, a few weekends a month I'm back in a small town environment like I grew up in, with complete solitude.

The drive itself is peaceful as we pass sugar cane fields, orange groves, cattle farms, and some spectacular view of the lake. However, the moment I walk into the house, my entire attitude shifts and I have a sense of calm. The yard has over 40 palm trees, wonderful breeze from the lake, and incredible wildlife all around. It's a weekend of writing, relaxing, watching movies ... a great sense of tranquility.

Of course everyone doesn't have a yearning to move to another city or buy a weekend place.

Rather, we need to be intentional about changing our environment, whether that means limiting our time in toxic situations, going for walks or the gym, seeing a movie, creating a sanctuary in a room or garden, scheduling a weekend trip, or all of these. Natural law requires that we engage in the process. It helps to understand the Yin Yang Theory.

Balance and the Yin Yang Theory

How does Yin Yang correlate with balance?

According to Felice, *Yin, the receptive principle, means to receive. Yang, the creative principle, means to contribute, or give.* The Yin Yang Theory forms the foundation of the most basic principle in nature—balance—formulated more than five thousand years ago. Thus, according to the ancient Chinese, this theory is the foundation of everything in existence.

Balance refers to the harmonious flow or rhythm of life. It isn't a static, attainable goal to achieve, and it can't be put on autopilot. Rather, it's a way of living that maintains equilibrium between the yin and yang aspects of our lives—between what we receive and what we give out to others and the world.

Felice suggests doing this simple exercise: "Divide a sheet of paper in half. Then look at your week. On one side of the paper, list every activity you did that contributed to others. On the other side, list everything you did that was about receiving something for yourself."

Mind expanding—and revealing.

Most of us find we have a *much* longer list on the giving side. It might include activities such as driving the kids to school, making meals, doing the project at work the way the boss wants it, and so on. In contrast, on the receiving side, the list usually has a minimal number of activities, such as taking a bubble bath, going for a run, sitting quietly sipping tea, and reading a book.

"The longer list normally reflects *yang* energy going outward from self. We usually short-change our *yin* lists of activities that involve going inward to self. To change this unfortunate state, we must be willing to spend more time with ourselves and do more things with and for ourselves.

"We must evaluate what we're doing and support ourselves in embracing changes. If we don't do that, we'll perpetuate the imbalance we're struggling with. This imbalance *forces our brains to focus on the external*, attempting to 'save' us from perceived threats. We end up feeling numb and unable to properly digest our food—or our emotions," Felice explains.

I can see how the Yin Yang Theory affects every component of our lives. Take money, for example. Yin and yang exist in our checkbooks and in our bank accounts. Saving is yin; spending is yang. And spending beyond our means throws balance out the window because it reflects excessive contribution on the yang side.

Regarding our work-home balance, Felice says, "If you give too much at the office, you don't have enough to give at home. Some men commonly take a half-hour to themselves after they come home and sit quietly with their feet up to recharge (yin) before they go and interact with their families (yang). Women generally override that healthy urge and set about making dinner or tending to the children.

"But if I'm stressed all the time," says Felice, "I don't receive love well. My body doesn't receive nutrients efficiently so I become undernourished. I don't feel happy in my life and I act like a bitch. That's the stress response."

Restoring Energy Within Ourselves

So how do we find, restore, and preserve balance within ourselves in terms of energy? "The simplest way is *to start with structure*," Felice recommends. That means structuring into our day three activities for ourselves to ensure that the stress response *won't* be the only game we are participating in. For example, plan a peaceful activity for twenty or thirty minutes at the beginning and end of each day.

This could be reading while the kids are playing, turning off (or at least on vibrate) the phone and e-mails so you only respond to them two or three specific times during the day, and/or going to the gym or taking a walk after work. I even enjoy movie nights when I go to the theater by myself, or with someone, and take my favorite Chinese foods in with me.

One exercise Felice recommends consists of taking three to seven minutes as many times as necessary during the day and allowing yourself to *feel utterly and completely exhausted*. Close your eyes. Focus on how you feel. Completely cave inward and become aware of self. Do this *at least* once, and she strongly suggest three times—at your desk, in the bathroom, or in your car. Your exhaustion becomes evident when you are still and focus within. Give yourself enough time for that awareness to surface. Actually allowing yourself to feel the exhaustion inadvertently directs your attention to where it is needed the most.

A very powerful practice … Give it a try for yourself; it's truly insightful.

At times, we require support and assistance from others, as Felice explains, "We can't always achieve balance by ourselves because we've been thrown off for so long. We might need to call a friend for advice and support, or even call for marriage counseling or psychotherapy. We can lose ourselves. And when we do, we don't have to go it alone.

"After all, balance involves the interplay between people. It's not only about your own energy but about how much energy you allow to come to you from others. The majority of people live in a giving mode about seven-eighths of the time. Sometimes someone else has to intervene and contribute. That person's action can bring you out of stagnation or imbalance."

Felice offers three major suggestions for achieving a healthy mind and body while maintaining a balance of yin and yang in our lives.

THREE COMPONENTS FOR ACHIEVING AND MAINTAINING BALANCE

1. **Go to bed early.** *One hour of sleep before midnight is equivalent to sleeping three hours after midnight.* Yin Yang Theory suggests that polarities must be continually adjusted to achieve balance. The sun rises from midnight to noon. Once the sun reaches the apex of the sky at noon, it begins to drop and continues dropping until midnight. Patients were once urged to sleep while the sun was going down because the body benefits from the quiet of the yin or darkening/quieting half of the 24-hour cycle.

   For example, you could record your favorite late night TV shows and watch them in the morning (or on the weekend) when you're bright-eyed, rather than at night when you're blurry-eyed. The sleep cycle of early to bed, early to rise may be a helpful rhythm for you.

2. **Take regular breaks from your life.** Even if your home feels like a sanctuary and has a gentle energy, it can be a reminder of life's stresses. No matter what your obligations are and to whom, you're wise to consistently remove yourself from your home environment. Feeling relief from stress reveals more of who you are without those burdens. As you discover what that feels like, it helps you define your no-stress baseline. You may be surprised at the contrast. Consistency is more important than the amount of time you take or how far away you go. Will you give yourself one night a month to sleep away from home? Can you take one evening a week? Four days each quarter? Look at your calendar and mark the dates you plan to be unavailable to the world. Create islands in time upon which you can rest your soul.

3. **Write yang and yin lists.** Your yang list includes everything you did on an "average" day that provided service for or contributed to others. The yin list includes all your activities on that day that you did for yourself, your peace, and your happiness. Then compare your lists. How much of your day is dedicated to serving others? How much is dedicated to serving yourself and your own needs? Does your lists reflect the way you want to be living? Are you walking your talk? Is it time to make some adjustments in both activities and time management? Devoting too much time to others' needs and not enough to your own (or vice versa) creates stress that you can avoid with minor scheduling changes.

A Way of Living

Remember that balance isn't a finite goal, but a way of living everyday using the Yin Yang Theory to focus your intention—and attention. It's the process of flow that avoids stagnation or neglect of any aspects of ourselves. It involves maintaining equilibrium between giving and receiving within our relationships, our roles, our duties, and ourselves.

What I learned from the ancient principals is that, as we look at our responsibilities in life—our partner, children, career, physical and spiritual health, finances, and community—it is critical to *give ourselves permission* that we don't have to be perfect in every area. Perfection is a culturally imposed super hero myth.

The first step is to gain clarity as to what is important to you. These responsibilities then become your primary areas to give your focus intention, and then you become much more realistic how much time you have left to give the other responsibilities in your life.

To help I've designed the *Living Inside-Out Workbook* and *Clarity & Focus Journal* as tools to assist in evaluating your life from an inside-out perspective with a foundation of creating balance. (For details visit www. EddieMiller.com)

I've begun to *visually* understand the idea of yin and yang. When I feel like my life is out of balance, my health feels compromised, I feel anxious, begin to self-soothe in ways that lead to more imbalance, I can "see" how the yin is shrinking in me and I can consciously raise awareness of how I must restore the energy I invest in taking care of myself. That's the true balance we can maintain by being aware of the cycles in our lives—the ins and outs and ups and downs—adjusting when needed and enjoying the process.

"When people live from the inside-out, they have the courage to recognize their need for balance and to construct their lives with that in mind. There is wisdom and authenticity leading their actions. Self care is recognized as imperative for positively impacting the world."

— Felice Dunas, PhD

Living Inside-Out Lessons from Chapter 16

- Yin and yang is the foundation of everything in life.

- Yin is the receptive, receiving. Yang is the creative, contributing.

- Balance is a flow or a rhythm to life. It's a way of living that maintains an equilibrium between the yin and yang aspects of our lives, and equilibrium between what we receive and what we give out to others and to the world.

- Balance isn't just how you live your life within yourself. Balance is also how much energy you allow to come to you from others.

- By doing calming things, grounding things, restorative things, can teach our system, our brain and our body to stop reacting as if there were a threat and to start relaxing from the inside-out.

17
LIVING FROM THE INSIDE-OUT

The Spirit Within

"Living with authenticity means that who you appear to be to others is who you really are. Your beliefs, your values, your commitments, your inner realities are all reflected in how you live your life on the outside."

— Barbara De Angelis, PhD

By this point, I hope you're becoming more aware of how your core beliefs drive your behavior and have created the life you currently experience. Now you have powerful tools to delve more deeply within yourself, ask more potent questions, shift your awareness, and consciously decide how you want to show up in life.

In the beginning of the book, I introduced the Inside-Out Philosophy™ and its premise that, as human beings, we have the *innate wisdom and capacity* to transform and create the life of our dreams.

Through these chapters, we've probed our beliefs and stories, our perceptions and habits, and examined areas that may be out of balance with what we desire.

Now, how do we access the innate wisdom we all possess?

How do we *know* that we know, and then *trust* that we know despite what others say or our own negative, self-limiting voices? How do we know we aren't fooling ourselves or that our minds aren't continuing to travel down pathways that no longer serve us? How do we find our essence, our spirit within?

We are Fully Spirit

To navigate the vastness of the idea that we are fully spirit, I called on Barbara De Angelis, PhD. Her messages of how to live authentically, shine in adversity, and be ripe for an awakening spoke to me and aligned with my Inside-Out Philosophy™.

One of the most influential teachers in the field of relationships and personal growth in the past twenty-five years, Dr. De Angelis has reached tens of millions of people worldwide with her positive messages. She is the author of 14 top-selling books, which have sold more than eight million copies and have been published in twenty languages.

One of Barbara's recent books, *How Did I Get Here? Finding Your Way to Renewed Hope and Happiness When Life and Love Take Unexpected Turns,* gives practical insights on how crises, great or small, become our greatest learning tools to better ourselves.

In discussing the spirit within, Barbara says, "To define spirit is actually redundant because the truth is this: *Everything* is spirit. All of what is, what we see, what we experience, and who we are, is a manifestation of the invisible thread of consciousness that runs through everything.

"A lot of times, people talk about spirit as if it's a topic, a thing, a place, something to contact. But the truth is for those who study spiritual texts and go deep into a spiritual practice, *everything* is the manifestation of spirit, the essence and definition of everything, the true Source. Although it's perhaps invisible in terms of how we define, touch, and feel things, it's the core reality of everything."

The Quest from Fear to Faith

I began to search for understanding of my own spiritual truth when I was in my late teens and early twenties. In contrast, as a kid, I remember sitting in a little one-room country church that sat on a hill, where month after month I would listen to stories about this big scary guy in the sky. The ultimate Authority Figure who I would consistently disappoint if I didn't follow the rules and watch my every step—but worse, a Force that would punish me.

It was hard for me, as a small child, to trust fully in a God who I thought could hurt me. I would later understand my relationship with the Divine in an entirely different light, but as a young person, I had some very conflicted feelings and beliefs about faith.

Part of it was that I was taught that I had to ask God to come into my heart, to pray for God to help me, to ask God to watch over me—all of which created this disembodied perception that God was something *outside* of me.

When I went to college, I began my own discovery process. As I set out to study theology and spiritual teaching, I lifted the veil for myself. I realized that God is the *constant presence in my fluctuating life*—that even if *I* didn't see the value in who I was, this greater presence did. I came to discover why God is referred to as a *Higher Power* and *Source*.

When I became consciously aware of this presence and source of unconditional love, it was a turning point in my life. It changed my whole stance on how I perceived myself in the world, with others, and what I thought was important.

The day my life dramatically shifted was the Sunday before Thanksgiving, in 1994; I was 26 and living in Kansas City. Prior to this I had been searching for answers, but hadn't discovered a clear path to take. By this time I was practicing self-acceptance, my dad and I were in the process of rebuilding our relationship, and trying, everyday, to live authentically in my own skin.

I had heard about a minister by the name of Mary Omwake, so I decided to check out the church for myself. I remember that day so clearly. The church was packed, the sun was illuminating the windows, and as I was listening to the music and Mary's message, I was suddenly embraced with a sense of peace and affirmation for what I was experiencing within myself. I knew that, *for me,* I had found what I was looking for ... a clarifying message that God lived and breathed within me, the true essence of *spirit within*.

When I understood 'spirit within,' I no longer had to *ask* God to come into my heart, pray for God to *help* me, or ask God to *watch over* me — because I now knew that God, Source, Higher Power, is *always present, always within.*

I shifted from my head to my heart, from thinking to feeling. I shifted from fear to faith. That meant having faith that everything didn't actually fall squarely on *my* small shoulders, and that living out the ultimate vision of what I was supposed to be doing here on planet earth was actually being co-created with the Divine.

Another critical break through was I realized that I'm a *spiritual being having a human experience.* And this revelation has become the foundation of what it means to live from the inside-out.

This is what Paul Scheele is referring to when he talks about abundance being our "natural" state. If everything is spirit, if everything is Source, then how can we 'not' have access to wisdom, to knowing, to truth? We have all those things and so much more because, spirit and Source are infinite!

As I've mentioned, my purpose in this book is to neither justify nor negate anyone's spiritual or religious beliefs or practices, but rather to offer my insights on how and why we have infinite innate wisdom and capacity.

We all have lungs. We may or may not know how our lungs work to convert oxygen into carbon dioxide, which allows us to think, move our muscles, and makes our food digest, but if we want to know the facts, we can glean them from any medical text.

But, what or who initiates that first breathe within us, that desire to breathe in the first place? Who or what decides when our breath leaves our bodies and which allows us to finally let go of this world and physical reality?

For me, that *who* or *what* is the same *divine intelligence* that created the sun to rise each morning and the flowers to bloom exactly on schedule. For me, that divine intelligence is called God, and, for me, God is closer than my next breath, not something *out there* to only call on for help when needed, or to fear, but the entity that lives and breathes within me — in all of us.

So no matter how tough things get in life, I always know I am loved, supported, and guided to the best of my ability to *receive* that love, support, and guidance.

How do I know this?

Listening to Our Innate Wisdom

I listen.

I can only listen well when I can silence the *other* voices, the ones inside my head warning, chattering, filling my mind with worries and what-ifs, the voices from my past, the ones from the critics or people who held themselves back with their own fears and tried to convince me of the same. I cannot hear anything beyond that noise when I only focus on the noise.

But when I manage to quiet my mind and enter the gap—the space between my thoughts, I can hear something else.

I can hear … my own wisdom. It isn't an ego thing. It's an infinite intelligence thing. When I feel connected to my own wisdom, it's really that I feel truly human and able to cope with and endure through the many challenges of life. I feel like I have the whole Universe on my side. And vice versa. That, to me, is how I share my spirit. And that's where resilience lives.

Our human resilience comes from our spirit. So does our courage. Our character. Our determination. Our purpose and passion.

As Barbara offers, "The truth is there is nothing closer to us than that voice. People expect that *inner voice* to be just that—a voice in their head sounding like Jesus or Gandhi or a saint. And that's not the way it is. Truth speaks in whispers, and wisdom rarely reveals itself with a bang over the head. Wisdom is in knowing. It's something much subtler than the way we normally perceive things.

"People *do* have an inner voice of truth speaking to them, but they often don't hear it because it's not as loud as the voice of desire, the voice of the ego, and certainly the voice of fear. But it's there."

In effect, we've been learning to identify the voices Barbara refers to—those of desire, ego, and fear—throughout this book.

Underneath any negative limiting self-talk, Barbara says there are moments when "we are ripe for an awakening." That ripeness occurs "when we're uncomfortable enough that we question things in an attempt to relieve ourselves from our misery. We *will question* because we can't *not* question anymore."

The awakening occurs when we hear our innate inner voice whispering one word—*NOW!* It's the voice Barbara calls "the voice of the assignment you were given because you are needed."

So, I suppose the question becomes ... how do we honor this voice and allow others to see our gifts?

The Process of Divine Discomfort

In her teachings, Barbara addresses the role of crisis in our lives, saying, "The whole purpose of life is the journey toward *remembrance and wholeness.*"

Remembrance and wholeness is reference to the true essence of our being, we are a creation of the Divine, whole and complete. Remember if everything is spirit, if everything is Source, then how can't we have access to wisdom, to knowing, to truth? Spirit and Source are infinite ... infinite intelligence, infinite abundance, infinite supply, infinite creativity, infinite power, infinite potential.

Barbara shares, "Even though things, at times, seem difficult, at the core, we are challenged to retrieve what's important, remember something, move into a different way of being."

What's the result? A perceived crisis becomes a great learning opportunity. Barbara calls this process of turning crisis into learning "divine discomfort."

I know it can be a hard concept to wrap one's head around in the midst of a crisis, but divine discomfort is an important process to understand. I think of times when I felt lost, inadequate, and frustrated that things weren't happening fast enough or regret that I didn't make better choices. It's been hard to tolerate my own discomfort.

But, as you might have heard or read elsewhere, the Chinese symbol for crisis means "opportunity." Pain and conflict are powerful teachers. From them, I've learned to look for the opportunity in my struggles. And even if it took time and produced anguish, I always found it—in every instance.

"Either the Universe is benevolent and everything makes sense, or it doesn't," says Barbara. "If you look at nature, everything has a purpose. Everything. Even the tiniest, tiniest thing. Everything is so intricately designed with creative intelligence. There is nothing haphazard in our Universe. Nothing."

A protist, for example, is one of the smallest living things, each made of a single microscopic cell. An average protist is twenty times smaller than the dot on this *i*. And yet, there's nothing insignificant or random about it. Certain varieties of the protist are vital to the ecosystem—particularly in the ocean, while others are responsible for a range of serious human diseases.

Taking it one step further, what would it mean if we knew that we, as human beings, were not created in a haphazard way? That means whatever happens to us—even the things we can't understand at first—are not haphazard. The same intelligence that designs the beautiful miracle of a flower growing from a seed is operating in the creation of who we are. It's present in everyday of our lives ... whether we perceive it or not.

"The crises we go through contain tremendous intelligence and alignment with the highest," says Barbara. "That's why we're here—to learn, to grow, and to remember who we are. If we look for the goal—the purpose—then we will turn these crises into not just opportunities but *liberation*."

A crisis is not always about difficulties or deficits.

Barbara describes the kind of crisis we can find ourselves in *when we actually achieve our goals*. "We begin to panic, thinking, maybe this isn't our dream house, maybe it needs to be bigger or we need better relationships or more money," she says. "So we run after the next accomplishment or acquisition, assuming it will resolve our current issue. The crisis arrives when we get what we thought would make us happy and discover that 'something' still feels like it's 'nothing.' What a fantastic moment this can be on a soul's journey.

Barbara reminds us that we don't need our lives to be perfect or even look perfect. "Everything is within you, so you find a way to trigger it yourself. That's real power, that's real mastery, that's real freedom."

"It's in this moment of awareness that we can go, 'Wait a minute. Let me turn within. It's not what's on the outside that will fulfill me deeply; it's more a knowing or remembering' who I am on the inside."

Turning Within to Fill the Emptiness

It comes down to a willingness to try another way to fill the *emptiness,* the feeling that something's missing or disconnected.

But how do we do more than fill that emptiness. How do we experience the fullness of living?

For some, looking inward can be scary, as Barbara notes, "We are afraid of the unknown … and there is nothing more unknown than going within. We tend to focus on our senses. We like to touch things, see things, hear things. When we begin to turn within, it's uncharted territory. Where's the GPS for the inner path? Where's the road sign to indicate you're 'here'? We like to define and control, yet there's nothing more undefined and uncontrollable than the reality within.

"Here's the irony. Operating from within *is* the place from which you can control everything. *Real change always and only occurs from deep within.* When I begin to operate from that level (within), miraculous things happen on the outside that cannot be explained."

Consider these five keys to enhance the process of going within:

FIVE SPIRITUAL KEYS TO REMEMBER

1. **Spirit.** Everything is spirit. All of what is—what you see, what you experience, who you are—is a manifestation of the invisible thread of consciousness that runs through everything.

2. **Inner Voice.** There is nothing closer to you than your own inner voice. However, it's important to understand that your truth speaks in whispers and your wisdom rarely reveals itself with a bang over the head.

3. **Crises.** The crises you go through contain tremendous intelligence and align with your highest good, which is to learn, to grow, and to remember who you are. If you look at crises this way, you can shift your thought process and look for your purpose, identify your goal, and turn a crisis not only into an opportunity but into *liberation.*

4. **Remembering.** What you're looking for isn't found in what you accomplished on the outside; it's more of a knowing or remembering. Remembering that you come from the Divine and therefore you are whole and complete. When you have feelings of emptiness or disconnect by going within you can access the cause. And by remembering that you come from Source and therefore you are whole and complete, you tap into your inner wisdom to discover unconditional love and endless possibilities.

5. **Consciousness-Awareness.** The only way change happens is by being awake and aware—and paying attention. That's when you naturally and spontaneously make adjustments toward having more hope and more freedom. The more conscious you become, the more you see, the more you will move in a positive direction. You understand that your inner work needs to be a daily part of your life—a commitment.

Overcoming Resistance

Over the years, I've noticed my own resistance to being still and quiet, and listening to my inner wisdom. I've wrestled with restlessness. Other times, I've avoided 'going within' because I feared what I might uncover. I've also resisted the quieting process for fear of making the changes that would have to occur as a result of what I found.

Where do we find the confidence to look inside and follow our inner voice? Yet, where *else* do we find our true power? Our vision? Our essence? Our passion for living?

It's all within. Once we learn to tune in to our inner voice, the other distracting voices will no longer diffuse our energies and block access to our wisdom.

Going within actually becomes comforting and enjoyable.

One of my favorite lyrics is from Tim McGraw's song *Still*: "When the world gets crazy and tries to break me and I've had all I can stand. I can close my eyes no matter where I am and *just be still*."

I can just be still.

Daily Practice

Here is how I start my day ...

I'm a big fan of the *Life is Good*® brand—you know hats, tee-shirts, etc. I've developed a practice of starting everyday with gratitude. I typically wakeup and grab my *Life is Good* hat to go to the gym or just wear it around the house. I even have one in the back window ledge of my car as a backup.

It may sound corny but I always start everyday with a thankful heart, for the day, my partner, my work, my life. Rain or shine, I almost always say "what a beautiful day." It's not a pie-in-the-sky attitude but rather a really simple pleasure for me. That kind of gratitude just seems to ground me and prepare me to receive whatever the day has in store.

That's another layer of 'knowing and remembering.' When I see the day as a gift, it's a kind of remembering my wholeness as a human being who has been given this gift of living and I pause, even for a moment, to take inventory of that. It puts everything in perspective.

Barbara explains what happens to us, as a society and individually, when we don't allow ourselves to notice the moment as were are focused on the speed to get things done and the outcome.

"In our society of instant gratification, people like instant enlightenment. 'I did this once, I did that one, I saw that, I got it, I read that, I had a session and I got cleared.' It doesn't happen in that way. The habit of pulling yourself out of the moment is the cause for our greatest suffering.

"You get it, you lose it, you get it, you lose it. You remember it, you forget it, you remember it, you forget it. Until you forget less, remember more, understand it more, then over time, your remembering and your knowing becomes much greater than your forgetting.

"That is the path to enlightenment. Once you are awake, you will never fully go back to sleep. It's impossible to pretend you don't know something that you know—it's just impossible," Barbara states.

It's essential to remember that going within takes practice—day-by-day, situation-by-situation, and moment-by-moment. It requires being present, being aware of what we're doing and why we're doing it. It also requires being still long enough to hear those guided whispers. A good friend once said, "Presence can't be put on autopilot."

Barbara explains, "Some people have this odd idea like 'I took a seminar once' or 'I read a book once' and 'I had this fantastic awakening and I really grew after that.' I look at them and ask, 'What did you do *last week*?' To me, there has to be a commitment to understand that this inner work—living your life from the inside-out—means not just visiting it but *living* it. It means adding an element of the inner connection to everything you do.

"It's as much a part of your life as bathing, eating, and sleeping. Being conscious, visiting that place inside of you, meditating regularly, praying—the technique doesn't matter. What matters is being aware that going within is a repetitive process."

You can begin by choosing how you want to experience your life, and you can choose to make everyday a time you experience love, wisdom, and making a difference. Barbara advocates making each day a time that you can SHINE.

S — Share your unique gifts.

H — Harness your passion.

I — Identify your authentic voice.

N — Never imitate; know and be yourself.

E — Enlighten others with your energy.

As I contemplate Barbara's challenge, I'm immediately reminded of the day my good friend and expert in chapter 4, Lu Hanessian, called and said, "I just heard this and had to call you ... What if the first person you meet in heaven isn't God. *What if it is the person you were meant to be?*"

I think my heart actually skipped a beat.

And it really made me think.

We are all called to share the amazing gifts that we have been given—to SHINE everyday. To celebrate life fully. When we embrace that we are spiritual beings living a human experience, it is easier to grasp that the crazy *outside* stuff we deal with can all be resolved by *going within*. We move into possibilities and being who we are meant to be.

So, who are you meant to be?

"When I begin to operate from that level (within), miraculous things happen on the outside than cannot be explained. Going inside shifts everything

— Barbara De Angelis, PhD

Living Inside-Out Lessons from Chapter 17

- You are 100% spirit.

- Spirit and Source are synonymous with God.

- Your wisdom rarely reveals itself with a bang over the head. It's in knowing.

- People do have an inner voice of truth speaking to them, but they don't hear it because it's not as loud as the voice of desire, the voice of the ego, and certainly the voice of fear.

- The whole purpose of life is the journey toward remembrance and wholeness.

- You can turn your crises not just into learning opportunities but into liberation.

- Practice, practice, practice; presence can't be put on autopilot.

- The habit of pulling yourself out of the moment is the cause for your greatest suffering.

- Once you are awake, you will never fully go back to sleep.

- Everything is within you, so you find a way to trigger it yourself. That's real power, that's real mastery, that's real freedom.

18

Move to Action

"It is never too late to be who you might have been ... starting now!"

— Eddie

With any philosophy or plan you might embrace, all the theory, examples, and pointers don't mean anything until you apply what you've learned. Sometimes, though, it also requires allowing your soul, your core self, to evolve and synthesize from the inside-out. This could happen in seconds, days, and even years. This evolution is the Soul's Journey.

The Soul's Journey

In the five years that have passed since I first got the idea to write this book—and especially during the last three years of focusing on the content, interviewing, and crafting these chapters—my life has changed dramatically.

At times, the words of wisdom shared by these remarkable experts have been a breath of fresh air. They were exactly what I needed to create a shift or gain an awareness that provided the critical next piece in my own journey.

Some of the nuggets of wisdom allowed me to make giant leaps forward, while others helped me to take the baby steps I needed along the way.

Yet, some words of wisdom left me frustrated as I would say to myself, "Well, I've tried that before and it didn't work." As I dug deeper, I began to uncover the same points of tension that I struggled with most of my life. No matter what I tried the underlying challenges continued to surface. Some of these points of tension even revealed the secrets I was guarding deeply within. I realized that first I had to *face my fears in order to gain a deeper understanding of the importance of this journey.*

And there lies the breakthrough for all of us.

We've learned from the various experts that behind the adversity, the struggle is an undeniable power and inner strength at our core. Yet it's only by leaning into our own challenges and facing our own fears that we access our true power.

Originally, I thought it would take a year to finish this book, but it took several more. Although I have been working to improve my writing skills for years, the stories of the kid with dyslexia, who to this day still doesn't read really well out loud, and my other limiting beliefs were playing full blast in my subconscious mind.

It was the process of my own soul's journey.

Elements of the Journey

In the last chapter, Barbara De Angelis shared another critical component of what is meant by living inside-out, and the essence of what is meant by the soul's journey, *the importance of remembering who we are.*

We've learned from this book that our lives are a tapestry of our thoughts and actions of the past and the stories that we've created, and how these stories often keep us from realizing our true potential, hold us back from our 'ultimate' lives of good health, thriving relationships, and worry-free prosperity, and perpetuate our struggles, conflicts, ruts, and regrets.

We also, with great hope, learned that we can discover, through these mythologies and "self-impeding" beliefs, *a pathway to personal growth.*

And therein lies our freedom.

By shifting our awareness to this present moment and embracing *our unique truth,* we arrive at an amazing place—a window of opportunity— that's totally available to us at our fingertips.

So today, with the wisdom of these chapters, we can address any aspect of our lives by being open to the vast possibilities all around us and begin to make the conscious sustainable changes we desire.

Our Highest Vision on Earth

Over the years, it finally dawned on me that the biggest, highest vision for my life was something I could create in the present, not some distant future. I released myself from the burden of potential being something way-way down the road, and realized that I could fulfill my potential this morning, this week — now.

On the soul's journey — our journey — we've learned suffering is optional. That means we *can* choose to live everyday with a *heaven on earth — heaven within* consciousness.

When I chose to become accountable for my own life, things changed radically. Granted, it wasn't an overnight decision. I waved no magic wand. I simply realized I had to stay focused on the intension I desired each day in order to create a new mental pathway — a new habit that would lead to my goal. As a result the way in which I saw others, myself, and the world around me changed.

Imagine, *we each can create a heaven on earth consciousness!*

Years ago, I dreamed of living near the water in a tropical climate with palm trees; *today* I live in one of the most beautiful cities of the world, Miami. I consciously chose to live out this vision. Although I didn't know Miami would be the destination, I imagined this life of abundance and warmth, of possibility and beauty, and over time, it has unfolded by staying open to my WOO — window of opportunity.

I've been extremely fortunate to grow up with parents who are in love with each other, and, even today, they act like school kids always holding hands, being silly, and enjoying their life together. I dreamed of that for myself, too. After nearly two decades of searching, waiting, and anticipating, *today* I have a relationship that fills my life with joy, balance, abundance, and a sense of fulfillment.

I've spent years working various jobs just to make a living and doing whatever it took to keep moving in the direction of my goals; *today* I'm achieving my goals, passionate about the contribution I'm making, and earn as much in some months as I once made in a year.

For over twenty years, I lived in the story of how my dad should and shouldn't be. Regardless of how he attempted to express his unconditional love for me, I blocked it. *Today*, we have a stronger relationship than ever and recently enjoyed a seven day family vacation. We had a great time and are talking about what to do next.

I was the kid that others would make fun of in school because I tripped over words when I read out loud—and still do—and writing was a challenge for me too. *Today*, after years of focusing to improve my writing skills, the use of spell check, amazing friends to support me, and the help of a wonderful editor, I've written this book.

All this didn't happen overnight.

Not every moment was joy and bliss.

Sometimes, life appeared to be intolerable!

Yet that's the point. The soul's journey is a process of learning, growing, and remembering, it isn't always joyful and bliss, and sometimes life can appear to be intolerable.

QUESTIONS THAT MOVE YOU TO ACTION

Your soul's journey is about the constant evolution of your being—to experience your highest good. You are on earth to grow and learn; therefore, you have no idea what life has in store for you and the length of time—divine timing—it will take for your desire to appear. So I ask you to answer these questions for yourself.

How do you show up when ...

- you haven't reached your expected career goals and keep struggling to keep your business going?
- your relationships with your partner, kids, family members, co-workers, and/or others are full of conflict and misunderstanding?

- you're confronted with losing your home when the economy takes a downward turn?
- you've put your health and fitness as a last priority and you're dealing with high blood pressure or a chronic illness?

Many of us who are faced with these challenges tend to have one common reaction—we run. We run from the situation, from our circumstances, from the ones we love, and, most importantly, *we run from ourselves*.

However we have a choice, it is in these times that we've learned to turn within to tap into our inner wisdom and truth and consciously choose how we are going to *show up*—who we are going to be. How we will—or won't be—*present*. Regardless of the obstacle, we are all called to *look for the gift* and reach our highest good—our highest potential. We are called to live heaven on earth.

You and I have the same Source, Higher Power, as did the Wright Brothers, Thomas Edison, Dr. Jonas Salk, Alexander Graham Bell, Martin Luther King, Gandhi, Mother Theresa. We, like them, have *an innate wisdom and capacity to transform our lives and the world*. At our core is an immeasurable strength and power. Many of us say we can't see it. We complain of foggy minds—overwhelmed. Of scattered thinking overworked. Of multi-tasking—overcommitted—so much, we can't recall what our priorities are anymore.

So the question is how can we gain *clarity and focus*?

Clarify Your Focused Intention

We can start by thinking about the various aspects of our lives that we've covered in this book. Identify one or two that really charge you and get you excited. What resonates?

Then use the method below I created and use on a daily basis to gain clarity and focus. See what happens for you if you use it at the beginning of each day and at night as you are falling asleep. Although I prefer to spend

20 minutes or more, you can still see a shift within yourself even with just 5 to 10 minutes a day, as you build up to 20.

I use this method:

- To increase concentration in stressful situations
- Before making difficult life choices
- To resolve relationship challenges with loved ones
- To keep it together when I might feel like I'm at my breaking point
- Anytime I need to clear my mind and hone in on my focused intention

Six Steps to Clarity and Focus

Here are my *Six Steps to Clarity and Focus*. You may just discover answers to questions that have been heavy on your mind. As well as how to release limiting beliefs and negative self-talk, how to be more productive, how to know what's most important to you, and how to tune in to your intuition. All this leads to the critical next move—taking action to accomplish your goals.

Let's go through the steps...

1. **Breathe and become still.** Find a comfortable place where you won't be distracted. It could be on the couch or bed, in the backyard, at your desk, in your car. Typically, I find a comfortable chair in the back yard and start this process by becoming aware of the radiant beauty around me.

   Once you have found a place that works for you, then close your eyes and *while focusing on your heart* breathe in deeply for a count of six, hold it six counts, and exhale slowly over six counts. Do this several times until you become calm and relaxed. As you are breathing in and out, continue to bring your focus to *your heart*. Throughout these steps, move your attention from your mind "thinking" to your heart "feeling." Your intention is to go within to connect with our Source, God, Higher-Power, Mother/Father God, Divine, Universe, use the term you are most comfortable with.

2. **Go to gratitude.** Being thankful for all you have in your life is critical to this process; as being in the state of gratitude is one of the highest vibrations to most easily connect with Source. When you come from a space of gratitude you in turn will find ideas and opportunities that positively impact your life will appear at a faster pace.

Continue to focus by breathing deeply through your heart, focusing your thoughts to connect with your feelings. This may seem to be an unusual request, but I promise you it has a big payoff. Begin by recalling everything that gives you joy, satisfaction, peace, love—it could be your husband/wife/life-partner, kids, parents, friends, job, home, where you live, free time, your pet, your favorite vacation spot. Express thankfulness for all you have received as you continue to breath in and out through you heart, getting in tune with the feeling of pure joy.

I spend time going through my *gratitude list* one by one, in no particular order and at a relaxed pace in this way: "Thank you God for my life-partner, thank you for my parents, thank for my family, thank you for our special friends, thank you for our incredible team, thank you for the home we live in, thank you for the car I drive, thank you for my desire to be of service, thank you for the answers revealed, thank you for the beautiful day, thank you, thank you, thank you." I continue until I reach a state of what I call *authentic appreciation*. In this state of absolute gratitude, all concerns of the day disappear.

3. **Ask for what you want.** You're now ready to go to a deeper level to connect with Source and ask about everything and anything that is of concern, be it your relationship, kids, job, finances, life purpose, how to handle a situation, a request for guidance, and so forth.

In this moment, you tap into your *'inner wisdom.'* The part of us that is always present, but that we're not always aware of. This is where Source reveals our *truth*.

Know that you are absolutely free to ask for *clarity and focus* regarding anything you need. Once you have asked for your needs to be met, know that they will be. In that moment, consider the peace in that trust.

From the deepest place in your heart and soul, ask for what you *want*. Ask for these yearnings and callings to be answered. Ask for this *without* apology or fear of the result. Sit with this for a few moments.

4. **Let worries speed by.** If we want to be more productive and enjoy life to the fullest, learn to *let go of the negative self-talk* that can run rampant in your mind. As we become more attuned to our inner wisdom we will become more *aware* of just how many times a day these limiting beliefs pop into our thoughts—and how determined they are to stay there! The key is to *be aware and know* that these are not your true attributes.

    As you are asking for what you want, random thoughts, limiting beliefs, and negative self-talk will likely show up unannounced and uninvited. To overcome them, try these two simple techniques I use:

    First, when these thoughts occur it is a good indicator that you are *thinking* and *not feeling.* Move from your head back to *your heart* by concentrating on breathing through your heart. When you do, you're better able to keep the focus on *asking for what you are requesting.* I find it helpful to take my right hand, pointing straight up, and bring it right in front of my chest with my thumb pointing at my chest to bring my focus back to my heart.

    Another method you may want to try, while your eyes are still closed, is *go to the river.* By that I mean imagine a beautiful flowing river just to the right. Up ahead, you see a bright yellow speedboat coming your way. As it passes you, throw those negative thoughts on the boat and watch it speed away.

Every time a new limiting belief or random thought appears, imagine another speedboat flashing by. Toss your negative thoughts onboard so you can focus once again on the answers you desire.

Think I'm kidding? These techniques work. Try them. I've used these techniques over and over again, and today I rarely have a negative thought enter my mind during this process.

5. **Listen to what is revealed.** When you focus on your heart, breathe, quiet your mind, and *go within*, you'll be amazed at what will be revealed. You'll begin to decipher what is and what isn't important. Your priorities will fall into place. You'll be reminded of things you have forgotten. You'll discover solutions to problems and allow creative ideas to appear.

Don't be discouraged if the answers don't come immediately; just keeping applying this method five to 20 minutes twice a day. I guarantee 100% you'll begin to experience positive changes if you start everyday and fall asleep at night with this process.

Throughout the day, don't be surprised if answers are suddenly revealed when you least expect them. They may appear in the form of a message delivered by a friend or stranger, an article, an advertisement, even a thought while in the shower or at a traffic light. You never know.

If you find it difficult to gain clarity and focus, then I suggest the next time you go through these steps, ask for insight as to *what is holding you back from moving forward*—what is blocking you. You will likely discover an underlying factor holding you back that you first need to focus on.

The key to making it work? *Ask for what you want and truly ask from you heart*. Allow the Universe to collaborate with you, providing answers that help you attain your highest good.

6. **Write it down and take action.** I always have a pen and *Clarity & Focus Journal* next to me to write down key points at the end of each process. I encourage you to do the same as you may easily forget these important nuggets. Review your thoughts, ideas, and realizations in your journal over the course of the month.

Ultimately, the final point is that you have to *take action*. All the brilliant ideas in the world are of no value unless you *act on them*. When you act on what is revealed from within, you will gain momentum and see results.

(A downloadable version of these steps is available at www.EddieMiller.com)

As I've shared with you throughout the book, the Inside-Out Philosophy™ is based on the universal premise that, as human beings, *we have within us an innate wisdom and capacity to transform our lives on any level*, whether it's accepting and loving ourselves, achieving our dreams (health, relationships, family, career or finances), living with passion, or understanding our divine purpose.

When you make the *Six Steps to Clarity and Focus* your daily ritual, you can easily tap into your innate wisdom and begin to create a life filled with happiness, health, and prosperity.

Start Now!

In each chapter, I've outlined practical steps to apply to your daily life based on the Inside-Out Philosophy™ and its key principles:

1. *Focus Your Intention*

2. *Embrace Change from Within*

3. *Be Present to Possibilities*

4. *Know Your Truth*

5. *The Questions are the Answers*

6. *Awaken to Your Natural Abundance*

Now it's important to apply the seventh and final principle—*Move to Action*.

Although it may appear to be paradoxical, there is a critical first step to the seventh principle.

See, for years I've searched for and focused on what was the *next action step* in order to accomplish my goals. *What should I do next?* And what I've learned is that before I can take action, I have to get quiet, go within, and listen to what is revealed.

By connecting with Source through the *Six Steps of Clarity and Focus*, I'm able to get clarity on what's waiting to be expressed. That's part of taking *100% responsibility for my life*.

We're often running around working really hard to make things happen we become overworked, overwhelmed, and overcommitted. When we just start to take action we are typically working on the wrong thing. Because we haven't slowed down enough to open ourselves up to the ways in which we are being guided.

If 'life' *is not* going in the direction we want it to, often it isn't life that's not cooperating—*it's us not cooperating with life*.

Here's the paradox. Only when we are in motion can we be steered in the right direction. By slowing down enough to gain guidance, in response, we are given direction, insight, and clarity. That's when we learn to *access, listen, trust, and follow our own inner wisdom*. It helps us overcome our mental and emotional blocks, negative self-talk, and perceived fears while providing everything needed to take action and in the process become the person we were meant to be.

The first key is to tap, once again, into your dreams, desires, and potential. In that process, you will rediscover the 'ultimate side of you.'

What *is* that ultimate side?

It's the side of you that's your biggest cheerleader, willing to embrace change and find solutions. The side that intrinsically knows you can ask and will receive, and make a positive contribution to the world. And, it's the side of you that's open to possibilities you have not yet considered.

Thank you for allowing me to share my own inside-out journey with you. I hope you keep this book close at hand—your desk, car, office, or night stand—and that it proves to be a friend, a guide to steer you back, to remind you, as to who you really are at any point on your soul's journey.

I encourage you to focus first on those areas that give you the most energy and move your focused intention on the nuggets of wisdom shared in these pages.

You are a remarkable, one-of-a-kind spiritual being having a human experience—embrace your truth and begin to live the life of your dreams. When you move into what is possible, it becomes your reality.

"Living inside-out isn't a destination, it's a choice. Embrace what you fear the most and your inner power and strength will emerge."

— Eddie

Living Inside-Out Lessons from Chapter 18

- The highest vision for your life is heaven on earth—a heaven within consciousness.

- The soul's journey is about the constant evolution of our being, to grow and learn.

- You have an innate wisdom and capacity to transform your life and the world.

- Clarify your focused intention with the *Six Steps to Clarity and Focus*.

- Take action—only when we are in motion can we be steered in the right direction.

- First however, we go within to gain guidance and are given direction, insight, and clarity.

- Tap into your dreams, desires, and potential to rediscover the ultimate side of you.

HOW TO USE THIS BOOK

These 12 amazing steps have been compiled here to help you create the conscious, sustainable changes you desire. Enjoy!

1. *Review all of these chapters and determine where you want to place your focused intention*—happiness, health, finances, relationships, balance, spirituality, and so on. You can always address more than one area at a time.

2. *Use the Six Steps to Clarity and Focus (from chapter 18) to become absolutely clear on what you want.* Breathe and become still, go to gratitude, ask for what you need and want, let worries speed by, listen to what is revealed, write it down, and take action. You will know the right path to take when you can actually see it, *feel it,* and taste it.

3. To know what it feels like to accomplish your focused intention, *let your feelings be your guide.* Remember, how we feel at any given moment directly responds to our connection with Source energy, to our vibrational field. Our feelings give us a clear understanding of the direction of our vibration, our focused intention. They guide what we become aware of and create whether it's positive or negative. When we consciously move our focused intention into feelings of happiness, then that's what we create.

4. *Remember that you're a spiritual being **playing** in a human experience.* As Byron Katie puts it, "When we want reality to be different than it is, there is no way we're going to be anything but unhappy and disappointed—it's hopeless." The stress we feel is caused by arguing with "What Is." By that, she isn't saying never be angry, fearful, anxious, or sad. Rather, she advocates using those emotions to find your truth and embrace your power within.

5. Having listened to your inner voice, *create a daily "action" list* to help you to stay on course with your focused intention, move into action, and make the most of your time. Review the key steps in each chapter to focus on and write down your action plan. You can use a simple Word document or calendar on the computer or a task list on your handy BlackBerry or iPhone. At the end of everyday, remove all of the items you have accomplished and write down key tasks for the next day.

6. *Arrange tasks in order of importance.* For example, if you're on a deadline or someone has asked you to do something important, list these items first. Then add to the list of other tasks that will help you move forward with your focused intention. Depending on the size of the task or steps, don't list more than five top priorities for each day, even if 20 are waiting. In implementing this approach, the most important question to ask is this: "What is the best use of my time? What can I accomplish today? How can I do things for myself that balances the yin and yang?"

7. *Set a targeted amount of uninterrupted focused time* to accomplish your priority tasks. This means no e-mails, phone calls, or interruptions of any kind. Only answer e-mail—and phone calls if possible—at specific times and for only a certain amount of time so you can keep focused on your five priority items.

8. *Select one person who is focusing on similar goals to be your accountability partner.* Everyday Monday through Friday, you commit to call each other (the call typically last five minutes or less), report on your progress, and share the next top three priorities that will move you in the direction of your goals.

9. *Set up a support system.* The five people we hang out with most tend to have the greatest influence on our lives and affect our mental, emotional, and financial well-being. What groups, organizations, or clubs can you join to help you move in the direction of your desired focused intention?

10. Be patient, knowing it takes *21 to 30 days to shift habits and create conscious sustainable changes.* Use the words of wisdom shared by the incredible experts in this book to keep your focused intention on the steps that will help you succeed.

11. *Apply the principle of Move into Action without tension.* Remember Marci Shimoff's rule of three in chapter 8? The rule of three — intention, attention, no tension — means letting go and allowing Source to guide you.

12. *Live your truth in the present moment and create from it what is possible.* Identify your stories and replace them with your empowering truth. When facing your perceived fears, negative self-talk, and limiting beliefs, step into them. In the process, you'll step into your creative power and *tap into your natural abundance. Don't waste time worrying about the past or the future.* Instead, use what you've learned in these chapters to focus your intention on today to live your life to the fullest.

Discover your radiant beauty within.

— *Eddie*

ABOUT THE AUTHOR & FEATURED EXPERTS

About the Author

 **Eddie Miller says, "Perception is everything!"** On our path to achieving our ultimate potential, it's what we *believe* about ourselves and our lives that actually drives our choices—not our life vision.

Eddie is creator of the "Inside-Out Philosophy™," CEO of Miami Property Solutions LLC, a motivational speaker, best-selling co-author of *The New Masters of Real Estate,* and host of the popular Answers Are Within teleseminar series.

By learning to tap into our own inner wisdom, we can dismantle internal blocks, break through the ceiling of our self-limiting beliefs, and change the perceptions that have held us captive. Only then can we truly create conscious, sustainable change.

Eddie's transformative Inside-Out approach inspires and motivates people to conquer their fears, make more informed and intuitive choices, and achieve a state of inner and outer balance to live the life of their dreams.

He also uses the Inside-Out Philosophy™ in business. His company, Miami Property Solutions LLC, is one of the fastest growing private real estate investment companies in South Florida.

As a leader in the nonprofit sector for more than a decade, Eddie is chair emeritus of the Center for Advancement in Cancer Education and the former COO of the National Foundation for Alternative Medicine. **www.EddieMiller.com**

Foreword

Jack Canfield is co-founder of the *Chicken Soup for the Soul* series, which introduced inspirational anthologies as a genre and helped it grow into a billion-dollar market. As the driving force behind more than 112 million *Chicken Soup* books sold, Jack is uniquely qualified to represent and promote success. He is the best-selling author of *The Success Principles: How to Get from Where You Are to Where You Want to Be; The Power of Focus; The Aladdin Factor;* and *Dare to Win*. He is also a contributor to the acclaimed movie and *New York Times* bestseller *The Secret*. **www.JackCanfield.com**

Featured Experts

Listed in alphabetical order are the 16 experts who share their wisdom in *Living Inside-Out*.

MIND — Unleashing the Power of the Mind

Doug Bench, MS, JD, AAAS, is a noted educational brain-science research based author and speaker. Armed with a degree in physiology and a doctor of law degree, he became an expert in the area of brain-science research after his mother's diagnosis and eventual death from Alzheimer's disease. Since then, Doug has spent years researching and analyzing the findings of more than 1,000 cutting—edge neuroscience research studies and books on the brain to develop techniques and skills that help people to maximize the performance of their brain, reduce memory loss, as well as the risk of Alzheimer's disease. He has presented this advanced information on brain-science to over 240,000 people, receiving rave reviews for the results his information has created. He is author of *Revolutionize Your Brain!,* and *Do It Yourself Brain Surgery!* **www.TheBrainTrainingAcademy.com**

PURPOSE — Be Present to Possibilities

Brian Biro is one of the nation's foremost speakers and teachers of life balance, leadership, and team building. He is characterized as "having the energy of a ten-year-old, the enthusiasm of a twenty-year-old, and the wisdom of a seventy-five-year-old." Brian was rated number one among more 40 speakers at four consecutive *Inc. Magazine* international conferences. This former radio talk show host of *The Unstoppable Spirit* wrote the internationally acclaimed bestseller *Beyond Success!* as well as *It's Time For Joy!*, *Through the Eyes of a Coach*, and *Motivational Leaders*. **www.BrianBiro.com**

SPIRIT — The Spirit Within

Barbara De Angelis, PhD, is one of the most influential teachers of our time in the field of personal and spiritual development. For the past 35 years, she has reached tens of millions of people with her positive messages about love, happiness, and the search for meaning in our lives. Author, television personality, and sought-after motivational speaker, Barbara was among the first to popularize the idea of self-help and personal transformation in the 1980s. She is the recipient of one of the highest honors in the world of public speaking as the 2007 winner of Toastmasters International's *Golden Gavel Award*. Barbara has written 14 best-selling books, which have sold 10 million copies and been published in 20 languages, and offers seminars and coaching to help people create transformation from the inside-out. **www.BarbaraDeAngelis.com**

BALANCE — Ancient Wisdom for Modern Living

Felice Dunas, PhD, is an international lecturer, best-selling author, and coach. She has worked in over 60 countries around the world enhancing the lives of individuals, couples, and corporate executives. Dr. Dunas helps people understand human behavior and energy and as it pertains to health, intimacy, and authentic leadership. She is also a founder of the acupuncture industry in the United States and has maintained a clinical practice for over 40 years. **www.FeliceDunas.com**

RELATIONSHIPS — Building Relationships that Last

Jane Greer, PhD, is a marriage and family therapist in New York. She has written: *What About Me? Stop Selfishness from Ruining Your Relationship, How Could You Do This to Me: Learning to Trust after Betrayal,* **and** *The Afterlife Connection.* **Dr. Greer** is a media consultant and contributing editor for *Redbook Magazine*. She has appeared on numerous national television shows including *The Today Show, The Early Show, Anderson Cooper 360,* and *The Oprah Winfrey Show* and has been interviewed for publications such as *People* and *Us*. She hosts a weekly internet radio show, *Doctor On Call*, featuring, "Let's Talk Sex" every last Tuesday of the month and is a newscaster for *Heroes and Happy Living* at www.HealthyLife.net Monday through Friday, 7 a.m. and 7 p.m. **www.DrJaneGreer.com**

STORY — Know Your Truth

Lu Hanessian is an award-winning newspaper columnist, former NBC anchor, Discovery Health Channel host, and author of the acclaimed book *Let the Baby Drive: Navigating the Road of New Motherhood*. For five years, she hosted *The Science Show*, syndicated in 110 countries. Lu is the founder of Know Better Parent, LLC and "Parent2ParentU." Her extensive studies over the last 25 years have lead her to a certification with renown neuroscientist Daniel Siegel, MD in his Integrative Program in Interpersonal Neurobiology (IPNB). Lu is the founder of a new 'socially conscious' company called WYSH—Wear Your Spirit for Humanity. She has been a guest on *CNN, FOX News Channel, The View, The Today Show*, and *NPR*. Her essays and articles have been published in *The New York Times, Mothering, Fit Pregnancy*, and *Child Magazine*. **www.Parent2Parentu.com & www.WearYourSpirit.com**

FITNESS — Emotional & Physical Fitness for Life

Jim Karas is a nationally recognized fitness and weight loss expert. A graduate of the Wharton School of Business, he applies classic business principles to helping people look and feel their best. Jim is a three-time *New York Times bestselling author*, which includes the controversial blockbuster, *The Cardio-Free Diet*. He has been the Fitness Contributor for ABC's *Good Morning America*, is frequently seen on *The View* and *FOX News* and has been profiled in countless publications such as *O—The Oprah Magazine, Vogue, Time*, and *Glamour*. He oversees Jim Karas Personal Training in New York and Chicago and his "Who's Who" client list includes Diane Sawyer, Hugh Jackman, and Stacy London. **www.JimKaras.com**

LIVING IN TRUTH — The Questions are the Answers

Byron Katie, founder of The Work, has one job: to teach people how to end their own suffering. When Katie appears, lives change. As she guides people through her simple yet powerful process of inquiry called The Work, they find that their beliefs radically shift. Katie is the author of the bestselling *Loving What Is; I Need Your Love—Is That True?; A Thousand Names for Joy; Question Your Thinking, Change the World; Who Would You Be Without Your Story?;* and, for children, *Tiger-Tiger, Is It True?*. **www.TheWork.com**

NUTRITION — Skillfulness the Path to Conscious Eating

David Katz, MD, MPH, FACPM, FACP, is an internationally renowned authority on nutrition, weight control, and the prevention of chronic disease. He is associate professor, adjunct, of Public Heath Practice at the Yale University School of Public Health, and director of the Yale University Prevention Research Center. Dr. Katz has published over 100 scientific papers and 12 books to date. In 2009, he was a widely supported nominee to the Obama Administration for the position of U.S. Surgeon General. He has an extensive media portfolio, and is currently a regular guest on the *Dr. Oz Show*; a blogger for *Prevention Magazine*, and a health contributor to *Huffington Post*. He is the principal inventor of the Overall Nutritional Quality Index (ONQI) algorithm used in the NuVal System—www.NuVal.com. **www.DavidKatzMD.com**

FINANCIAL MANAGEMENT — Creating a Lasting Financial Foundation

Mackey McNeill, CPA, PFS, RIA, is the President and CEO of Mackey Advisors, Wealth Advocates who passionately pursue their client's prosperity. She is a CPA, Personal Financial Specialist, Registered Investment Advisor and Certified Enneagram Teacher. Mackey has been quoted in such publications as *The Wall Street Journal, TIME, Money* and *Reader's Digest*. Mackey shares her ideas in her award-winning book, *The Intersection of Joy and Money,* which was named "Most Life-Changing Book and Outstanding Book of the Year" by Independent Publisher. Her personal mission is to passionately expand prosperity in her community, in her life and in her relationships. Mackey is a leader in the sustainable living moment, and resides at RedSunflower Farm, an organic, permaculture homestead in Independence, Kentucky. **www.CultivatingProsperity.com**

LOVING OURSELVES — Loving Ourselves & Empowering Our Children

Lisa Nichols is the CEO of Motivating the Teen Spirit, LLC, best-selling author of *No Matter What* and co-author of *Chicken Soup for the African American Soul*, as well as a featured expert in the best-selling book and movie *The Secret*. A transformational coach and advocate of personal empowerment and emotional healthiness, her audiences include teens, educators, business professionals, CEOs, and parents. Her no-holds-barred conversation, witty sense of humor, and business savvy have made her a popular guest on radio shows and a sought-after speaker. **www.Lisa-Nichols.com**

PROSPERITY — Creating Financial Abundance

Bob Proctor is a direct link to the modern science of success and The Law of Attraction, stretching back to Andrew Carnegie, the great financier and philanthropist. Carnegie's secrets inspired and enthused Napoleon Hill, whose book, *Think and Grow Rich*, in turn inspired a whole genre of success philosophy books. Napoleon Hill, in turn, passed the baton on to Earl Nightingale who has since placed it in Bob Proctor's capable hands. Featured in the blockbuster hit, The Secret, Bob Proctor has worked in the area of mind potential for over 40 years. The author of two international bestsellers, *You Were Born Rich* and *It's Not About the Money,* Bob travels the globe, teaching thousands of people how to believe in and act upon the greatness of their own mind. **www.BobProctor.com**

NATURAL ABUNDANCE — Awaken to Your Natural Abundance

Paul Scheele has activated the natural brilliance within millions over the past thirty years. His dynamic programs cultivate human potential in all audience types, awakening the genius mind in everyone. Paul is the CEO of Scheele Learning Systems which offers advanced technologies to support human development. He is also the founding partner of Learning Strategies Corporation, a premier developer of self-improvement, education, and health programs. His expertise includes transformational change, neuro-linguistic programming, preconscious processing, accelerated learning, and universal energy. Paul has authored two best-selling books, *PhotoReading* and *Natural Brilliance*. His work has been translated into eighteen languages and used by enthusiastic clients in 185 countries. **www.ReclaimYourGenius.com**

HAPPINESS — The Power to Embrace Our Own Happiness

Marci Shimoff is the *NY Times* bestselling author of *Happy for No Reason: 7 Steps to Being Happy from the Inside Out*, which offers a revolutionary approach to deep and lasting happiness. Marci's also the woman's face of the biggest self-help book phenomenon in history as the co-author of the *Chicken Soup for the Woman's Soul* and *Chicken Soup for the Mother's Soul* series. Her books have met with stunning success selling more than 14 million copies worldwide in 33 languages and have been on the *New York Times* bestseller list for a total of 108 weeks, making her one of the bestselling female nonfiction authors of all time. In addition, she's a featured teacher in the international film and book phenomenon, *The Secret* and a regular television and radio personality. She is a celebrated transformational leader and renowned expert in happiness, success and the law of attraction. **www.HappyForNoReason.com**

VITALITY — Health & Vitality for Life

Susan Silberstein, PhD, is founder and Executive Director of the Center for Advancement in Cancer Education, through which she has counseled more than 25,000 cancer patients and coached over 50,000 prevention-seekers. Susan is a sought-after expert and national lecturer on nutrition, cancer prevention, and the psychology of health and disease. She is the author of the acclaimed books *Hungry for Health* and *Breast Cancer: Is it What You're Eating or What's Eating You?*, creator of the *Beat Cancer Kit* series, narrator of the popular video *Fight Cancer With Your Fork*, and editor of *Immune Perspectives* magazine. She has appeared on hundreds of television and radio talk shows. **www.BeatCancer.org**

CHANGE — Embrace Change from Within

Chris Waddell is a member of the Paralympic and the US Ski and Snowboard Halls of Fame. A thirteen-time medalist and World Champion in two sports, he considers his athletic success the platform for future contributions. Chris shares his message, *what happens to you is not as significant as what you do with what happens to you*, to inspire individuals to achieve their best. In 2009, he became the first paraplegic to summit Tanzania's 19,340-foot Mount Kilimanjaro, Africa's tallest mountain. *People* Magazine named him one of the "Fifty Most Beautiful People in the World." He has been a spokesperson for Hartford Financial Services Group, Time Warner Cable, DaimlerChrysler, Matrix Essentials, the Salt Lake Organizing Committee, and the International Paralympic Committee. **www.One-Revolution.org**

Visit

EddieMiller.com

Access these free life-changing tools that will empower you to live your life from the inside-out.

Interviews with Eddie Miller and •
Featured Experts

Blog updates and •
Monthly Newsletter

Inside-Out Minute Videos •

MP3 of the Clarity & •
Focus Meditation

Featured Handouts from •
Living Inside-Out

And much more . . . •

Plus, checkout the new
Living Inside-Out Workbook
and
Clarity & Focus Journal

BUY A SHARE OF THE FUTURE IN YOUR COMMUNITY

These certificates make great holiday, graduation and birthday gifts that can be personalized with the recipient's name. The cost of one S.H.A.R.E. or one square foot is $54.17. The personalized certificate is suitable for framing and will state the number of shares purchased and the amount of each share, as well as the recipient's name. The home that you participate in "building" will last for many years and will continue to grow in value.

Here is a sample SHARE certificate:

YES, I WOULD LIKE TO HELP!

I support the work that Habitat for Humanity does and I want to be part of the excitement! As a donor, I will receive periodic updates on your construction activities but, more importantly, I know my gift will help a family in our community realize the dream of homeownership. **I would like to SHARE in your efforts against substandard housing in my community!** *(Please print below)*

PLEASE SEND ME _____ SHARES at $54.17 EACH = $ $_____

In Honor Of: _____

Occasion: *(Circle One)*   HOLIDAY   BIRTHDAY   ANNIVERSARY

      OTHER: _____

Address of Recipient: _____

Gift From: _____ *Donor Address:* _____

Donor Email: _____

I AM ENCLOSING A CHECK FOR $ $_____ PAYABLE TO HABITAT FOR HUMANITY OR PLEASE CHARGE MY VISA OR MASTERCARD *(CIRCLE ONE)*

Card Number _____ Expiration Date: _____

Name as it appears on Credit Card _____ Charge Amount $ _____

Signature _____

Billing Address _____

Telephone # Day _____ Eve _____

PLEASE NOTE: Your contribution is tax-deductible to the fullest extent allowed by law.
Habitat for Humanity • P.O. Box 1443 • Newport News, VA 23601 • 757-596-5553
www.HelpHabitatforHumanity.org

Printed in the USA
CPSIA information can be obtained
at www.ICGtesting.com
JSHW012014140824
68134JS00025B/2412